MAN RAY

PHOTOGRAPHY AND ITS DOUBLE

Edited by Emmanuelle de l'Ecotais and Alain Sayag

With essays by :

Jean-Jacques Aillagon

Serge Bramly

Michel Frizot

Floris M. Neusüss and Renate Heyne

Michel Sanouillet

Werner Spies

Lucien Treillard (Interview)

Translated from the French by Deke Dusinberre

from the German by Donna Wiemann

Editor, English language edition Herbert R. Lottman

GINGKO PRESS

Exhibition

This book was originally published to coincide with the exhibition,
Man Ray, La Photographie à l'Envers, organized by the
Musée National d'Art Moderne
Centre Georges Pompidou
and held at the Galeries Nationales du Grand Palais in Paris,
from April 29 – June 29, 1998.

Exhibition Curators : Emmanuelle de l'Ecotais and Alain Sayag
Production Manager : Cathy Gicquel
Transport Manager : Delphine Davenier
Exhibition Design : Laurence Fontaine
Framers : Bruno Bourgeois, Sébastien Rodorera
Restorer : Véronique Landy
Photographers : Jacques Faujour, Jean-Claude Planchet, Bertrand Prévost,
Daniel Valet, and Jean-Luc Piété (platinum prints).
Public Relations : Carole Rio, Emmanuelle Toubiana
With assistance from Adriana Loundine and Silvia Labanchi

Book

Photo Selection and Editorial Supervision :
Emmanuelle de l'Ecotais, Alain Sayag, and Gilles Mora
Graphic Design : Ernesto Aparicio, assisted by Caroline Gautier
Editorial Secretary : Claire Marchandise
Copyright : Claudine Guillon and Mathias Battestini
Publicity : Danièle Alers and Anne-Marie Ferrieux

Centre National d'Art et de Culture Georges Pompidou
President : Jean-Jacques Aillagon
General Manager : Guillaume Cerutti
Director, Musée National d'Art Moderne : Werner Spies

Published by

GINGKO PRESS Inc.
5768 Paradise Drive, Suite J, Corte Madera, CA 94925
Phone (415) 924–9615, Fax (415) 924–9608
email gingko@linex.com

3–927258–66–0

Copyright for the original version
© Centre Georges Pompidou / Éditions du Seuil, Paris, April, 1998

Copyright for the English version
© Gingko Press, Inc., Corte Madera, CA, August 1998

Cover design by Julie von der Ropp

Printed in France

CONTENTS

Calvin Klein

The Man Ray Exhibition was made possible by support from Calvin Klein,

and with the aid of the
Association des Amis du Centre Georges Pompidou.

This exhibition could not have taken place without the help of all those who generously contributed advice or art works. Our acknowledgments go to :

Mme. Nocton, Bibliothèque de l'Institut Poincaré
Marcel Boiteux, Fondation Electricité de France
Mme. Kysslia, Fondazione Marguerite Arp
David Travis, The Art Institute of Chicago
Timothy Baum
Mme. Beaumont-Maillet, Philippe Arbaizar, (Cabinet des Estampes et de la Photographie, Bibliothèque Nationale de France)
Ken Browar
Jane Corkin
Marcel Fleiss, Galerie 1900*2000
Barry Friedman
Sandra Pinto, Galleria Nazionale d'Arte Moderna
Manfred Heiting
Weston J. Naef, The J. Paul Getty Museum
Galerie Kicken
Frank Kolodny
Antony Penrose, Lee Miller Archives
Peter Galassi, The Museum of Modern Art, New York
Gérard Lévy
Harry and Ann Malcolmson
Reinhold Mißelbeck, Museum Ludwig
Sylvio Perlstein
Alain Paviot
Arturo Schwarz
Michael Senft, Jack Banning
Galerie Natalie Seroussi
Roger Thérond
Thomas Walther
as well as to those lenders who wish to remain anonymous.

We would also like to thank Eric and Gregory Browner, Harouth Bezdjian, Jean-Michel Bouhours, Agnès de Bretagne, Nathalie Cattaruzza, Pierre-Henri Carteron, Guy Carrare, Jacques Faujour, Bertrand Prévost, Pierre Ronceray, and Anne-Marie Zucchelli, as well as Serge Lemoine, who supported the estate settlement plan. Thanks also to Jean-Hubert Martin and Germain Viatte, who steadfastly defended Man Ray's oeuvre, and most especially to Lucien Treillard, who constantly made his intimate knowledge of Man Ray's work available to us.

Furthermore, we would like to acknowledge Calvin Klein Incorporated, Calvin Klein Cosmetics, Calvin Klein Underwear, cK Calvin Klein Jeans, Calvin Klein Eyewear, and cK Watches.

Finally, thanks are due to Jean-Pierre Marcie-Rivière, president of the Association des Amis du Centre Georges Pompidou.

"Man Ray, n. masc., synon. de joie, jouer, jouir" *

All attempts to provide an account of Man Ray's immense, versatile production invoke, at one time or another, the definition proposed by Marcel Duchamp : *Man Ray, n. masc., synon. de joie, jouer, jouir.**

There is perhaps no better illustration of this definition than the exhibition presented at the Grand Palais by the Centre National d'Art et de Culture Georges Pompidou as one of the "external" shows being organized in Paris and abroad during renovation work at the center.

Whatever the case, this show adopts an original approach insofar as it aims to present the full spectrum of an oeuvre that constantly stretches and oscillates between commissioned work on the one hand (portraits, fashion pictures, photojournalism), and exploration, speculation, and experimentation on the other.

"I'm not a photographer of nature, but of my own imagination," Man Ray declared in 1951. This exhibition hopes to show that he was, in fact, both. It is precisely this two-way movement that supplied his photographic achievement — shown here for the first time as a whole — with its capacity for formal renewal and its playful, jubilatory power.

The artistic stakes behind the show are matched by cultural and institutional stakes of equal importance. The Musée National d'Art Moderne/Centre de Création Industrielle now boasts a Man Ray collection of unique wealth and variety, thanks to the 1994 estate settlement following the death of Juliet Man Ray (which transferred his archives to the nation in lieu of inheritance taxes), and to the bequest made by Lucien Treillard in 1995.

This exhibition, "Man Ray, Photography Inside Out," is the result of an exhaustive investigation of the Man Ray archives. That task, as documented by this catalogue, represents one of the key roles played by the Centre Georges Pompidou — to enhance and enrich France's national collections of twentieth-century art in a scholarly and historical manner, and to present and share this wealth of material with the widest possible public.

Jean-Jacques Aillagon

President
Centre National d'Art et de Culture Georges Pompidou

* Loose translation : noun [masculine] synonymous with joy, jest, exhilarate.

Preface

Visitors who had an opportunity to see Man Ray's darkroom never got over it. They discovered a scene of incredible concoctions. This has prompted me to utter a conclusive judgment: although Walter Benjamin — lauded by historians of photography as the profession's evangelist thanks to two little words, "aura" and "reproducibility" — argued that the question of original prints was meaningless, Man Ray's rich work strikingly refutes that argument. At an early date, Man Ray tried to grant photography a status that would free it from technological obsolescence and repetition, which explains the complicated, singular games of chance that he played in his studio. The effects he obtained from photography are most adequately categorized as surrealist. Man Ray provided his surrealist friends with powerful images capable of demonstrating their ideas and their vision through the medium of photography, whose proof was incontrovertible (at least apparently).

The pages of their magazine, *La Révolution Surréaliste*, show that explorers of the nocturnal, invisible realm would turn to Man Ray when seeking plunder. One is struck by his prodigious sensitivity to the epiphany of things, something that could never be repeated. And finally, there is perhaps no finer defense of surrealism's central theme of transgression via eroticism than Man Ray's wanton nudes, who point more to death than to sexuality.

Man Ray once declared that he had never executed a "recent painting," and the same thing could be said of his photographs. He meant that he sought staying power, in contrast to the avant-garde's immediacy and situationism. It was a reaction against the spirit of the times which — unlike Man Ray himself — was more comfortable with instant snapshots.

Werner Spies

Director, Musée National d'Art Moderne

Noire et Blanche, 1926

From One Show to Another   *Introduction*
Alain Sayag

Yet another Man Ray show, people will say — and they are right insofar as this is the third exhibition that the Centre Georges Pompidou has devoted to Man Ray since it was founded. The implication is that the number of artists worthy of exhibition is highly limited, or that institutions justify previous choices through a stubborn persistence as simplistic as it is suspect.

Explanations are therefore in order. In earlier shows, Man Ray remained frozen in his standard pose of a brilliant "jack of all trades," a talented dilettante who claimed to do only what he pleased, rejecting all financial and social constraints. This attitude became widely popular, giving rise to an immense cohort of "official artists with patrons, surviving in tepid security, claiming to wield the torch of novelty, boldness, charm, and spontaneity. All that remains of their elusive Marxism is a touching belief that the new remains invincible, that the future is on its side and the wind of history is in its sails." [1]

Man Ray, meanwhile, whatever he may have claimed, was first of all a professional photographer. Thus his work belonged not only to the avant-garde movements of the day but also to the mass culture then emerging. He quickly became a successful *photographer*, as opposed to a successful *artist* like Picasso or Matisse, whose fame and standing were assured by the end of the First World War. No trace remains of his commercial transactions, alas, but the lifestyle he was leading by 1925 attests to the high fees he could charge his clients. Access to the entire collection of 12,000 negatives turned over to the French government by the heirs of Juliet Man Ray, along with Lucien Treillard's generous bequest of another 1,500 negatives that had gone astray — all systematically studied by Emmanuelle de l'Ecotais — has disclosed the extent to which his production was nourished by the tension between everyday commercial activity and the desire to produce "artistic" work. It demonstrates that the hundred or so images selected over time and set apart by Man Ray represent just one side of an achievement of rare complexity.

His selection of images was constantly revised with a view to improvement and reduction, ultimately becoming limited to a few dozen constantly reproduced pictures. Although this reduction effectively promoted his work it disguised its reality, further distorted by another factor, namely Man Ray's adopted pose of amused dilettante, as echoed on every page of his autobiographical *Self Portrait*: "The artist [is] that privileged being who [can] free himself of all social constraint — whose only objectives should be the pursuit of liberty and of pleasure." Several pages later, he even added that he refused to make a film "unless it could be effortless and a pleasure, as making a painting or a photograph had become ...." [2]

Man Ray cultivated this carefree attitude, of course, displaying refined hedonism even in the way he furnished his Rue Férou studio. The bed, which occupied almost the entire space of the "bedroom," was endowed with a plethora of swinging tables that enabled him to carry out his business without ever leaving it. He remained in a horizontal position all day long, like some slothful do-nothing king of yore.

1) Philippe Muray, Exorcismes Spirituels, Paris : Les Belles Lettres, vol. 1, p. 218.

2) Man Ray, Self Portrait, Boston : Little, Brown, 1988, pp. 171 and 177.

Perhaps La Rochefoucauld was right in thinking that "laziness is the least known of all the passions," that it is "a bliss which consoles every loss." Perhaps it provided the only solace for the loss of the craft of painting, made more complete by the practice of "modern" photography, as though it is better to display laziness or ignorance of the craft, rather than a penchant for a mechanical apparatus.

Man Ray's willing admission of laziness nevertheless reeks of pretense. One need merely flip through the thousands of negatives and contact prints recently acquired by the Musée National d'Art Moderne to realize how difficult it sometimes was to take these pictures, not to mention the task of printing, which was often the object of laborious attention.

There were multiple phases in Man Ray's work. The first concerns the sitting itself. Even though the number of pictures taken was relatively limited, increasing only slightly over time with the change from glass plates to celluloid film, his labor was not restricted to simple mastery of the technical imponderables (such as the aperture/light relationship). Examining, for example, the portrait of Meret Oppenheim, titled *Érotique Voilée* (published in *Minotaure* in 1934, taken in 1933 or 1934), we discover no fewer than nine negatives, showing the patient work of refining the scene. Oppenheim is shown nude, "hands and arms smeared with the black ink of an etching press in Marcoussis's studio." The artist Louis Marcoussis, according to Man Ray, "wore a false beard to hide his identity," but in fact one of these negatives shows him without the bowler and phony whiskers that made him resemble a Landru-type figure. [3] It is the contrast between the ridiculous figure of the malefic petty bourgeois and the vulnerability of the model that make this "very disturbing [photograph] a perfect example of the Surrealist tendency toward scandal." [4]

On other occasions, the final image was honed once the picture had been taken. The artist Max Ernst, who arrived in Paris at roughly the same time as Man Ray, was photographed at least three times in 1935. Man Ray, fascinated by Ernst's "pale eyes and thin beaked nose [that] gave one the impression of a bird, a bird of prey," [5] in fact took just two pictures at each sitting, using a different camera each time. The two first photos, taken frontally and in three-quarter profile, seem to have been eliminated. Of the next two, one was solarized and reworked during printing, as the contact print shows. In the third series, Ernst's torso is placed at a three-quarter angle, but the face is turned to the camera. One of these images was skillfully re-worked : after having made a contact duplicate of the negative through a plate of glass, Man Ray altered the emulsion (by heating ?) to create a particularly successful crazed and fuzzy effect.

Many examples of this slow process of maturation could be cited, revealing the extent to which Man Ray's dilettantish pose disguised the work of the professional photographer. If he denounced "craft," and if he stressed chance effects (which he claimed led to his finest breakthroughs, solarization and rayographs), it was simply to emphasize the absolute freedom of the creative artist. It was designed to remind us, in the most elegant way possible, the extent to which photography is just a technique or tool for achieving an artistic goal. Otherwise, photography is at best a record, at worst mere anecdote.

3) *Henri Landru was a notorious French criminal who was arrested in 1919 and accused of murdering ten young women. Despite his claims of innocence, he was guillotined in 1922 [Translator's note].*

4) *Man Ray,* Self Portrait *(1988), p. 203.*

5) *Man Ray,* Self Portrait *(1988), p. 201.*

Noire et Blanche, reverse negative print, 1926

Model holding Giacometti's *Objet désagréable*, 1931

DUPLICATING REALITY

The Profession of Photographer

As early as 1921, Man Ray could be described as a "professional"
photographer. He was using photography in a standard, utilitarian way — to
duplicate reality. First came his "commercial," commissioned work
(reproductions of art works, magazine spreads, fashion pictures and portraiture), followed by more personal images that simply reflected reality, such
as still lifes and pictures taken during travels. These images offer a different
angle on Man Ray's photography, namely the little-known one of the
"piecework" photographer. Rather than demystifying his work, they help
to explain both its diversity and its rigor. Man Ray's way of making pictures
can be understood through study of the cropped contact prints and
original negatives shown here full-frame, most of them published for the
first time.

Man Ray's "documentary" and "commercial" work appeared extensively
in the press at the time, proving that he was highly appreciated for
pictures that he later tried to dismiss when he claimed that "photography is
not art," by which he meant that artists can not limit themselves merely
to duplicating reality.

Tristan Tzara and Jean Cocteau, 1921

Lampshade, 1920

Jean Cocteau sculpting his own head in wire, circa 1925

Rideau Diaphane [*Curtain*], 1933

21

How I Became Man Ray:
The Piecework Photographer Michel Frizot

The status of photographer is even less stable and codified than that of artist, especially when the individual concerned attempts to balance or combine these two occasionally antagonistic roles by inventing for himself a vaguely hybrid status. Emmanuel Radnitsky was one such individual, and in order to become Man Ray he had to pass from the acquired convictions of painting to the precarious uncertainties of photography via a narrow, initiatory path along which an ancient, noble alchemy was replaced by a coarse concoction of hypo and lenses. And that chemistry of blackness could stain the fingers for a whole lifetime, in such a way that a highly refined artist had to resign himself to working in the photographer's back room, because that was where the work truly materialized.

Man Ray the painter became a photographer only because he needed to preserve a photographic record of his canvases. That, however, is part of the onto-logical nature of the medium — while people may paint out of desire, out of faith, or out of excitement, they take photographs "in order to" (initially, at least, even if they find better reasons later). People take photographs in order to please someone, in order to perform a given objective task, or in order to disseminate an image designed for a specific function, use, or role. Despite having frequented Stieglitz's gallery in New York, which was mainly devoted to art photography, Man Ray had not been drawn to a medium that, in those days of pictorialism, seemed to flaunt grand airs without really possessing the means. The young Man Ray commented on the way Stieglitz took an impromptu portrait during a visit to the gallery in the following terms: "It lasted about ten seconds." [1] He admired the ease yet lamented the fashionable pointlessness of a personal image. It was certainly not this incident that spurred Man Ray to imitate the master. He was much more enthusiastic, on the other hand, about the idea of obtaining photographic reproductions of his paintings in order to publicize them, keep a record, or provide an illustration. "There was no question of using a camera ... except as a means of recording the [paintings]." [2] He went on to add, probably impressed by Stieglitz's obvious mastery, that "it was much simpler than [he had] imagined." Shortly after separating from his first wife, deciding to face up to the inevitable realities confronting an unknown, penniless artist, he told his new acquaintance Berenice Abbott that he was "taking up photography."

He only really "took it up" when Katherine Dreier, co-founder of the Société Anonyme with Man Ray and Marcel Duchamp, exclaimed, "So, [you're] a photographer." [3] Being a photographer was ultimately the effect of recognition alone, as though technique, practice and title (even usurped) had not sufficed. Dreier, the patron, went on to suggest that Man Ray photograph the works in the society's collection so that they could print "postcards of the works exhibited" which, Man Ray added, "would add to the income." [4] Thus a photographer was born, behind the scenes — as it were — of a desired activity; the tinkering novice was waiting in the wings for a still-unobtainable artistic role.

1) Man Ray, Self Portrait, Boston: Little, Brown, 1988, p. 26.

2) Man Ray, Self Portrait (1988), p. 55.

3) Man Ray, Self Portrait (1988), p. 78.

4) Man Ray, Self Portrait (1988), p. 78.

Vu, n°10. 23 May 1928, cover

The Little Review, winter 1926, vol. XI, n° 2, p. 73
The Little Review, winter 1926, vol. XI, n° 2, p. 74

5) Letter from Man Ray to Katherine Dreier, February 20, 1921

Man Ray felt he had already been waiting too long when he arrived at Saint-Lazare train station in Paris. He was met by Duchamp and soon joined a merry band of artists even more dubious than him (Tzara, Picabia, Rigaut, Breton, Aragon, Soupault) ; he was accepted as *dada* (although dada was in full crisis) and as a painter, which mattered little since he was never even asked to prove himself. Instead, he was asked to take photographs, because it seemed he was a photographer — in other words, unique. This individuality was highly useful in the eyes of his new companions, who were little inclined to familiarize themselves with precision mechanics, optics, and chemistry. Most of the photographers associated with the Parisian art scene of the time — Kertész, Krull, Brassaï, Eli Lotar, Berenice Abbott, Lee Miller — were immigrants. Young Frenchmen, more disposed toward poetry and literature, willingly abdicated less noble tasks : photography was perhaps not worthy of a great intellectual calling. Man Ray was therefore the first to benefit from the sincere incompetence of poet friends who left the way clear for him. He benefited all the more since, like other immigrants, he managed to make a substantial living from it (given his inability to craft words, catalogue libraries, recite on stage, or edit ephemeral reviews, as the likes of Breton, Eluard, Crevel, Aragon, Desnos and Tzara would do).

By chance, coincidence, necessity and good fortune, Man Ray was a photographer when he arrived in Paris — or at least, he knew how to take photographs. This role provided him with a back door or service entrance for joining a group of clever, carefree intellectuals, the way a back staircase provides access to a grand mansion. He aimed to use his camera like a typewriter,[5] and so his photography enabled him to shine among those who really knew how to use typewriters. Man Ray thus became official portraitist to these gentlemen, first based in his hotel room on Rue Delambre, then on Rue Campagne-Première, where he soon installed a studio and darkroom. There is no point asking whether he displayed exceptional skill or adaptability — it is in the nature of photography and notably portraiture to respond to demand, to expectations, and ultimately to commissions. And it was in the nature of the demands of his artist and poet friends to choose the carefree, innovating and droll attitude of a dadaist friend over a strait-laced, bourgeois portrait studio (which would have been unthinkable, in fact).

The singularity of the photographer was sometimes due to his status of plodding pieceworker, of someone who knows how to perform simple tasks alien to others (literati completely flummoxed by a screwdriver). In a way, a photographer knows how to marvel at little things, directing his gaze toward insignificant details, never regretting the grandiose inner debates that others indulge in. Photography has thrived on this difference since its beginnings, as recognized by Delacroix and Baudelaire, on its servile yet protective mechanical particularity that keeps evanescent artists at a distance.

Man Ray had no choice but to invent a style for a profession already chosen by his peers — within the Paris art scene of 1921, however, photography was a vacant new field just waiting to be occupied. This was especially true since the professionals — heirs to the major nineteenth-century studios, namely Reutlinger, Paul Nadar, Seeber, Manuel, and Harcourt — had banked on massive adaptation to general public taste, on standardization, on a single style for a chosen class. Given an artistic microcosm easily impressed by common skills and vernacular culture, the best innovation would be to adopt the amateur techniques stemming from the miniaturization of cameras and simplification of processes, something that professionals could never permit themselves. All photographic avant-gardes of the 1920s, whether constructivist or surrealist, relied on self-proclaimed technical competence, on inflated authority and on wariness of professionalism, which resulted in a straightforward, casual technique that until then had been the mark of an amateur. Neither Moholy-Nagy, Rodchenko, Kertész, nor Man Ray attended schools of photography and darkroom technique, nor studied the science of artificial lighting. They acted instinctively, sliding unperturbed into what would be considered, elsewhere, professional errors — (systematic) diagonal framing, visual puns, exaggerated physical features, overlapping images, the blur of movement, and superimposition or double exposure of negatives (Man Ray's 1921 portrait of Tzara). The top of a sitter's skull might be photographed, or the sitter lathered with shaving cream (Duchamp by Man Ray); the photographer need not wait for the sitter to be properly installed, could confine the subject to a fragment of the picture, exaggerate distance or nearness, wield the camera without really aiming it, crop the figure, or abandon the fully equipped studio for private places, everyday situations, and naked eroticism. In every case, this meant subverting the real, calculated, optimal potential of an industrialized system; instead, chance was raised to the level of a creative principle — an avant-garde credo in both literature and photography. Soon, darkroom accidents like rayographs (or photograms) and solarization became a special mark of artistry. It was therefore not surprising that Man Ray, the amateur, provided dada artists and poets with images displaying stylistic rupture, ignoring outmoded constraints and exploiting the freedom of the untrained. Photography, much more than painting, transformed every gesture into a fortuitous throw of the dice, which could only delight those lovers of the poetry of randomness and risk.

It was therefore also natural that Man Ray began to take pictures "in order to.... ," that is to say allotted a predefined function to the practice of photography (without excluding later, deflected uses). He took pictures of the work of his painter friends (notably Picabia), and of his own objects (which often disappeared, leaving photographs as the sole record of the work, thereby becoming file records). At the end of a session, he would save one plate for a portrait of the painter, aware of the unavowed narcissism behind the financial imperatives. It was only later that his shot of Duchamp's dusty "Large Glass" — taken purely out of friendship — became *Élevage de Poussière* [Dust Breeding], a work by Man Ray, in a symmetrical but similar relationship to Duchamp's tonsuring of himself, which became an artwork thanks solely to photography.

Yet the photographic portraits not only fed off personal satisfaction and professional schism, they also responded to a need for publicity, in the form of dedicated prints or postcards — the equivalent of todays "p.r." — used for articles in periodicals, the frontispieces of books, the walls of book stores, or shop windows. If Man Ray moved to Rue Campagne-Première in July 1922, it was precisely to handle "the increasing amount of work." *Vanity Fair* was publishing portraits by the "American painter" as early as 1922 (the one of the marquise Casati appeared in October). And if Man Ray became a society portraitist despite himself, it was due to the almost therapeutic nature of the rage for images of oneself; the choice of a practitioner's office partly accounted for the curative effect, as Man Ray

Art et Médecine, October 1931, n.n., p. 20-21
Art et Médecine, October 1931, n.n., p. 30-31

Ballet Russe, *Jack in the Box*, 1926

understood when he stated that people came to him "as though [he] were a doctor."

Man Ray's photographs generally had — at the outset, at least — an assumed goal and destination, and like those by Kertész and Brassaï, they performed an illustrative role. This is witnessed by the extensive publication of his photos not only in *Vanity Fair, Variétés, Vogue*, and *Harper's Bazaar* — great consumers of portraits — but also in *Der Querschnitt, Les Nouvelles Littéraires* and, more surprisingly, *Art et Médecine* (for which Kertész worked) and the racier *Paris Magazine* (where Brassaï's nudes were more likely to be found). Despite his status of painter and artist at the service of the *Révolution Surréaliste*, Man Ray deigned to send pictures to an illustrated weekly like *Vu*, if only on commission (the September 26, 1928, issue announced Man Ray as special correspondent assigned to the steel plants at Saulnes, in Lorraine). Several covers resulted from this collaboration — the dancer Escudero, Miss France, Mademoiselle Dorita the Snake Charmer, and Magda Schneider.

There is probably no mutually exclusive manichaeism in Man Ray's work between bread-and-butter photography (to which he certainly succumbed at certain times) and an essentially artistic and creative achievement. To the contrary, his work extends across various categories, all open to being recycled or deflected into another role or meaning, each feeding off the other, reaching different audiences. What they all shared was the de-sanctified technique of the modest amateur who skillfully seized every opportunity to adapt his approach to his ends.

"Everyone will tell you that I am not a painter. That is true. At the beginning of my career, I at once classified myself among the photometrographers. My works are purely photometric," wrote Man Ray in a 1959 pastiche of Erik Satie's haughty modesty. [6] But his systematic rejection of the label of "photographer" covers only the split with the shameful model of the tame and affluent professional photographers of the 1920s with their main-street studios. Man Ray, as "faultographer," was obliged to assert the simplicity of his origins and the modest, artisanal, and amateur roots of an entire sector of twentieth-century art.

6) Man Ray, *catalogue of the exhibition at the Musée National d'Art Moderne, Paris, 1972, p. 19. English version is reprinted in Man Ray,* Self Portrait *(1988), p. 304.*

Antoine, "Le sculpteur de masques", 1933

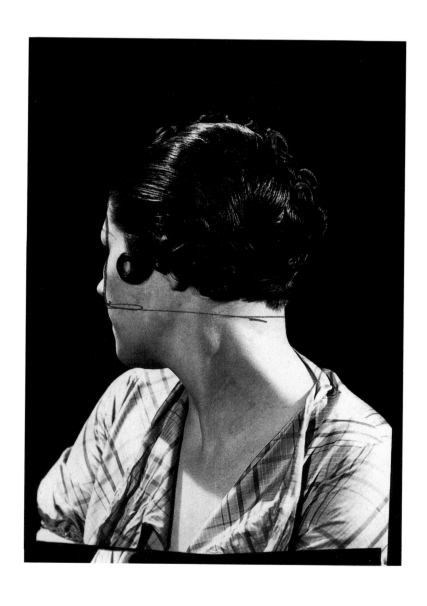

Antoine, "Le sculpteur de masques", 1933

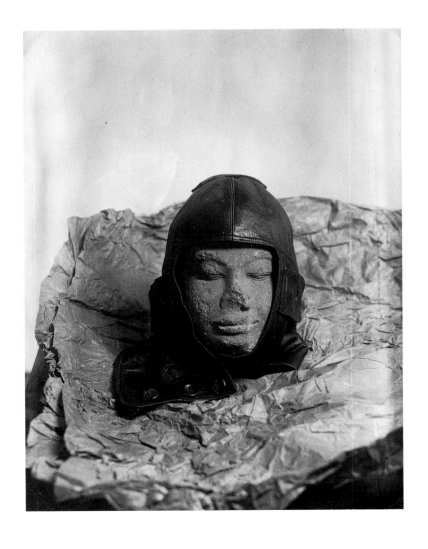

A head of Buddha, stolen from Angkor by Titaÿna, 1928

Titaÿna, 1928

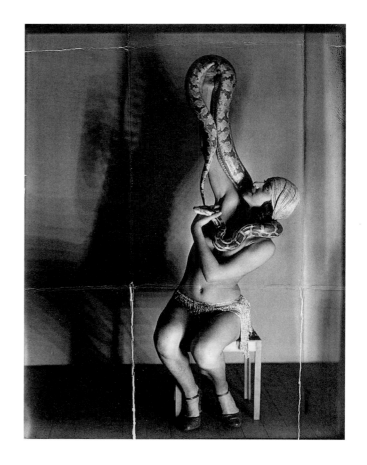

Mlle Dorita, Charmeuse de Serpents [Snake Charmer], 1930

Mlle Dorita, Charmeuse de Serpents [Snake Charmer], 1930

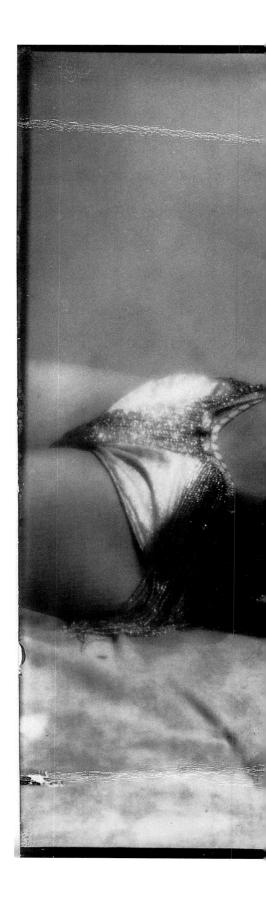

Mlle Dorita, Charmeuse de Serpents [Snake Charmer], 1930

Mlle Dorita, Charmeuse de Serpents [Snake Charmer], 1930

Untitled Advertisement, 1925

Jewelry, for *Harper's Bazaar*, 1935

With its elegant pose and refined setting, the 1936 *Self Portrait as a Fashion Photographer* presents a highly stylish image somewhat in the manner of George Hoyningen-Huene. The irony of the title furthermore suggests that Man Ray was happy to play this role. After all, he enthusiastically produced other self-portraits in costume : animal-tamer, woman, jazz musician, priest, and fakir.

Although this portrait represents just one facet of his work — Man Ray reportedly succumbed to the game of superficial frivolity without ever being taken in — it also reflects the real state of affairs at the time. Whether he liked it or not, Man Ray was a successful commercial photographer whose services were actively solicited on both sides of the Atlantic ; and although fashion and advertising invaded and overwhelmed his existence, they offered fine rewards in exchange — affluence, fame, women. Studio business was so good that Man Ray had his suits made in London, drove a new Voisin car, and bought himself a country house in Saint-Germain-en-Laye. Never again would he earn as much money as he did during the worldwide depression. Yet he was dismayed by these ambivalent circumstances, this particular success, because he desperately wanted to be appreciated for his painting !

So how did he find himself in this situation ? To begin with, imagine a young, ambitious, penniless artist arriving in Paris in the delightful tumult of the post-World War I era. Not speaking a word of French, he pins his future on a few acquaintances made in New York. Not just *any* acquaintances, all the same, for they included Marcel Duchamp and Francis Picabia, the latter having already published Man Ray's early photographic efforts in his review, *391*.

Not a single work was sold at Man Ray's first Paris show at Librarie Six. So how could he keep the dream alive ? "I now turned all my attention to getting myself organized as a professional photographer, getting a studio and installing it to do my work more efficiently. I was going to make money — not wait for recognition that might or might not come." [1]

He wrote that photography initially interested him only as a way to make a living, and that as his resources dwindled, he turned increasingly to this occupation. This confession surfaces as a leitmotif throughout his writings.

He began by making photographic reproductions of his friends' art works, a not very lucrative business that he extended by doing their portraits (out of friendship and to build up a file). Yet he took his first true steps in the world of popular photography in 1922, less than a year after his arrival in Paris, when Picabia's wife, Gabrielle Buffet, introduced him to Paul Poiret, the "fabulous" fashion designer.

Man Ray has described in detail how, thanks to a second-hand camera, a few plates and make-shift lighting (concocted by the concierge), he launched himself in business ; and how, on one occasion, printing his photographs in the bathroom,

1) *Man Ray, Self Portrait, Boston : Little, Brown, 1988, p. 100. Unless otherwise specified, all quotations are from this autobiography.*

Advertisement for Man Ray's portrait studio, 1935

he discovered the virtues of photograms, which he called "rayographs." Apart from its anecdotal appeal, this tale has the advantage of developing the three main lines of Man Ray's success: a) Display originality (produce, following Poiret's advice, something different from the stuff that ordinary photographers churn out); b) Combine fashion and art (say, a gold brocade hobble skirt with a gilded bronze bird sculpted by Brancusi, *Maïastra*); c) Fill every image with line, color, substance and, above all, "sex appeal."

Whenever he entered a new, untested field, Man Ray did not grope as someone else might, because he at once discovered unexpected sources of inventiveness in himself. Now he was to outdo himself all the more insofar as fashion houses were a breeding ground for pretty young women. He learned to dance in the same way, driven by a combination of desire, natural brio, and stubbornness.

His career decision was all the shrewder in that photography was just then entering a new era which radically altered and extended its use. Since the 1880s, a series of inventions and technical developments had continually improved the process of mechanical reproduction, to the point that magazines, newspapers, books, and advertising could finally offer vast new perspectives for photography. Printing made mass dissemination possible, and demand grew accordingly.

Fashion imagery, meanwhile, was still wavering between society photo spreads and hand-drawn plates. Although photographs were winning more and more space in women's magazines, and although they were no longer systematically converted into engravings, it was drawings — and the spirit of drawing (of which photographic pictorialism was an incarnation) — that continued to influence both public taste and editorial policy.

"Make your pictures different," Poiret urged Man Ray. His ignorance of the rules of the game immediately enabled Man Ray to bypass the conventional, hieratic, and dully pompous approach. The introduction of a certain spontaneity into his fashion photographs, whether due to inexperience and lack of resources or not, was no less original than his use of art and sex appeal. One need merely look at what was being published at the time.

During this first phase of his career as a commercial photographer, between 1922 and 1934, Man Ray nevertheless operated on several registers. Although he worked simultaneously for *Vu, Paris Magazine, Harper's Bazaar, Jazz, Vogue, Variétés, Art Vivant, Minotaure* and *Femina*, he submitted highly different pictures to each periodical, ranging from portraits to rayographs. His fashion work was only occasional.

The magazines themselves practiced eclecticism in those surrealist days, willingly mixing genres. During the major Art Deco exhibition of 1925, when Man Ray photographed dresses worn by stylized dummies nearly ten feet tall, placed in the garment section of the Pavillon de l'Élégance, his pictures appeared not only in the August issue of the new French *Vogue*, but also on the cover of the July issue of *La Révolution Surréaliste*, the only difference being that the former carried the caption, "And Siegel has created a new approach to the art of fashion dummies," while the latter bore the title, "And war on work," which could be interpreted in various ways. Conversely, *Vanity Fair* was one of the first magazines to publish a page of rayographs in its November 1922 issue ("A New Method of Realizing the Artistic Possibilities of Photography").

Advertising agencies, already in search of the unusual, were similarly interested in the arts. Never had art been so fashionable. McKnight Kauffer had Man Ray work for London's Charnaux Corset Company in the late 1920s, just as, several years later, Kauffer would employ the leading advocate of the American avant-garde, Francis Bruguière.

Man Ray is thus known to have worked on several advertising campaigns, including ones for Wrigley's chewing gum and Pond's cold cream. Not all is known, however. Significantly, although he kept his files more or less in order, Man Ray saved few traces of these various commissions (in Hollywood, during the war, he had to hunt through book stores and clip newspaper pictures in order to constitute a file of past work). Nor does his autobiography place much emphasis on them, mentioning almost no fashion houses, advertising agencies, or women's magazines by name. Man Ray merely skimmed over such things, as though they merited no further attention, whereas today this work no longer seems out of keeping with the rest of his output.

As a fashionable photographer before becoming a fashion photographer, Man Ray led a lonely but creative double existence. On the one hand he was an artist having difficulty making a breakthrough, and on the other he had a brilliant, busy social life stemming from his "bread-and-butter" work.

Yet he hardly complained at the time. According to Duchamp, the term Man Ray was synonymous with "joie, jouer, jouir", which loosely translates as joy, jest, exhilarate. The great hedonist was a fortunate and highly consenting victim of his own success. The French were convinced that he always kept his eye on the ball, and he took advantage of it by accepting proposals to make repeated forays into film and other genres, without becoming attached to a single one.

This versatile creativity nevertheless wound up doing him "more harm than good." In 1929, following the stock market crash, he was seized with a kind of panic. "People were saying I had given up photography for the movies, few sitters presented themselves for portraits. The magazines shunned me ...."

A series of exhibitions featuring his rayographs — in Paris, in Cannes, and at the Julien Levy Gallery in New York in 1932 — eventually re-established his reputation. This time there would be no half-measures : when *Harper's Bazaar* sought his services, he entered into a contractual arrangement with the magazine. From 1934 to 1940, he worked regularly for *Harper's Bazaar*, insidiously becoming a fashion photographer full time.

"I believe that a magazine must have surprises," declared Carmel Snow, the new editor of *Harper's Bazaar*. [2] She handed artistic direction of the magazine to Alexey Brodovitch, a graphic artist of Russian stock, who immigrated to the United States in order to found a department of advertising art at the Philadelphia College of Art. He taught his students to innovate by being "alert for new visions and techniques."

Brodovitch had known Man Ray in Paris. Their collaboration, which had been Brodovitch's idea, began in startling fashion in September 1934 with *Fashion by Radio*, a "photographic impression" of the French fashion shows. Man Ray employed the photogram effect to screen and stylize the model to an extreme, suggesting

2) The World of Carmel Snow, *New York : McGraw-Hill*, 1962, p. 100.

images transmitted by short wave. The following month, a photograph signed by hand like an art work presented the designer Augustabernard's new line by employing a distortion effect emphasizing a "gown [that] billows at the bottom." [3]

These pictures — purified until they gave no more than an overall impression of the garment, and then magnificently enhanced by the layout — appeared extremely experimental. In the fashion realm of the day, one could go no further.

Although much more substantial, Man Ray's subsequent contributions were also much more restrained even if, faithful to his initial principles, they continued to display sex appeal and a range of avant-garde techniques (notably the panoply of his own special effects : solarization, inversion, colorizing, photogram technique, superimposition). His photographs continued to combine art and fashion (as prop or setting, he would successively employ the *Winged Victory of Samothrace*, a Leonardo sketch, white plinths inspired by Brancusi, birds commissioned from Giacometti, even some of his own works such as *A l'Heure de l'Observatoire — Les Amoureux*). [4]

Yet as his mastery of the genre grew, that mastery almost seemed a handicap. He was becoming weary and eventually began to repeat himself. By the time of the Second World War, he was sending *Harper's Bazaar* old images, like the solarized negative of a nude, colored during the printing stage ("Beauty in Ultra-violet," October 1940).

This lassitude affected not only the work itself. When passing through New York after fleeing occupied France in the summer of 1940, he turned down flattering offers on the grounds that he needed a vacation. As soon as news of his return got around, he "was solicited by magazines to go to work at once. Advertising agencies offered [him] a studio and all facilities. [He] begged off, saying that [he] . . . needed a rest for a couple of weeks." He only wanted to retire to Hawaii or Tahiti where, like Gauguin, he could devote himself to painting and live on coconuts.

In fact, he got no further than California. He supplied a few pictures to *Harper's Bazaar* as late as 1944, but no longer bothered with the constraints of fashion imagery. The caption, for which he must have been partly responsible, of a close-up of a face published in November 1942 is revealing in this respect : "Man Ray, who has been painting in Hollywood, returns to his former medium, photography, with this extraordinary study of a woman's face for the beauty issue." [5]

The return was brief. It would seem that the commissioned work he executed throughout the 1930s — the decade he went from artist to fashion photographer — somehow discouraged him from all future photography. Launched in Poiret's fashion house under the aegis of haute couture, his career as photographer thus ended with fashion, as though fashion had underpinned and illuminated it all along. Exhausted by one, he rejected the other. His cameras henceforth stayed in their cases except on rare and very private occasions.

3) Reprinted in John Esten, Man Ray : Bazaar Years, New York : Rizzoli, 1988, p. 2.

4) Similar inspiration was provided by the African mask in Noire et Blanche (French Vogue, May 1926), one of Man Ray's favorite pictures, and Oscar Dominguez's upholstered wheelbarrow (Minotaure, no. 10, 1937).

5) Reprinted in Esten, p. 66.

Composition, 1936

Meret Oppenheim, fashion photo for *Harper's Bazaar*, 1935

Fashion photo, circa 1936

La comtesse de Beauchamp, Vionnet evening gown, 1933

Fashion photo, circa 1930

Untitled fashion photo, circa 1925

Pavillon de l'Élégance, 1925

Nusch au miroir [Nusch with a Mirror], 1935

Nusch au miroir [Nusch with a Mirror], 1935

Fashion photo, circa 1935

Advertisement for Bergdorf Goodman, 1930. Emily Davies wearing a Vionnet gown

Fashion photo, circa 1935

Fashion photo, circa 1935

From the series *À l'Heure de l'Observatoire, les Amoureux* [*Observatory Time — The Lovers*], 1934

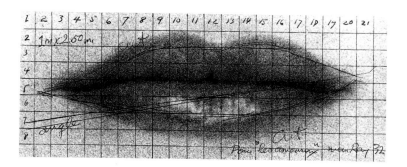

Study for *À l'Heure de l'Observatoire, les Amoureux* [*Observatory Time — The Lovers*], 1932

From the series *À l'Heure de l'Observatoire, les Amoureux* [*Observatory Time — The Lovers*], for *Harper's Bazaar*, 1936

Since Man Ray is now considered to be one of the most important twentieth-century photographers, it is startling to realize that his work has rarely been studied in a "scholarly" manner.

That is what this author now proposes to do, relying principally on the Man Ray estate settlement (i.e., his personal archives of negatives, contact prints, and documents now deposited at the National Museum of Modern Art in Paris, or MNAM), as well as on extensive consultation of periodicals of his time. Such study makes it possible to distinguish between two kinds of work — "commercial" photographs, and more personal, "artistic" work. Beyond the purely formal distinction, however, it is worth stressing the simplistic and restrictive nature of such delineation.

This article will try to show what our examination of the MNAM archives has revealed about the way Man Ray worked, based on examples drawn from "documentary" and portrait photography, his two main sources of income after moving to Paris in July 1921.

DOCUMENTARY PHOTOGRAPHY

Reproducing art works

Man Ray was a self-taught photographer. It is well known that the need for reproductions of the canvases in his first one-man show at the Daniel Gallery in New York in 1915 prompted his purchase of the necessary equipment. "I decided to do something in the way of preparing reproductions of my work for catalogues and the press. The few reproductions that professional photographers had made of some paintings were unsatisfactory. Translating color into black and white required not only technical skill but an understanding as well of the works to be copied. No one, I figured, was better qualified for this work than the painter himself." [2]

By 1917 Man Ray was photographing works for the Société Anonyme, which he founded with Marcel Duchamp and Katherine Dreier. At Dreier's request, he undertook a series of photographs which were subsequently to be sold as postcards by the Société. Dreier felt that Man Ray, as a member of the society, should execute this task without payment, so he was simply reimbursed for expenses incurred.

The negatives and contact prints in the MNAM archives reveal that Man Ray photographed art works by himself and his friends not only on arrival in France but also, more surprisingly, right up to the end of the 1930s. On occasion he even exhibited photographs of his works, notably enlargements of drawings, as happened twice in 1937. [3]

Two letters now in the Lucien Treillard collection demonstrate that André Breton often asked Man Ray to photograph works for reproduction in *Littérature* :

1) Excerpted from Emmanuelle de l'Ecotais, Le Fonds Photographique de la Dation Man Ray, étude et inventaire, PhD dissertation, Université de Paris IV (Sorbonne), 1997.

2) Man Ray, Self Portrait, New York : Little, Brown, 1963, p. 56.

3) "Youthful Drawings by Man Ray, 1908–1917," an exhibition at the Galerie Jeanne Bucher in Paris, November 1937, and "E.L.T. Mesens Presents Three Surrealist Painters : Max Ernst, Man Ray, Tanguy," at the Palais des Beaux-Arts in Brussels.

Detail of a
Salvador Dalí painting, *Les Désirs Liquides*, 1932

Paris, December 19, 1922

Dear friend,

It has been agreed that Max Ernst's painting will be brought to my place tomorrow morning. Do you think you could manage to drop by Rue Fontaine with your camera *around noon*? I hope I am not troubling you too much. Only the Picabia and the Duchamp remain to be shot. I don't really know what you can do with the former (*Feuille de Vigne* from the Salon d'Automne). As to the Duchamp, I am still somewhat vexed."

Man Ray executed these commissions for what was probably a modest sum. Breton, for that matter, ended one of his letters by suggesting to Man Ray : "If you have something to publish in *Littérature* (a drawing or something), you know that it will always be very welcome. Perhaps you could send it to me before January 5th?" Man Ray accepted Breton's offer with delight, since the February / March 1923 issue of the magazine published his rayograph titled *Monsieur...., Inventeur Constructeur, 6 Seconds*.

Contact prints in the MNAM archives show that Man Ray photographed Breton's *Rêve-Objet* in 1935 for publication in *Cahiers d'Art*.[4] Such images went unsigned, since their role was purely documentary, which was also the case with a reproduction of Valentine Hugo's painting, *Les Surréalistes*, published in the same issue of *Cahiers*.[5]

An inventory of negatives in the archives reveals that Man Ray also photographed works by other painters including Georges Braque, Giorgio De Chirico,

4) Cahiers d'Art, *no. 5–6, p. 125.*

5) Cahiers d'Art, *no. 5–6, p. 137.*

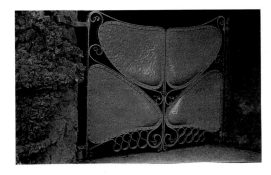

"*Les os sont à l'extérieur*"
["The Bones are on the Outside"], 1933

"*On pénètre dans les grottes par de tendres portes en foie deveau*"
["The grottoes are entered through soft, calf's liver doors"]1933

Architecture by Antoni Gaudí in Barcelona

6) Man Ray, "*Sur le réalisme photographique*," Cahiers d'Art, no. 5-6, 1935, p. 120.

7) Spring 1922, vol. VIII, no. 2. p. 41.

8) 1932, no. 8–10, pp. 337–342.

Salvador Dalí, Max Ernst, Jean Hugo, Marie Laurencin, André Masson, Francis Picabia, Pablo Picasso, Henri Rousseau, Yves Tanguy.

He seems to have systematically photographed his own art works, notably all his objects (most of the originals having vanished, this visual material was used to reconstitute those objects in the 1960s, as illustrated in the exhibition catalogue, *Objects of My Affection*).

The "documentary" category also covers some of the photographs that Man Ray produced at the request of magazines such as *Vogue*. Perusal of this publication indeed shows that Man Ray was sometimes required to execute purely commercial work. The French issue of *Vogue* dated December 1924 features several Christmas gift suggestions for "Madame" (a lamp, a tea service), for "Monsieur" (a car blanket, a magazine stand), and for the children (a wireless radio, a breakfast service) — surprisingly, all of these images are signed Man Ray. With only one exception, none of the photos is original in any way. They are purely documentary, simply showing the object for sale. The one exception is the shot of the magazine stand, for which Man Ray employed a soft focus highly inappropriate to this type of advertising. The sole point of the soft focus, however, was to enable Man Ray to underscore the title of a magazine peeking out from the bottom shelf — which of course was none other than *Vogue*, the true subject of the photo. Compared to the other images in the series, this shot is astonishing. One is inclined to think that if Man Ray had not displayed the magazine so visibly, the photograph would have been judged a failure, and never published.

It is nevertheless worth noting that Man Ray had been publishing fashion photographs and portraits in *Vogue* since August of that same year. The pictures of furnishings and gadgets were probably explicit commissions from the magazine. Yet as he wrote in his article, *Sur le réalisme photographique*, "those with the most selfish reasons for profiting from photography — magazines driven by obscurely mercenary motives, which tried to bend me to their needs — ... [ultimately] wasted their efforts on me."[6] It would seem that Man Ray produced this kind of imagery for magazines only on very rare occasions.

Man Ray's "Documentary" Eye

Man Ray himself left a crucial indication as to whether or not he considered a photograph an artistic creation. If he signed his photographs, he wanted those works to be recognized as such. When he did not sign — and thanks to archive negatives, contact prints, and other documents we now know which reproductions were his handiwork — he felt he was performing a purely technical task.

When *The Little Review* reproduced Picabia's *L'Oeil Cacodylate*,[7] the photo remained uncredited. When Giacometti's sculptures appeared in *Cahiers d'Art*, on the other hand, they bore Man Ray's mark.[8] Here Man Ray's work was not just a straightforward, faithful reproduction of his surrealist friend's work, since he had endeavored to offer a special vision, which was simultaneously his own and the one Giacometti aspired to convey. Taking the photo of *Pointe à l'oeil* as an example, Yves Bonnefoy has demonstrated how "in Man Ray's photograph, the shadow cast on the figures on the ledge affects in a striking and certainly uncoincidental way the form of this praying mantis who devours her male mate and who so fascinated almost everyone in the avant-garde world at the time. Giacometti placed great importance on photography for the way it represented works by other artists and other periods as well as for the way it displayed his own work; and since he and Man Ray were friends, there is no reason to doubt that this sinister shadow became part of his little sculpture and reinforced its meaning."[9]

Man Ray's collaboration with Marcel Duchamp yielded numerous photographs that could hardly be described as "documentation." When it came to portraits of Rrose Sélavy or to Élevage de Poussière ("Dust Breeding," an "aerial" photograph of a section of Duchamp's "Large Glass" in gestation), Man Ray did not limit himself to faithful reproductions of Duchamp's oeuvre.[10]

Nevertheless, a photo like Élevage de Poussière seems to have been conceived as a straightforward reproduction of part of The Bride Stripped Bare by her Bachelors, Even. Man Ray explained in his Self Portrait that he had asked Duchamp's permission to make this picture: "It would be good practice for me, in preparation for the work I was to do for Miss Dreier."[11] The fact that Man Ray and Marcel Duchamp both signed the picture, and that the photograph became another element comprising the Green Box, confirms the fact that Élevage de Poussière was above all a photographic record of the development of the "Large Glass."

The image was published for the first time in October 1922 in the fifth issue of Littérature, but bore a different title from its current French title (which Man Ray claimed that Duchamp coined much later).[12] The 1922 title read: "Voici le domaine de Rrose Sélavy / Comme il est aride — comme il est fertile — / Comme il est joyeux — Comme il est triste!" [This is the estate of Rrose Sélavy / How arid it is — how fertile it is / How joyous it is — how sad it is!"] It was signed, in French, "Photo taken from an airplane by Man Ray — 1921." This particularly poetic title was probably composed by Man Ray, but it is known that he spoke not a word of French at the time. The only person likely to translate — or even, perhaps, devise — such a title was Paul Eluard. A manuscript exists, for that matter, proving that Eluard translated texts that Man Ray wanted to publish.[13] Although the manuscript post dates the photograph, nothing rules out the possibility that they collaborated as soon as they met.

The original title recurs in a letter that André Breton sent to Man Ray: "Rather than taking the frame off the Duchamp photo ("Voici le domaine de R.S."), I would be delighted if you would supply me with a new print, for which I will pay you, naturally."[14] Image, title, and signature all lent an acrobatic feel to Man Ray's technique,[15] allowing viewers to believe that the geometric pattern beneath the dust represented the boundaries of the fields of Rrose Sélavy's "estate." What was initially designed as practice for Man Ray in recording a work in progress became a work of art in its own right. Man Ray framed it and André Breton wished to buy a print of it.

In 1933, Duchamp advised Salvador Dalí to ask Man Ray to take the photographs for an article by Dalí on Gaudí's architecture, to be published in Minotaure.[16] In theory, a photo spread highlighting the features of Gaudí's architectural style constituted a purely documentary exercise. Yet the photographs published in Minotaure are signed Man Ray. The two artists truly collaborated on the article, Man Ray's images being considered as important and creative as Dalí's text.

9) Yves Bonnefoy, Alberto Giacometti, Biographie d'une Oeuvre, Paris: Flammarion, 1991, p. 206.

10) Man Ray also performed the task of documentation — the negatives held by the Musée National d'Art Moderne include all his reproductions of works by Marcel Duchamp.

11) Man Ray, Self Portrait (1963), p. 91.

12) Even ten years later, the picture was reproduced in Cahiers d'Art with the caption, "Photograph by Man Ray of the glass composed by Marcel Duchamp from 1917 to 1921, titled The Bride Stripped Bare by her Bachelors, Even. Cahiers d'Art, no. 1–2, 1932, p. 60.

13) This document, currently in Lucien Treillard's collection, is Eluard's translation of a Man Ray article published under the title of "Sur le réalisme photographique" in Cahiers d'Art, no. 5–6, 1935, p. 120.

14) Letter dated December 29, 1922. Lucien Treillard collection.

15) In Self Portrait, Man Ray described how he took a bird's-eye shot of Duchamp's flat panel. Since it was lit by a single, bare bulb, he was obliged to leave the shutter open for an hour (during which time he and Duchamp went out for a meal).

16) Salvador Dalí, "De la beauté terrifiante et comestible de l'architecture Modern 'Style," Minotaure, no. 3–4, 1933, pp. 67-76.

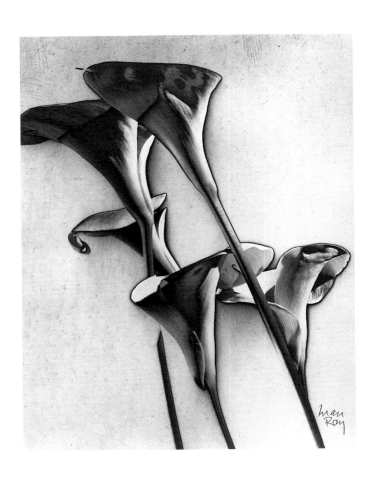
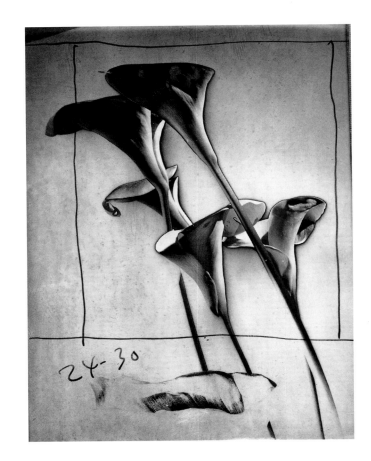

Les Arums [Arum Lilies], 1930

Study for *Les Arums* [Arum Lilies], 1930

Les Galets [Pebbles], circa 1933

"Holiday Snaps"

MNAM's Man Ray archives include many vacation pictures. It is probable that not all of them were taken by Man Ray — in the 1930s, the surrealists often vacationed together in the south of France, and Man Ray would lend his camera and develop photos taken by his friends. Included among the photographs taken on such occasions are a number of studied, carefully composed images of still lifes (a sunflower, for example, or the shadow of a balustrade). Some of those taken by Man Ray were published, notably in *Photography Is Not Art* (1937). Others, including highly successful portraits like the one of Eluard talking to Picasso, were published with no mention of the photographer. [17]

The part of this series that features card games and swimsuit poses on the beach reflects a vacation atmosphere devoid of originality, except on one point. The difference between surrealists and "ordinary" people probably owed much to the sexual freedom that reigned among the group. A certain amount of swapping and ostentatious debauchery went on — a few of Man Ray's contact prints show a tangle of nude bodies in positions that make it difficult to distinguish who is who.

Some of the photographs that have been classified as "documentation" were taken by Man Ray during boat trips. For example, he took a steep upward shot of the mast and rigging of a sailboat which was subsequently used as the cover of Lise Deharme's magazine, *Le Phare de Neuilly* (1933). Photographs produced in a "documentary" context, then, might subsequently turn out to be "artistic." The advantage of photography over other arts is its swiftness of execution. Man Ray appreciated this swiftness because it enabled him to concretize an idea the instant it came to mind.

PORTRAITS BY MAN RAY, ARTISAN AND ARTIST

Portraits make up the largest part of MNAM's Man Ray collection, giving the lie to a widespread belief that his portraiture was just a "sideline," [18] even though Neil Baldwin long ago stressed the fact that Man Ray not only possessed voluminous "files" but also proudly "claim[ed] to have 'taken' virtually everyone of note in [Paris] or passing through." [19] Until now, however, it has not been possible to verify this claim.

Man Ray liked to promote the idea that his portraiture was purely and simply a commercial affair. It is nevertheless worth recalling that Man Ray had already been enthusiastic about portraits when he was still a young man acquiring an interest in art and hanging out in museums. "Emmanuel was voracious in his appetite for portraits. More than anything else, he wanted to understand the play of light and color upon the contours of the human face." [20] As early as 1910, "he began to take commissions for portraiture in his studio room at home. His first client was a Mrs. Medvedev, who came by only once or twice to pose. . . . He began to dream of becoming a society painter who would do only beautiful ladies." [21]

It is therefore hardly surprising that, beginning with his earliest experiments in photography, Man Ray attempted portraits. It should be stressed that while necessity triggered his photographic career (i.e., the need for reproductions of his

17) London Bulletin, no. 1, April 1938, p. 17.

18) Janus, Man Ray, Oeuvres 1909–1972, Paris : Celiv, 1990, n.p.

19) Neil Baldwin, Man Ray, An American Artist, New York : Da Capo, p. 102.

20) Baldwin, p. 10.

21) Baldwin, p. 11.

Les Trois Fleurs [Three Flowers], 1931

paintings), it was interest and financial gain that spurred his first portraits. His models were his wife, Adon Lacroix, and her daughter, Esther. Man Ray reported in *Self Portrait* that he was "quite pleased" with the results, and that he felt the trade of portrait photographer would not impinge on his work as a painter insofar as his "painting had evolved to a degree where [he] would never consider painting a portrait."[22] Yet money was apparently not the sole motive behind this decision, the proof being the inclusion of a very early portrait — of Berenice Abbott — in an annual photography exhibition. It was Alfred Stieglitz himself, to whom Man Ray had shown the result of his photographic efforts, who advised him to participate in the Fifteenth Annual Exhibition of Photographs in Philadelphia in March 1921. Man Ray's portrait of Abbott was presented under the title of "Portrait of a Sculptor" (catalogue no. 648). He won honorable mention for this photograph, earning him a ten-dollar prize and publication in a local newspaper.[23]

This indicates that Man Ray was interested in portraiture from an *artistic* standpoint right from the start. Otherwise, why show his photographs to Stieglitz (who, more than anyone else at the turn of the century, promoted photography as an art),[24] and why participate in a photography show where only "artistic photographers" exhibited?

Man Ray stated — in *Self Portrait* once again — that while artists, painters, and writers posed for him, he charged no fee, which contradicts his purported desire to make portraiture his money-earner.

It was at this time, moreover, that he began to make a little money; Katherine Dreier asked him to photograph her collection and to serve as the official photographer of the Société Anonyme. The society also purchased his *Lampshade*, a work he showed at its first exhibition in 1920. Man Ray himself admitted that, for once, his "larder" was full.

Relatively few portraits from that period exist, among them several of Marcel Duchamp (starting in 1916, and as Rrose Sélavy from 1921), a double portrait of Duchamp and Joseph Stella (1920), Edgar Varèse (1920), and Mina Loy and Djuna Barnes (1920). In his autobiography Man Ray described how he sought distraction by inviting people to his studio "as a means of obtaining subjects for portraits. One day it was two handsome young women writers, Mina Loy and Djuna Barnes, the one in light tan clothes of her own design, the other all in black with a veil. They were stunning subjects — I photographed them together and the contrast made a fine picture."[25] MNAM's Man Ray archives contain individual portraits of the two women, but the negative of the double portrait described above has disappeared, as have many pictures from that period.

Working Methods

When he arrived in Paris on July 22, 1921,[26] Man Ray had little or no income. He therefore began photographing the canvases of his painter friends. It was Francis Picabia who encouraged him to pursue such activity, after which a number of artists called on his services. Man Ray stated that he always saved one unexposed plate for the end of the session, in order to do a portrait — uncommissioned — of the artist. He "saved the best for last," as the saying goes, the portrait being done for pleasure.

22) *Man Ray, Self Portrait (1963), p. 87.*

23) *This information, taken from Baldwin, p. 71, has not be verified by this author.*

24) *Alfred Stieglitz founded the Photo-Secession group, which published the periodical Camera Work starting in 1903 and opened the 291 Gallery in 1905.*

25) *Man Ray, Self Portrait (1963), p. 98.*

26) *The often-cited arrival date of July 14 is erroneous. See Marcel Duchamp, Ephémerides, Milan : Bompiani, 1993, entry for July 22.*

Studios

Man Ray set up his first studio in the room he occupied in the Grand Hôtel des Ecoles at 15 Rue Delambre in December 1921. Several contact prints in the MNAM archives nevertheless suggest that he produced portraits as soon as he arrived in Paris. Whereas the Rue Delambre studio was already "professionally" equipped (Gertrude Stein's *Autobiography of Alice B. Toklas* records that Man Ray "had three large cameras, he had several kinds of lighting, he had a window screen, and in a little closet he did all his developing" [27]), several portraits in the archives were clearly taken in natural light only, with the aperture opened wide, as indicated by the artist on the contact prints : "F 5-5." These portraits, moreover, lack contrast and are rather dark, suggesting that Man Ray perhaps photographed several (unidentified) people when he was living either at the hotel on Rue de Boulainvilliers or, more probably, in the small servant's room above Marcel Duchamp and Yvonne Chastel's place at 12 Rue de La Condamine. These early portraits represent experiments ; Man Ray noted the f-stop on every image, in order to compare the prints later. Perhaps he was testing a new camera. It is known that Man Ray arrived in Paris with a Graflex as his sole photographic tool. By the end of his life, in contrast, he owned a great number of cameras. It is therefore possible that shortly after his arrival in Paris he had the opportunity to buy or try another one, these contact prints being the results of his tests.

Man Ray's installation of a veritable photo studio coincided with a show of his paintings at Librairie Six, December 3 – 31, 1921, where not a single work was sold. Only then did he realize that he would soon have to find a source of income other than painting. Photography, notably portraiture, which he had already been practicing for several years and for which his services were frequently solicited, seemed like the ideal solution.

Several contact prints in the MNAM archives date from this early period, recognizable by the use of an armchair that must have been part of the hotel furniture, plus a burlap curtain behind the sitter. The room's modest dimensions are indicated by the obvious closeness of photographer and sitter — here the frame never extends much beyond the armchair, whereas in later, improved circumstances Man Ray preferred to maintain greater distance from the person being photographed. Lee Miller commented that he was always at least ten to twelve feet from his sitter. [28] During a 1951 interview with Daniel Masclet, Man Ray stated that he used a long focal distance of 360 millimeters for his 9 x 12 plates — "that way, I can sometimes place myself a long way from my sitter, in order to obtain an absolutely perfect 'drawing,' with which Monsieur Ingres himself could not quibble." [29] He would then crop the face on the contact sheet and enlarge the final print, for he had observed that if he came too close to the face when taking the photograph, the sitter's nose assumed vast proportions in relation to the ears. Man Ray preferred to model the face through lighting rather than through optical distortion. It should also be noted that Stieglitz, who certainly must have acted as adviser during Man Ray's photographic debut, systematically cropped his own prints early in his career. Stieglitz deliberately took his photographs from a distance and subsequently used just part of the negative when printing.

27) Gertrude Stein, The Autobiography of Alice B. Toklas, Harmondsworth : Penguin, 1966, p. 212.

28) "My Man Ray — An Interview with Lee Miller Penrose by Mario Amaya," Art in America, May-June 1975, p. 59.

29) "Man Ray l'enchanteur—Interview de Daniel Masclet," Photo-France, no. 10, November 1951, p. 31.

Man Ray remained in the Rue Delambre hotel for only a few months, from November 1921 to July 1922. Yet that is where he seriously launched his "commercial" activities. Success came swiftly, since within six months the increase in clients justified and permitted investment in a studio. It was also on Rue Delambre that Man Ray discovered the rayograph technique, in late 1921 or early 1922. One rayograph, moreover, is composed of the key to his room, number 37, and a pistol — as though Man Ray, then aged 32, was giving himself five years to make it big or die.

Man Ray photographed the cream of Paris society before he even had his own studio. Usually, he photographed these celebrities in their homes, as was the case with Jean Cocteau (1921), the marquise Casati (winter 1921–1922), and Gertrude Stein (winter 1921–1922). For one thing, he liked to place them in their personal environment, which tended to produce an image of the sitter that was both intimate and "authentic." Further, he was probably embarrassed to receive such "important" people in his modest lodgings. Cocteau and Stein, for example, merited a certain consideration — Cocteau would provide Man Ray with an entrée not only to aristocratic circles, but also to theatrical and musical circles. Stein, meanwhile, introduced Man Ray to her many artist friends whose work she collected, including Georges Braque, Pablo Picasso, and Juan Gris.

With this latter group, Man Ray proceeded differently. As stressed above, he went to their respective studios to photograph their paintings. The contact prints in the MNAM archives nevertheless tend to demonstrate that in the case of Braque, it was the artist that Man Ray wanted to photograph. Then came the writers. It is not known how Man Ray met Sylvia Beach, but whatever the case, he was part of the crowd that filled Adrienne Monnier's bookstore on Rue de l'Odéon on December 7, 1921, to listen to James Joyce give a reading from his forthcoming novel, *Ulysses*. [30] In January 1922, Beach, as Joyce's publisher, sent him to Man Ray to pose for a portrait. Joyce is seen sitting in front of a burlap cloth, apparently uneasy before the camera, giving Man Ray the impression that he was performing a chore. Man Ray went on to photograph many American writers, and the walls of the bookstore Shakespeare and Company were covered with his portraits of Ezra Pound, T. S. Eliot, Winifred Bryher, H.D. (Hilda Doolittle), Marsden Hartley, Kay Boyle, Sinclair Lewis, Ernest Hemingway, Djuna Barnes, Robert McAlmon, Gertrude Stein, and more.

In July 1922, Man Ray moved to 31 bis Rue Campagne-Première, organizing the studio "to receive visitors and handle the increasing amount of work." [31] His business grew. By November 1923, he was in a position to rent several rooms that comprised "a charming little flat" in the Hôtel Istria, 29 Rue Campagne-Première. His studio was henceforth devoted solely to photographic work. In *Self Portrait*, Man Ray commented that it was Kiki who found the new apartment, complete "with heat and a bathroom, which was rare in Paris."

Taking the Picture

The quality of a photograph depends above all on the process of taking the picture. Man Ray managed to obtain a natural pose from his sitters swiftly and simply. Roland Penrose has described a session as follows : "It was as quick and

30) Baldwin, p. 100.

31) Man Ray, Self Portrait (1963), p. 146.

Terrain Vague [*Waste Land*], 1932

Study for *Terrain Vague* [*Waste Land*], 1932

Study for *Terrain Vague* [*Waste Land*], 1932

Nusch Eluard, circa 1935

32) Baldwin, p. 101.

33) "Man Ray l'enchanteur...", p. 32.

34) Meret Oppenheim interviewed by Billy Klüver and Jill Krauskopf, December 11, 1979, Lucien Treillard Collection.

35) André Breton, "The Visages of the Woman," Photographs by Man Ray 1920 Paris 1934, trans. anon., Hartford, Conn : James Thrall Soby, 1934. Dover reprint, New York, 1979, between pp. 42/43.

36) Man Ray, personal notes contained in the MNAM archives.

37) Robert Desnos, "Man Ray ou 'vous pouvez courir'," original typescript preserved at the Fonds Doucet. The text was first published in Paris-Journal on December 13, 1924, p. 5, then translated into English by Maria McD. Jolas and published as "The Work of Man Ray" in transition, no. 15, February 1929, pp. 264-266, from which this and following quotations are drawn.

38) Philippe Soupault, Mémoires de l'Oubli, 1923–1926, Paris : Lachenal & Ritter, 1986, pp. 29–30.

casual as bantering with him in a café. All he used to say was, 'Show your teeth'... he didn't fiddle forever with the lens or the lights." [32] Man Ray himself confirmed this approach in his interview with Daniel Masclet. "Don't tire your sitter, do everything quickly, in ten minutes, don't make it seem like work." [33] In fact, Man Ray prepared all his equipment (lighting, background, camera) before his "client" arrived.

A certain interventionism nevertheless emerges from Meret Oppenheim's account : "He didn't start shooting right away. He knew what he wanted — he'd say, 'Sit there,' and then he'd set up reflectors, umbrella, lights. 'Turn this way or that way ... Moisten your lips ... Open your eyes.' (Just before taking a picture, he asked you to close your eyes so that they seemed natural when you opened them ....) Then he changed the lights, and so on, all before taking any photos .... Above all, he was interested in the lighting. He was very professional. He had a precise idea of what he wanted. When he worked, his movements were paced ... he worked calmly and spoke little, except to ask you to shift your pose, and so forth." [34]

As Breton pointed out, Man Ray had "the eye of a great hunter, the patience, the sense of the moment pathetically right when a balance, transient besides, occurred in the expression of a face, between dream and action." [35] Surprisingly, the MNAM archives reveal that Man Ray was not a "machine-gunning" photographer — he took just a few shots during any given session. The number of images per sitter varies from two to 12, with a quantitative increase that corresponds to his growing success. By the late 1920s, clients were regularly entitled to a dozen shots, which is hardly excessive, reflecting Man Ray's comment that "if photographers wasted less film, they might perhaps think less of breaking even, and more of Art." [36]

Like Breton, Robert Desnos described Man Ray's "power" of capturing that moment between consciousness and unconsciousness. "He arrives between two shocks of an earthquake, stops creation on the peak of a plunge, immediately before the return to the normal position. He catches faces at that fugitive moment between two expressions. Life is not present in his pictures and still there is nothing dead about them. There is a pause, a stop, only : Man Ray is the painter of the syncope." [37]

It is significant that it was Desnos who provided this "definition" of Man Ray. The moment between life and death as represented by a "syncope," that is to say a faint or temporary black-out, is related to surrealist experimentation. When it came to their notorious occult seances, which they called "sleep experiments," Desnos was the most amazing participant. Philippe Soupault described how, one evening, Desnos "fell into a sleep [and] began to prophesy. He was highly excited, feverish even, beside himself. He spoke uninterruptedly, and seizing a pencil began to write phrases and puns ...." [38] Man Ray did not participate in these encounters, but they were well known. Moreover, he had a number of people pose first with their eyes closed, then open (Kay Boyle in 1934, Nusch Eluard in 1935), as though he wanted to "reveal" them in that instant of unconsciousness. Desnos explained how, as "a photographer, Man Ray derives neither from artistic deformation, nor from the servile reproduction of 'nature.' Your planes and humps will reveal to you a person you do not know, and whom you have never dared glimpse in your dreams. A new 'you' will spring from the delicate hands of the

Nusch Eluard, circa 1935

chemist in the red glow of the [darkroom]. It will bat its eyes out in the open air, the way night birds do." [39]

In his typically provocative manner, Man Ray explained his working method to Daniel Masclet. "First of all, little in the way of commercial smiles! If you look at a portrait for a long time (you know, of the 'now smile' variety), the smile soon becomes a nightmarish grin.... Naturalness? It's the height of artifice! I give all the orders, directing everything in the studio, I don't leave anything to the client's wishes. Why? It couldn't be simpler: the client knows absolutely nothing about it, since he has only been photographed twice in his life, whereas I study photography every day. So it's obvious that my opinion should prevail. This is the only method that has produced good results, but ... sometimes it takes years of study to know how to *recreate* naturalness." [40] Indeed, the MNAM archives confirm that Man Ray never instructed his clients to smile. There is even one series in which the only picture showing the young woman with a smile is crossed out.

Half-length oil portraits sometimes presented a "problem" for both artists and sitters in that the latter, not completely at ease, did not know what to do with their hands. In order to lend their sitters greater composure, painters (usually) gave gloves to men and a fan to women. As Walter Benjamin noted as early as 1931 in his "*Short History of Photography,*" photographic portraiture was not only influenced by painting, but also by the constraints of the young medium of photography. "The accessories of such portraits ... still recall the time when, due to the long exposure, the subject required supports in order to remain still." Although head braces and supports sufficed at first, famous paintings and a desire to look "artistic" soon spurred the use of other accessories. First of all came columns and curtains. The most enlightened critics denounced these abuses as early as the 1860s. Thus a specialized English review pointed out that whereas a column retained an appearance of authenticity in a painting, in a photograph it seemed absurd because it was usually set on a carpet. Yet no one believed that a column of marble or stone had a carpet for a base. [41]

Column and curtain are props that recur in the work of Man Ray. There is one major difference, however: instead of a marble column, he used a wine-press screw; rather than a superb velvet curtain, he used a plain burlap cloth. Furthermore, Man Ray's range of props was more extensive and more original. Above all, these props played an additional role — they gave his photographs a second meaning, or at least planted the seeds of additional significance, opening a window onto Man Ray's own imaginative realm.

One of Man Ray's frequently recurring props is a life-sized hand, or rather forearm, of dark wood, which he especially liked his female sitters to hold. These women — whether anonymous or known, such as Lise Deharme — present the forearm in various ways: placed vertically on a table, parallel to the bust, like the hand of justice (*Lise Deharme as Queen of Spades*, 1935); the palm of the wooden hand placed against the woman's cheek in a natural gesture, as though it were her own hand (itself hidden underneath a shawl); or held perpendicularly to the face, wooden fingers pointing at the temple. Jean-Charles Worth, posing bare-chested, placed the hand in front of his face, partly hiding it. This wooden hand, also seen in photographs of jewelry published in *Harper's Bazaar* (1935), probably came from a clothes dummy. The partial replacement of the human body by a

39) Desnos, p. 265.

40) "Man Ray l'enchanteur...," p. 31.

41) Walter Benjamin, "A Short History of Photography," trans. Stanley Mitchell, Screen, vol. 13, no. 1, Spring 1972, p. 18.

George Antheil, 1924

piece of wood denies photographic portraiture the realism normally expected of it.

Other props recur in Man Ray's portraits, notably the neck of a cello (nicknamed "Emak Bakia") on which he himself leaned in a self-portrait and which appears in several portraits of Jacqueline Goddard. Man Ray also used a simple stick of wood (a series of poses with Luis Buñuel shows how he employed it as a veritable compositional device). In both cases, however, it should be noted that the prop served the same function as head-braces in the previous century.

Man Ray's own musical instrument, the banjo, appears in a certain number of photographs. The portrait of Ernest Hemingway is the best-known example, but others exist, such as the singer Yvonne George, Juan Gris, and Kiki. Most of these portraits predate 1925. The banjo, usually independent of the sitter, is part of the background composition, a round shape recalling the sitter's head. In the case of Yvonne George, the musical instrument also functions as a reference to her profession.

As mentioned above, one of the most famous of Man Ray's portrait props was a press screw. The most celebrated use, of course, was for the portrait of Sinclair Lewis (1926), but the object recurs in portraits of Lucien Vogel (c. 1928) and the Spanish dancer Rolanda (c. 1928), among others. Just as in oil portraits, the column plays a compositional role here. Yet it is also tempting to ascribe a meaning to it — surely Man Ray used the press screw precisely because it related to his sitter in some way. Indeed, when Sinclair Lewis arrived in Man Ray's studio, he was drunk and thus his head was "spinning" (*le vis*, French for "screw," is perhaps a pun on Lewis). Lucien Vogel, meanwhile, "pressed" Man Ray for commissioned work for his magazine, *Vu*. And the Spanish dancer Rolanda would constantly spin while dancing, thereby turning the heads of her audience.

The use of various props furthermore proves that Man Ray composed his images with a great deal of care when it came to details and construction. His training as a painter played a key role here, and the influence of classical painting, visible for that matter in other aspects of his photography, is related to this way of working. Other examples of that influence exist : it is worth noting that Man Ray's portraits often incorporate a checkerboard pattern (which, when it comes to Man Ray, might be called a chessboard pattern), either as a backdrop (*George Antheil*, 1924), as a rug for full-length portraits (*Peggy Guggenheim*, 1925), or as a tablecloth for a half-length photograph (with the sitter's elbows on the table). The checkered floor evokes old masters who painted marble flooring in order to create perspective, although Man Ray was not seeking that effect when he used the pattern. Rather, he wanted to demonstrate his determination to produce a highly composed image orchestrated by what is the very essence of photography — contrasts in light, which are stronger than ever in black and white.

Man Ray's "do-it-yourself" approach is perceptible in many contact prints (whereas final, cropped prints exclude the paraphernalia required to produce the image). He clearly used everything at hand to produce a "good" portrait. He did not hesitate, for instance, to make a client sit on a trunk if necessary, or to use a camera tripod as an armrest.

There was nothing extraordinary about the furnishings in Man Ray's studio in the early 1920s — a simple upholstered armchair, a Biedermeier chair, and one of the gilded chairs commonly used by haute couture houses for guests at fashion

George Antheil, 1924

shows. Later, Man Ray would employ all kinds of wooden chests of varying heights, on which clients would lean or place an elbow, whether seated or standing. Using these chests meant that nothing inhibited the sitter's movements or crowded the image. And on certain occasions they could even serve as an integral part of the composition, as seen in a double portrait of Gala and Dalí (1936). By the late 1920s, the studio also boasted an armchair that Man Ray made himself. Only rarely did he use it in portraits, however, one of the sole examples being that of Balthus.

Man Ray and his assistants : darkroom work.

In the spring of 1923, Berenice Abbott knocked on Man Ray's door, in search of work. According to Neil Baldwin, Man Ray already had an assistant, a young man who "thought he knew everything" and therefore created problems. Abbott meanwhile, had everything to learn, and Man Ray hired her.

The darkroom upstairs was where, "for 15 francs a day, Berenice Abbott spent long hours 'doing everything after Man Ray took his picture' — [such as] developing and printing, which she learned quickly during just a few weeks of practice under Man Ray's subtle teaching-by-doing instruction."[42]

Starting early in 1923, then, Man Ray's assistants performed a fairly complete range of tasks ; from developing negatives to printing the final results, they followed instructions given by the artist. Man Ray thereby delegated a large part of the darkroom work at an early date. He took the pictures, which he then passed on to his assistant for developing. He was very meticulous, however, and his contacts, which he printed himself, bore notations concerning cropping (noted in pencil or ink, although sometimes the contacts were even folded[43]), the dimensions of the print, the type of paper, the contrasts to be brought out, and so on. His eye was so precise and surgical that his assistants had merely to execute the "master's" instructions. Man Ray's appetite for work nevertheless remained enormous. Baldwin even claims that he had an "an antipathy to idleness."[44] As a child raised in modest circumstances, he saw his parents work themselves to the bone. And the number of portraits he produced demonstrates that his studio was always busy. Thus it appears unlikely that the artist abandoned all darkroom work. He probably doubled up on darkroom sessions with his assistant. This does not exclude the possibility that Man Ray occasionally allowed his assistant to take the photographs of lesser clients. According to Lucien Treillard, when Man Ray found himself in the Basque country, he asked Jacques-André Boiffard (his assistant from 1924 to 1929) to handle one (or several) sittings.

The question of cropping is primordial to Man Ray's work. At first sight it would seem that he only thought about the final framing once the photograph had been taken, on studying the contact print, for the sole purpose of *composing* the image. Certain works, however — and not always portraits — reveal to the contrary that he already had an accurate idea of the ultimate frame he intended, proving that the goal of the operation was also to produce a grainier image. The almost total absence of sharpness produced a quality of softness in prints, often done on textured paper, that typifies Man Ray's oeuvre.

This was the case, for example, in the photograph of a nude seen from the

42) Baldwin, 115.

43) It might be added that Man Ray occasionally marked cropping indications on the negative, using the storage pouch to avoid defacing the original.

44) Baldwin, p. 103.

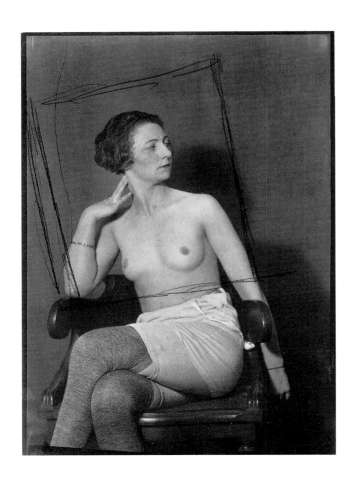

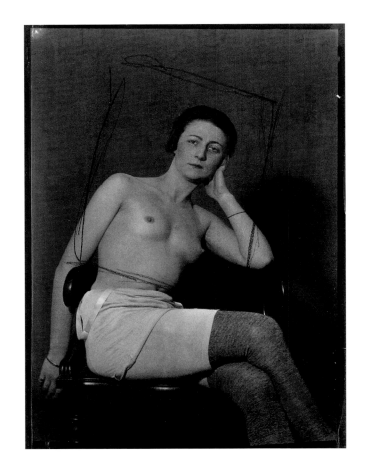

Madeleine Turban, circa 1925

Madeleine Turban, circa 1925

Detail from a self-portrait, circa 1930

back, commonly called *Dos Blanc* ("White Back"), published in James Thrall Soby's album in 1934.[45] The negative shows, on the one hand, that the model was kneeling (not apparent in the print) and that, on the other hand, her knees rested on a cushion for greater comfort. Since it seems obvious here that Man Ray never intended to show the model kneeling — had that been the case, he would have removed the cushion, which is pointless and even detrimental to the image — it can be concluded that right from the start he knew exactly how he was going to crop the image.

Retouching [46]

Man Ray practiced photographic portraiture differently from his contemporaries. They wanted to produce images that were sharp and pure, free from any touching up, often taken in close-up or from a particular angle. Man Ray, however, did not subject himself to any rule. In 1951 he told Daniel Masclet that he almost never did any touching up. "Retouching? I do it as little as possible, that is to say almost never…! That should be left to … photographers who are unable to sell a portrait without retouching it."[47] Here Man Ray was not being candid, for the MNAM archives prove the contrary: not only did Man Ray frequently touch up his negatives, but he did it especially for portraits, including self-portraits. At the time, however, retouching was considered shameful. Walter Benjamin even claimed in his 1931 *Short History of Photography* that when "the practice of touching up the negative became widespread (the bad painter's revenge on photography), a sharp decline in taste set in."[48]

Note, however, that the practice existed right from the birth of photography, since even paper negatives were retouched.

Retouching was done in pencil on the emulsion side of the plate, usually to eliminate wrinkles and minor skin blemishes. One of Man Ray's self-portraits is completely retouched — the face is literally furrowed with pencil lines.[49] The lines vary in heaviness, being light on the forehead but heavier under the eyes and around the mouth — a veritable face-lift! The delicateness of this retouching work (done with the aid of a magnifying glass) reveals Man Ray's exceptional deftness.

Although negatives in the MNAM archives occasionally contain retouching done in pencil directly on the emulsion, most of the time Man Ray first covered the entire negative with a greasy medium composed of gum and turpentine. Custom dictated that this substance be applied with an old cloth, using a circular motion from the center outward. But Man Ray flaunted custom, usually ignoring this principle by roughly plastering the product over his plates. His lack of interest in the technique can be explained by the fact that the effect remained absolutely invisible on the print. Usually Man Ray applied the substance only to the oval of the face. Remarkably, if unwittingly on Man Ray's part, this medium protected the emulsion from the air and spared the negatives from the chemical degradation of silver salts.

Although touching up was usually done to hide blemishes, it could also be an additive designed to modify the original model. This was the case, for instance, in a

45) Photographs by Man Ray 1920 Paris 1934, *Hartford, Conn: James Thrall Soby, 1934. Dover reprint, New York, 1979, p. 27.*

46) *The author would particularly like to thank M. Ronceray for his valuable technical explanations.*

47) *"Man Ray l'enchanteur," p. 31.*

48) *Benjamin, p. 18. André Gunthert's French translation of Benjamin's text ("Une Petite Histoire de la Photographie," Etudes Photographiques, no. 1, November 1996) nevertheless stresses in a footnote that, "In fact, the theory of the increase in retouching as a sign of photographic decadence… is clearly devoid of historical basis, and stems from the old curse that strikes the practice — ever shameful, but ever present — of manual intervention on the photographic subjectile." Benjamin, p. 33, note 34.*

49) *Negatives AM 1995–281 (74), (75), and 76 from the Lucien Treillard Bequest.*

50) Daniel Masclet's "Man Ray l'enchanteur," p. 26, quotes Man Ray as saying : "I don't know what a 'good' photo is. Unless it's one I like. (But I don't think a photo is bad simply because I don't like it.) To produce an authentic photo.... "

51) "Man Ray l'enchanteur," p. 32.

Untitled, circa 1930

nude image of Kiki. As Man Ray mentioned in *Self Portrait*, Kiki was distressed because she had no pubic hair. The artist remedied this situation by sketching it on the plate — the lines of black pencil are drawn in such a fashion that when printed, the area seems marked by shadow and light. It was more a question of discreet effect than of veritable drawing, for that matter.

Man Ray employed other retouching techniques, which entailed removing emulsion. The surface is scraped away to create a hole of light in the image (which becomes a black hole on printing). Man Ray etched the emulsion with the aid of a sewing machine needle with a beveled point. One of the most interesting examples in the MNAM archives is a negative taken when Man Ray visited the count and countess de Noailles in Hyères. After photographing their villa — designed by Robert Mallet-Stevens — he cut away part of the emulsion on the triangular flag flying from the roof.

It was also in this series, taken when he was making the film *Mystères du château de Dé* in 1929, that another negative was retouched with red chalk powder. Once again it was a photograph of the villa, but this time Man Ray wanted to give greater density to the sky by depicting clouds. This retouching was done, however, on the material substrate, that is to say on the glass side of the plate.

Man Ray thus violated one of the basic laws of what has been called "the new photography," which held that photographs should remain "pure." Instead, he worked as nineteenth-century photographers might have, or even neighbourhood studio portraitists. Yet he won almost instant recognition as an avant-garde photographer, and he participated in international exhibitions such as the *Film und Foto* show in Stuttgart in 1929. One of the reasons for his "popularity" is that Man Ray did not disclose his methods. He did so much later, but even then, as already noted, he was capable of lying. He thought that any means justified the ends when it came to a "good" photograph, or rather an "authentic" photograph. [50]

Thus he also employed over-exposure. "I often over-expose my portraits by a factor of three or four — the outcome is very soft on the face. I don't mean that I employ long exposure times. A hundredth of a second can be over-exposed threefold or more ; it depends on the amount of given luminosity ... [.] Just as I usually expose longer than other photographers, so I use blacks much less, the latter often being the consequence of the former. That's because, you see, too many photographers naively think that it's the blacks — "rich blacks," they say — that lend strength. In reality, blacks no more give vigor to a photo than "strong" drinks give a man strength ! So I've never added alcohol to my pictures." [51]

Kiki, circa 1924

Kiki, circa 1924

Étienne de Beaumont, 1925

Étienne de Beaumont, 1925

Jacqueline Goddard, 1932

Jacqueline Goddard, 1932

Yves Tanguy, 1936

Yves Tanguy, 1936

Nancy Cunard, 1926

Nancy Cunard, 1926

Jacqueline Goddard, 1932

Jacqueline Goddard, 1932

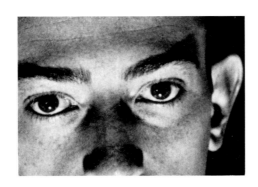

Salvador Dalí, 1929

Salvador Dalí, 1929

La Lune Brille sur l'île de Nias, circa 1924

Portrait of a woman with *La Lune Brille sur l'île de Nias*, circa 1924

Jean-Charles Worth, circa 1925

Untitled, circa 1935

Blanc et Noir [White and Black], circa 1929

Blanc et Noir [White and Black], circa 1929

Chevelures [Hair], 1937

Kiki, circa 1925

Le Baiser [The Kiss], circa 1932

Ady and Nusch, 1937

Lee Miller, circa 1930

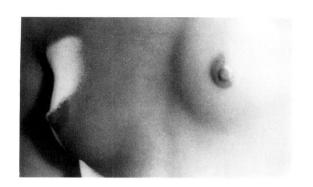

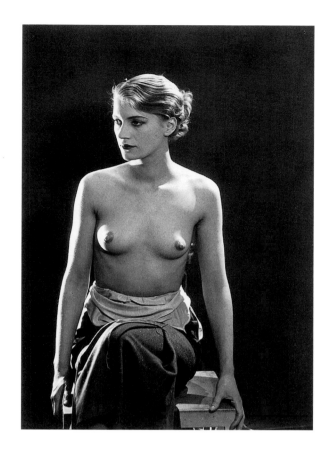

Lee Miller [Breasts], circa 1930

Lee Miller, circa 1930

Lee Miller, circa 1930

Meret Oppenheim, 1933

Self-Portrait with Meret Oppenheim, 1933

Self-Portrait with Meret Oppenheim, 1933

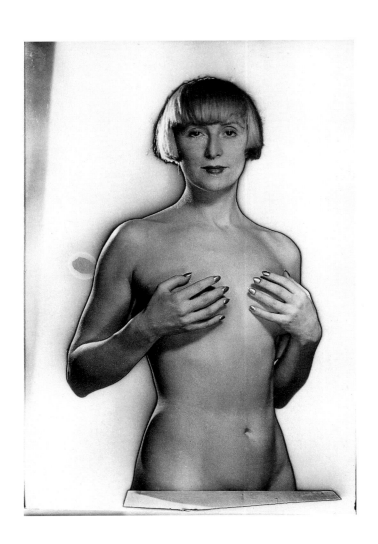

Suzy Solidor, 1929

Suzy Solidor, 1929

Nude, circa 1935

DELINEATING REALITY

Photographic Creativity

Alongside his everyday "commercial" work, Man Ray did his utmost to break the frame of conventional photography. His photographic "tinkering" and manipulations led to (re)discoveries such as rayographs in 1922 and solarization in 1929. He also implemented a range of effects like superimposition (of two exposures or of a screen over the negative), deformation created by moving the paper during printing, inversion of values, and more. He created illusion through props such as the drops of glass that he stuck below the eyes of the sitter in *Larmes* [*Tears*]. He constructed, composed, envisaged and invented a different photography, namely a surrealist one : pictures were veiled, blurry, or printed in negative ; the outlines of the sitter were electrified ; back became front, shadow overtook light. All means were justified in attaining his end — to delineate reality. There were no rules, no taboos, just the pleasure of playing with the very essence of photography. Creativity began where reproduction ended.

Kiki, circa 1926

Kiki, 1926

Edward James, 1937

Edward James, 1937

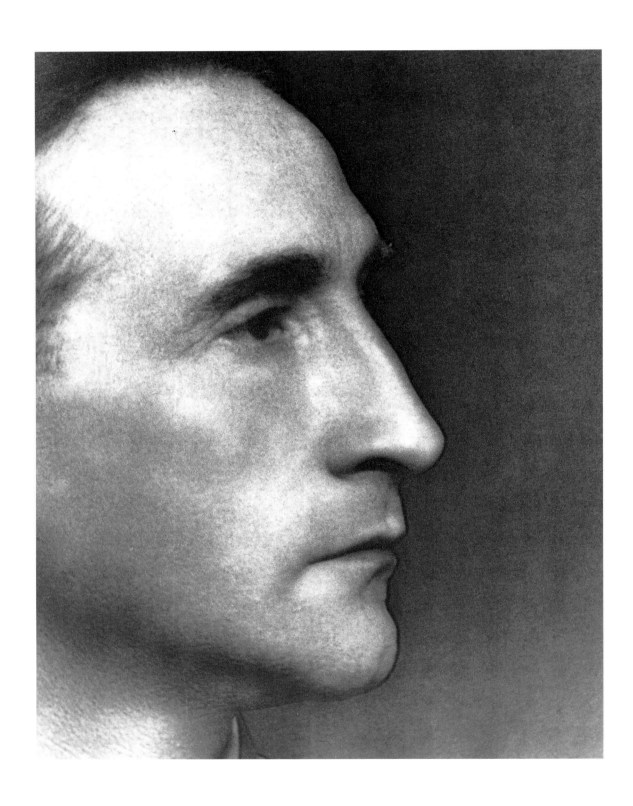

Marcel Duchamp, 1930

Untitled, circa 1930

1) Excerpted from Emmanuelle de l'Ecotais, Le Fonds Photographique de la Dation Man Ray, étude et inventaire, PhD dissertation, Université de Paris IV (Sorbonne), 1997.

2) Pierre Vaisse, "Portrait de société, anonymat et célébrité," in Michel Frizot (ed), Nouvelle Histoire de la Photographie, Paris : Bordas–Adam Biro, 1994, p. 499.

3) Vaisse, p. 499.

4) The practice of copying photographs has existed since the dawn of the medium. In Nouvelle Histoire de la Photographie, p. 361, Pierre Albert and Gilles Feyel stress that the first engraved copy of a daguerreotype was published in L'Illustration in 1848, while the first copy of a paper photograph appeared in 1853.

5) June 1922, p. 7.

6) July 1922, p. 76.

7) July 1922, p. 76.

8) August 1922, p. 72.

9) May 1923, p. 74.

10) May 1925, p. 75.

11) July 1926, p. 70.

12) May 1927, p. 79.

13) April 1930, p. 72

14) October 1922, p. 46.

Art and Portraiture

Emmanuelle de l'Ecotais [1]

The Impact of Illustrated Magazines

The expansion of Man Ray's portrait business owes a great deal to the rise of illustrated magazines. It is worth recalling that magazines were only just beginning to reproduce photographs at that time. It was the "discovery of photoengraving techniques that could finally be used for illustrating books and periodicals" which spurred a "new and massive demand" just after the First World War. [2] And "the launching of magazines specializing in high society, fashion, and entertainment — such as *Vogue, Vanity Fair*, and *Harper's Bazaar* — had a profound influence on portraiture." [3] It should be added, however, that the cost of paper prevented many magazines from taking advantage of the new process, which required a high quality paper that only lavish reviews could afford. As a consequence, in the early 1920s, weeklies such as *Paris-Journal* were still using more drawings than photographs. For this reason, it is enlightening to compare a few hand-drawn portraits to Man Ray's photographic portraits. Examining, for example, the portrait of Erik Satie drawn by Francis Picabia and published in 1924 in *Paris-Journal*, it is clear that Picabia used Man Ray's 1922 photograph as a model — pose, composition, and everything else seem "based" on the photographic image. The same is true for portraits of Tristan Tzara and Matisse. [4]

Things were different at *Vanity Fair*. The magazine was run by Frank Crowninshield (1872-1947), a man highly involved in the New York art scene as a member of the board of directors of the Museum of Modern Art. Crowninshield wanted *Vanity Fair* to reflect the artistic and technical developments of the day. It was thus a "society" magazine with a cultural bent, featuring music, theater, literature, painting, and photography. *Vanity Fair* was the first magazine to publish Man Ray's Paris portraits, starting in June 1922. Every issue featured artists or writers in a section headed, "We Nominate for the Hall of Fame." Thanks to portraits by Man Ray, the magazine presented, in the following order, Tristan Tzara, [5] Pablo Picasso, [6] James Joyce, [7] Gertrude Stein, [8] Augustus John, [9] Sinclair Lewis, [10] Sherwood Anderson, [11] André Derain, [12] Le Corbusier, [13] and more.

Furthermore, *Vanity Fair* devoted an entire page to various existing portraits of the marquise Casati, in which Man Ray's famous "blurred" photograph featured prominently alongside an oil portrait by Augustus John and a sculpted head by Jacob Epstein. [14] Photography was thus raised to the same level as other art forms, with a caption describing the "striking" portrait in which Man Ray revealed Casati's "gift of double vision." Study of the various painted portraits of the marquise, moreover, suggests that Man Ray's version of events (according to which his picture was the felicitous result of a technical error) is unlikely. Indeed, most portraits of the day reveal Casati's dark gaze, her heavily made-up eyes often marked by bags (see Romaine Brook's *La Marquise Casati*). It would seem more plausible to think that Man Ray, wanting to present the best possible image of his sitter, devised this way of simultaneously flattering the marquise and embodying her "gift of double vision."

Frédéric Mégret, 1929

Edward James, 1937   *Edward James*, 1937

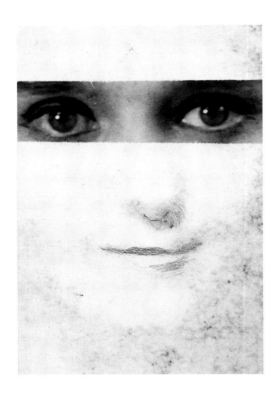

For Aragon's *Aurélien*, circa 1930

Vogue, meanwhile, only began publishing Man Ray's portraits in 1924. It should also be pointed out that this magazine was more devoted to Parisian high society life than to the arts. Here Man Ray mainly published portraits of marchionesses, countesses, duchesses and other "ladies" of the day. These portraits were mostly produced in what today appears to be a "classic," not to say pictorialist, manner — the female silhouette is generally set against a golden or shimmering background, the face bathed in soft light. Man Ray nevertheless worked to give his sitters a natural pose or posture, and it is precisely this "unaffected elegance" that made him so popular.

By the year 1925, Man Ray was able to charge 1,000 francs per sitting. Only a few eccentrics allowed him to follow his own inspiration when photographing them, as was the case with the marquise Casati, mentioned above, and Lady Abdy, "one of the foreign high society beauties residing in France" who was also a rather exuberant woman according to what was said here and there. Such a sitter tolerated a certain originality while Man Ray was shooting — she posed frontally, elbows on a table, face held in her hands. She even allowed the publication of this photograph in the pages of *Vogue*, an unusual gesture for that time. [15]

As we have observed, Man Ray's approach was adapted to the client. Theater personalities (Léna Amsel, Paulette Pac, and Marcel Herrand) and dancers were shown in costume, as exemplified by Vicente Escudero, a Spanish dancer photographed at the Rue Campagne-Première studio in 1928. Dressed in his stage costume, he seems to be "dancing" for Man Ray as opposed to simply posing for the photographer. Man Ray managed to reproduce the effect of movement through shadows cast by several lamps, creating sophisticated lighting designed to satisfy publications announcing the famous dancer's performance at the Pleyel concert hall. Movement thus assumes all its scope here not because it is decomposed, but rather because, lit by several lamps, Escudero's pose endlessly echoes across the walls, creating the impression of movement.

"Bread-and-butter" portraits

Two categories of portraits must be distinguished within Man Ray's work: those he did with interest, sensitivity, attention, and creativity, and those he produced mechanically. The distinction came naturally to Man Ray. Tourists — people who wanted "family portraits" or who, more generally, did not interest Man Ray — received a portrait that met their expectations: a good, technically competent likeness. The results were "fitting," but Man Ray invested little talent in them. Most of the unidentified portraits in the MNAM archives are of this type, totaling a third of the collection (1,651 unidentified portraits out of 5,004 contact prints preserved).

In contrast, other portraits betray all the artist's sensibility. Man Ray's sharp mind and eye created a veritable pantheon of men and women who left their mark on the times. Yet many of his fine portraits are of quite ordinary people. In both instances, however, Man Ray took a liking to a face, a character, or an achievement. Daniel Masclet has said that portraitists must have "an understanding and a love of faces." [16] Man Ray had that love of faces right from youth, but he had chosen to be an artist, and people whom he felt did not recognize him as such became

15) Vogue, vol. 6, no. 8, August 1, 1925, p. 26.

16) Daniel Masclet, Réflexions sur le Portrait en Photographie, Paris : Publications Photo-Revue, 1971, p. 15.

17) See previous chapter, "'Authentic' Photography," p. 71.

18) Roland Barthes, La Chambre Claire : Note sur la Photographie, Paris : Cahiers du Cinéma, Gallimard, Le Seuil, 1980, p. 18.

19) "Man Ray l'enchanteur—Interview de Daniel Masclet," Photo-France, no. 10, November 1951, p. 32.

20) "Man Ray l'enchanteur. . .," p. 26.

21) Letter preserved in the Man Ray archives, Musée National d'Art Moderne, Paris.

22) Pierre Mac Orlan (born Pierre Dumarchey, 1882–1970) was part of the group around Guillaume Apollinaire and Max Jacob. He wrote works in which reality merges with imagination (Quai des brumes, 1927) and was also greatly interested in photography of the day, having written a book on Germaine Krull (Paris : Gallimard, 1931). His letter is preserved in the Man Ray archives at the Musée National d'Art Moderne.

Jacqueline Goddard, 1932

"objects" to photograph, clients without interest for whom it was not worth mobilizing his talent. As has been said earlier, it appears that Man Ray occasionally allowed his assistant to take the photograph. [17]

It has generally been noted that, when viewing a portrait photograph, it is the sitter one sees. The photograph itself, as Roland Barthes pointed out, remains "invisible." [18] That is why a portrait of an anonymous sitter is necessarily less interesting than one of Picasso. Man Ray adopted a somewhat different attitude. "Often enough, my finest portraits were done with ordinary people — after all, Renoir and even Rembrandt himself had their maids pose for them. They did queens with maids, and sometimes maids with queens." [19] The MNAM archives contain a great many portraits of people who, even if they have been identified, are of little interest today. The collection is therefore partly a victim of history, which dictates that the memory of some people be cultivated, that of others forgotten. Yet in most cases, notably when research has turned up traces of these people, a minimum of information about the person reveals that Man Ray literally *revealed* his sitter. One of the finest — if least known — examples of his revelatory sensitivity is Man Ray's portrait of the Pitoëffs. One need merely compare his portraits of this theatrical couple with other portraits of them to realize (assuming one "knows" them) the extent to which Man Ray was able to capture their very essence, what Barthes called "a delicate mental texture, rather than mimicry," of which only "very great portraitists" are capable. [20]

Man Ray often received complimentary letters thanking him for the portraits he did. Sitters compared his portraits to paintings. In this respect, it is worth reproducing a letter written by the poet Max Jacob on September 21, 1922, just after he converted to Catholicism and withdrew to the abbey of Saint-Benoît-sur-Loire :

My dear Man Ray,

It's a painting! What colors! Or rather, what fine values! What external brilliance! What atmosphere! Not to mention that portraits by painters are never good likenesses whereas here I'm alive, myself! Not very handsome! Not too ugly! Not made younger. No longer very young! With a large concrete nose and the fairly devilish mouth of a woman.

I'm delighted with you and with the portrait. I've written to Cocteau that I know you. That I have a portrait by you and that everyone admires it and that he would be wise to ask you for it because I cannot bring myself to part with this authentic effigy.

Thanks a million, regal Buddha.

Warmly,

Max Jacob

PS : I'll come to Paris in a month to thank you and to advertise for you, if you like. [21]

Several years later, in July 1927, it was Pierre Mac Orlan who congratulated Man Ray for a portrait "more sensitive than countless paintings." [22]

Thus little by little, everyone who counted on the Parisian artistic and literary scene visited Man Ray's studio, from actors (Marcel Herrand, Catherine Hessling) to musicians and dancers (Serge Lifar), orchestra conductors (Ernest Ansermet),

Tristan Tzara, 1924

Study for the portrait of Tristan Tzara, 1921

Tristan Tzara, 1921

André Breton, circa 1930

composers (*Le Groupe des Six*), singers (Jeanne Bathori), poets, writers, painters, and sculptors (Jo Davidson), not forgetting collectors (Edward James, Gertrude Stein), gallery owners (Jeanne Bucher), publishers (Albert Skira), the night-club crowd (Louis Moysès, who ran *Le Boeuf sur le Toit*), and fashion designers (Jean-Charles Worth, Elsa Schiaparelli, Nicole Groult). All of avant-garde Paris came "to have a portrait made."

As Sylvia Beach said, "to be 'done' by Man Ray ... meant you were rated as somebody." [23] Even in London, tourists planning to pass through Paris were advised to make a date with the photographer. In June 1935, on acquiring a studio on Rue Val-de-Grace, Man Ray even advertised it in *Minotaure*. [24]

Despite this success, Man Ray adopted a provocative attitude toward his portrait work at the time. In 1929, Jean Gallotti devoted a column titled "Is Photography an Art?" to Man Ray. "There is an entire series [of photographs] that [Man Ray] discusses only condescendingly, which turn out to be portraits recalling the English Romantic school, or else modern women with shorn heads, or actresses in theatrical poses, all handled with broad modeling and fine tones. They are, in fact, admirable. All were shot on very small negatives, and later enlarged, a method that eliminates pointless details from the final print and produces a soft yet not affected feel. For Monsieur Man Ray, however, all this is nothing but fodder for the uncouth." [25]

The chief reason for Man Ray's derogatory attitude toward his own work can be explained by the fact that portraiture was then considered to be a minor art (regardless of the medium employed). The pursuit of a likeness — theoretically inherent to portraiture — had diminished the status of artists once photography was invented, for copying was no longer considered art. With the spread of photography studios in the nineteenth century and mass access to portraiture, even painters came to devalue the portrait genre. It is worth recalling Man Ray's comment that his "painting had evolved to a degree where [he] would never consider painting a portrait." [26]

It was also the case that ever since the invention of photography, photographers — especially portraitists — were usually looked upon as failed painters. The general consensus was that only bad painters became photographers, those who could not handle a brush well enough and therefore had to employ mechanical means to reproduce reality. Man Ray must have thought long and hard before adopting this career.

Given this context, Man Ray's talent lay in his use of techniques that marked both his period and photography itself, to the extent of giving portraiture back its letters of nobility, a development sparked by his use of superimposition and above all solarization.

Only rarely did Man Ray use superimposition in portraiture. The oldest and best known example is certainly the portrait of Tristan Tzara (1921), showing the dada poet sitting atop a ladder while the nude torso of a standing woman is superimposed on the image as though printed or painted on the nearby wall. The negative of Tzara is lost, and only a negative of the bare-breasted woman is preserved in the MNAM archives, demonstrating that Man Ray produced this superimposition by printing the two negatives simultaneously [27] (or one after the other) rather than exposing the same plate several times. [28]

23) *Sylvia Beach*, Shakespeare and Company, *New York : Harcourt, Brace & Co., 1959, p. 112.*

24) *Man Ray had rented an apartment on Rue Val-de-Grace since 1929, but did not use it as a photo studio ; the advertisement indicates that Man Ray no longer occupied Rue Campagne-Première but had not yet moved to Rue Denfert-Rochereau.*

25) *Jean Gallotti, "La photographie est-elle un art ?" L'Art vivant, no. 103, April 1, 1929, p. 282.*

26) *Man Ray, Self Portrait (1963), p. 87.*

27) *A certain number of negatives in the MNAM archives are literally taped together.*

28) *The MNAM archives contain items demonstrating that Man Ray also created superimposition effects by exposing a plate several times, as seen in a previously unknown version of* L'Aurore des Objets *("Dawn of Objects") combined with a seascape, and also in a fashion photograph which underscores the fluidity of a garment by combining two poses on the same negative.*

André Breton, circa 1930

29) Rémy Duval, "*Surimpression*," Photo-Ciné-Graphie, no. 15, May 1935, pp. 8-9.

30) From a letter discovered in MNAM's Man Ray archives, dated October 12, 1934.

31) It should be noted, however, that Lee Miller's father was an enthusiastic amateur photographer.

32) "My Man Ray — An Interview with Lee Miller Penrose by Mario Amaya," Art in America, May-June 1975, p. 56.

33) Dominique Baqué, Les Documents de la Modernité, Paris : Editions Jacqueline Chambon, 1993, p. 126.

34 The first was published in Arts et Métiers in 1933, the second in Photo-Ciné-Graphie in 1934.

Superimposition, like solarization, was never used solely for aesthetic ends. Rémy Duval described the effect of superimposition as follows : "Superimposition originates in the mental world. Like that mental world, it reflects the simultaneousness of ideas. It abolishes time and makes two different elements converge, like the play of memory projecting various profiles of a face onto a single surface. It merges two different dimensions, recreating the characteristics of each. It is the transposition of a musical chord into the visual sphere." [29]

Indeed, the meaning of the picture of Tzara mentioned above must not be overlooked. The superimposition shows the dada poet sitting with a hatchet and an alarm clock dangling over his head, as though time were a sword of Damocles. Yet Tzara seems unconcerned, oblivious even, and smokes a cigarette. The bare-breasted woman, far from being vulnerable, stands tall and faces front. One hand on her hip, she gazes down on the scene from her great height — the handle of the hatchet turned in her direction seems to suggest her power of decision. Since her image on the wall is transparent, she is simultaneously woman and ghost, thus representing both life and death.

Man Ray produced many solarized portraits, starting in the fall of 1929. Lee Miller claimed to have mistakenly turned on the darkroom light while negatives of Suzy Solidor were being developed. The result of such a darkroom accident had long been known under the name of the Sabattier effect, but had always been considered a defect. No one until that moment had thought of transforming it into an artistic statement. A number of studies suggest that Lee Miller and Man Ray discovered solarization together. Yet only Man Ray — an experienced, thoroughly dada artist — could have seized on chance (if indeed it was chance), error, and defect in this way. A letter addressed by Man Ray to the editor of the *New Yorker* provides a plausible explanation for the origin of his use of this darkroom effect : "I make no claims as a discoverer of outlined photographs, wrongly called 'solarizations,' which are the studied application of a phenomenon in the action of light on silver bromide, known to scientists for the past thirty years, who have tried to create emulsions to over-come it. Alfred Stieglitz is the only man I know of who fifteen years ago dared exhibit a print utilizing this violation of the photographic process." [30]

Man Ray had therefore long known of this effect. It is nevertheless possible that his "rediscovery" happened by chance, and it is probable that Lee Miller provoked the accident, since she was still a novice photographer. [31] Yet her story of being startled by a mouse in the darkroom — as recounted in an interview with Mario Amaya — is farcical. [32]

"Solarization, technically defined as a partial reversal of values in a photograph, accompanied by characteristic outlining," [33] can occur in negative or positive. Man Ray, as it happens, produced his solarizations on negatives, since the MNAM archives contain many solarized negatives and contact prints. For an artist like Man Ray, using the solarization effect on negatives allowed him to work the solarized image just like any other, on contact sheets, especially when it came to portraits, which he systematically cropped.

Although solarization presents certain technical difficulties, Man Ray always refused to disclose them. Furthermore, he was notably vexed when Maurice Tabard completely revealed the solarization process in two articles. [34]

Nusch and Sonia, 1935

Nusch and Sonia, 1935

André Breton, circa 1930

35) Man Ray, "On Photography," *Commercial Art and Industry, vol. XVIII, no. 104, 1935, pp. 65-69.*

36) *Photo published on the cover of* Time, The Weekly News Magazine, *December 14, 1936*

The truth is that Man Ray thought that, "as far as desires go, there is really not such a great gulf between the one who creates and the one who appreciates. Except, with the former his application may lead him too far into technical adventures, and thus create a momentary breach between himself and the spectator who, too impressed by *tours de force*, may lose sight of the original subject matter. And yet such *tours de force* when carried out without any special effort on the part of the artist, are merely means for making his subject matter more telling."[35] Technique is simply a way to express an idea. It is not a goal in itself.

In fact, Man Ray did not "solarize" everybody. On occasion, highly studied lighting during the sitting produced a portrait closer to the model's true character than solarization would have done. That was the case with Salvador Dalí, who was photographed in amazing lighting that gave his face an extravagant if not demonic effect prefiguring the legendary moustache that Dalí had not yet begun to wear.[36]

The MNAM archives contain a rich harvest of previously unknown solarized portraits, including those of Albert Skira and Tériade, confirming the popularity of the process.

It was thanks to solarization, then, that Man Ray raised photographic portraiture to the level of creative art. The technique enabled him to obtain a striking effect that astonished at the time, suggesting a materialization of a person's aura. The fact that Man Ray photographed and then solarized the most important artists of the day (Picasso, Braque, Duchamp, Breton, Max Ernst) reinforced the theory that some artists are geniuses who possess a special aura. According to the occult sciences, such auras are visible only to the initiated. Although Man Ray, unlike the other surrealists, was not a fan of seances, solarization surely played an important role in his work partly due to that phenomenon. Photography was no longer straightforward documentation, simply showing what people saw — it went further, rendering visible and materializing an individual's charisma, that invisible quality which people sense only when in the presence of someone endowed with that power. With solarization, Man Ray turned photographic portraiture into an almost magical art.

From photographing objects to "revealing" people, Man Ray therefore struggled to show everyone — from avant-garde artists to the man in the street — that photography was an artistic medium. Yet he practiced what he called the "debatable" art of portrait photography so well that he was swamped with commissions. It was precisely that success, that wealth of orders, that surfeit of portraits of people seeking notoriety — people with affectations who wanted to be photographed by Man Ray more for the signature than for the intrinsic quality of the work — that ultimately led Man Ray to adopt a somewhat cynical attitude.

Several years later, Man Ray gave vent to his disillusion. "Since I'd opened a studio where I began to practice the debatable art of photography — in order to survive, I told myself — I was invaded by all kinds of people who came to see me as though I were a doctor, in the hope that I'd heal them, through flattery, of their inferiority complex, or who came to see me because they needed photos, in the same way they went to the baker or butcher to get some bread or meat." [37]

Clearly, then, it is the "uncouth" for whom *photography is not art*.

37) Man Ray, "Impressions très personnelles sur les années 1920–1930," Objets de Mon Affection, Paris : Philippe Sers, 1983, p. 40 (undated text).

Lee Miller, 1929

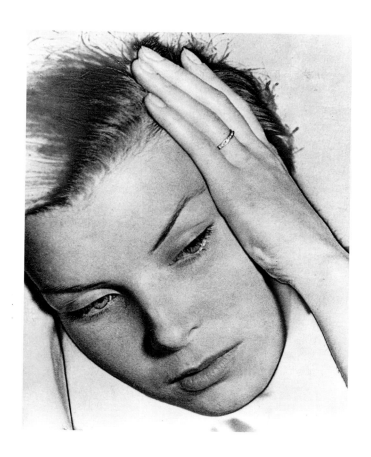

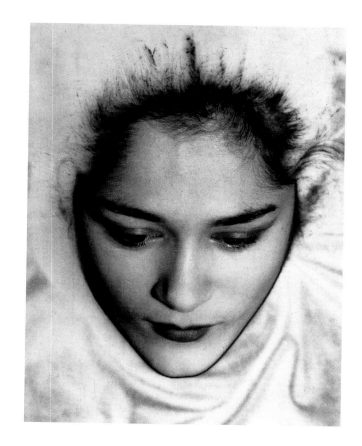

Untitled, 1929

Tanya Ramm, circa 1929

Dora Maar, 1936

Dora Maar, 1936

Lee Miller, 1929

Lee Miller, circa 1930

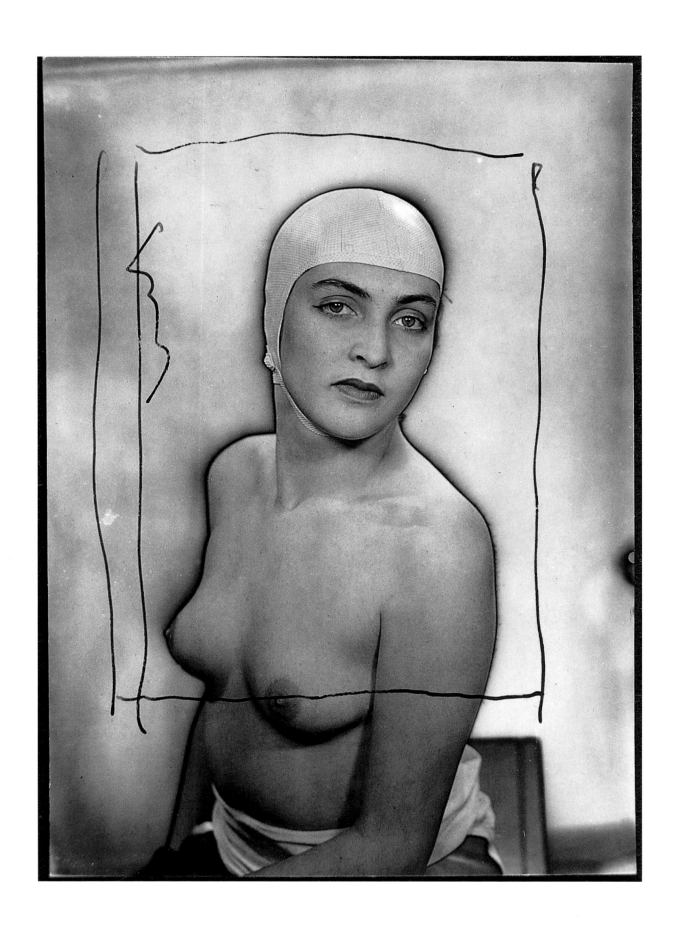

Meret Oppenheim, 1932

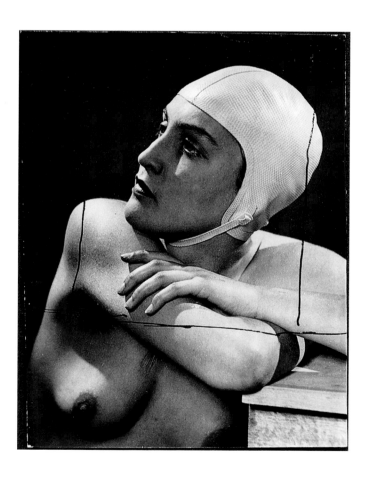

Meret Oppenheim, 1932

133

Lee Miller, circa 1930

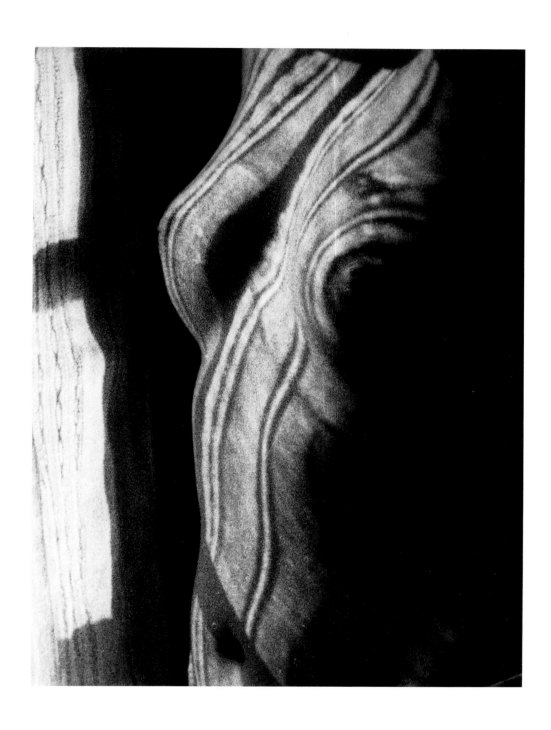

Retour à la raison [*Return to Reason*], 1923

Study for *Le Violon d'Ingres*, 1924

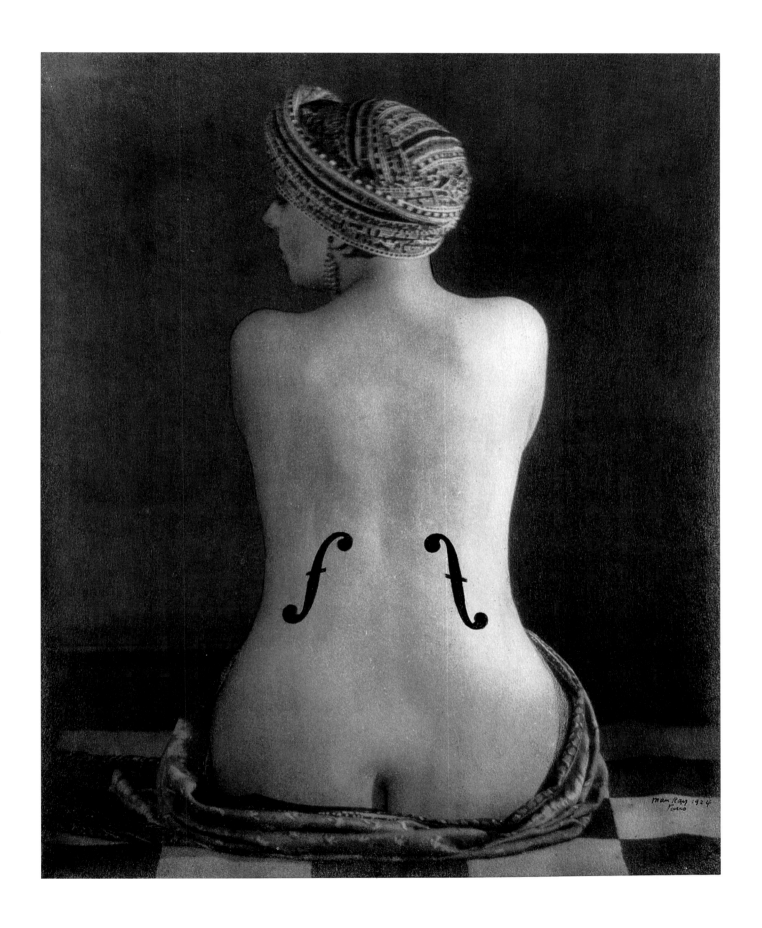

Le Violon d'Ingres, 1924

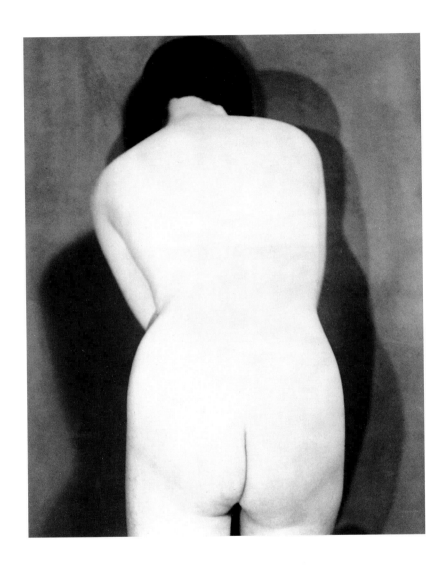

Untitled, 1927

Untitled, 1927

Kiki, 1923

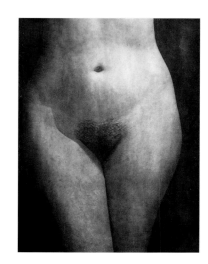

Untitled [Natasha], 1931

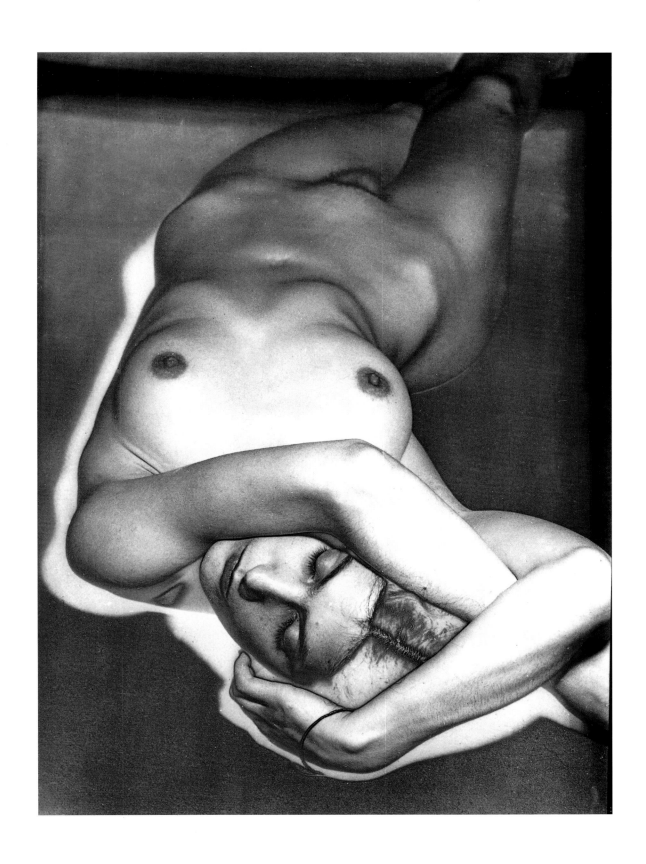

Untitled [Natasha], 1931

Jacqueline, 1930

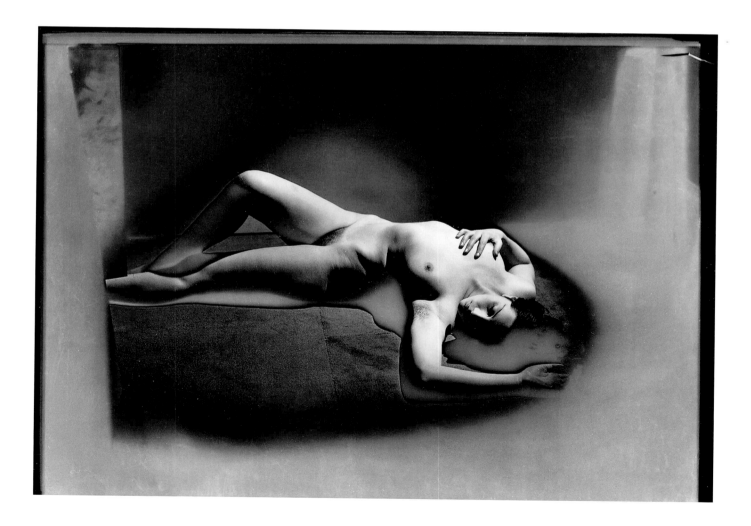

Primat de la matière sur la pensée [The Primacy of Matter over Mind], 1932

Lee Miller in Cocteau's film, *The Blood of a Poet*, 1930

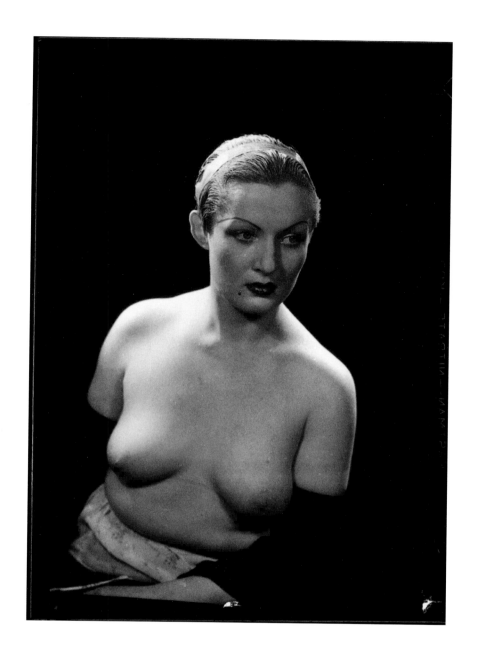

Nude, circa 1930

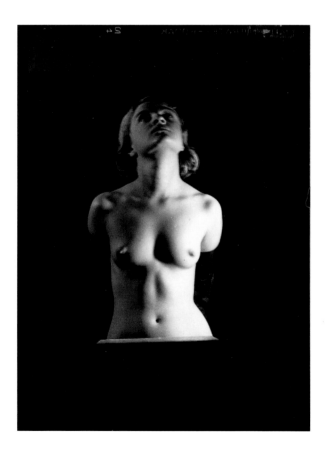

Nude female torso, circa 1930

Nude female torso, circa 1930

Kiki, circa 1925

Kiki, circa 1925

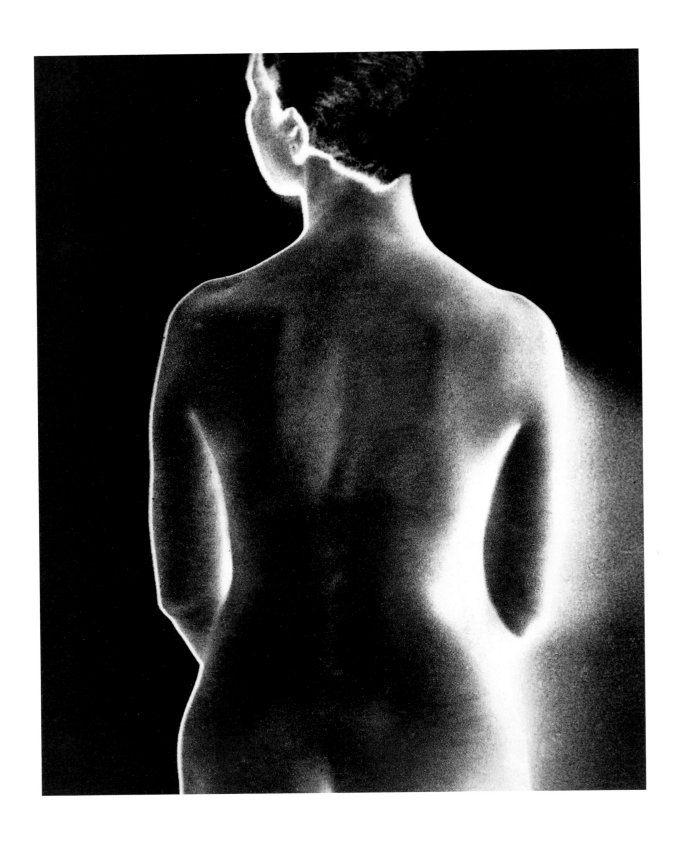

Untitled, circa 1930

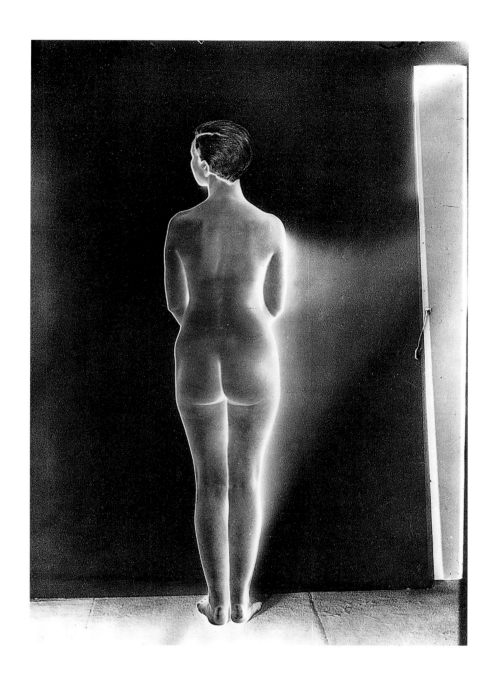

Untitled, circa 1930

Lee Miller, 1930

Lee Miller, 1930

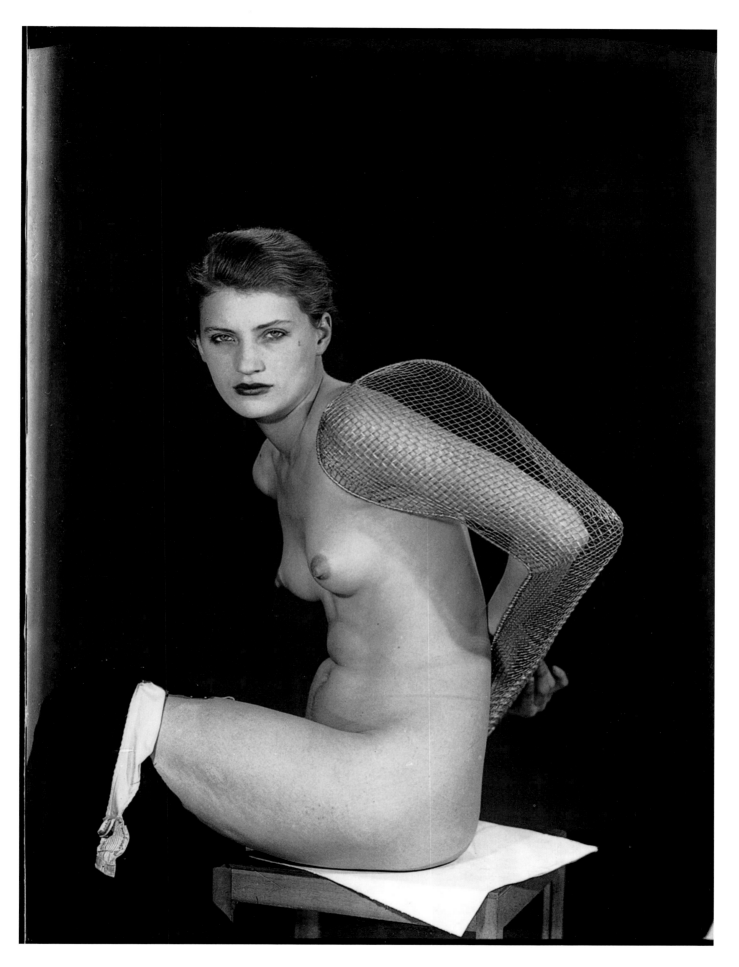

Lee Miller, 1930

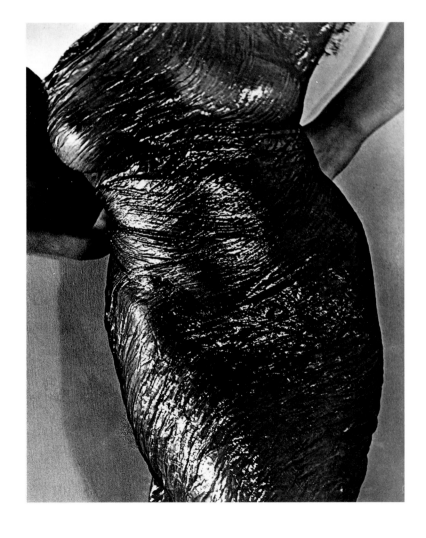

Anatomies, circa 1930

Study for *Anatomies*, circa 1930

Meret Oppenheim, 1933

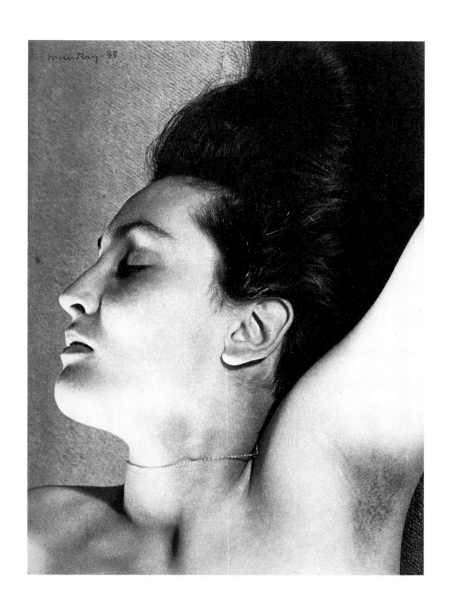

Meret Oppenheim, 1933

From the series *La Prière* [Prayer], circa 1930

From the series *La Prière* [Prayer], circa 1930

From the series *La Prière* [Prayer], circa 1930

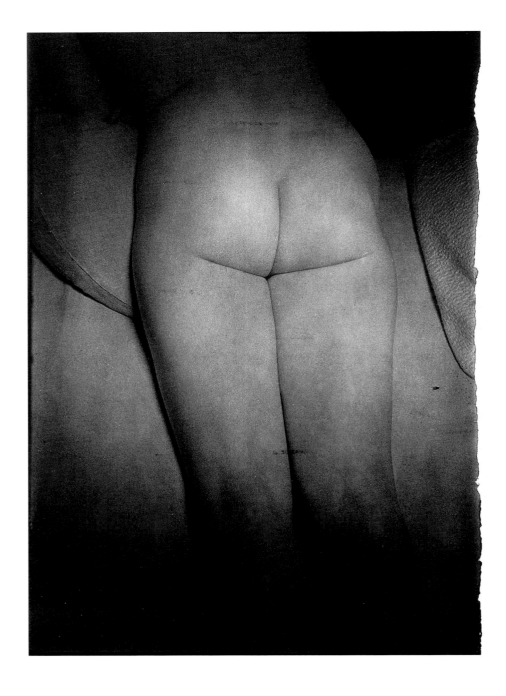

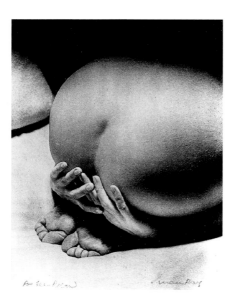

From the series *La Prière* [Prayer], circa 1930

La Prière [Prayer], 1930

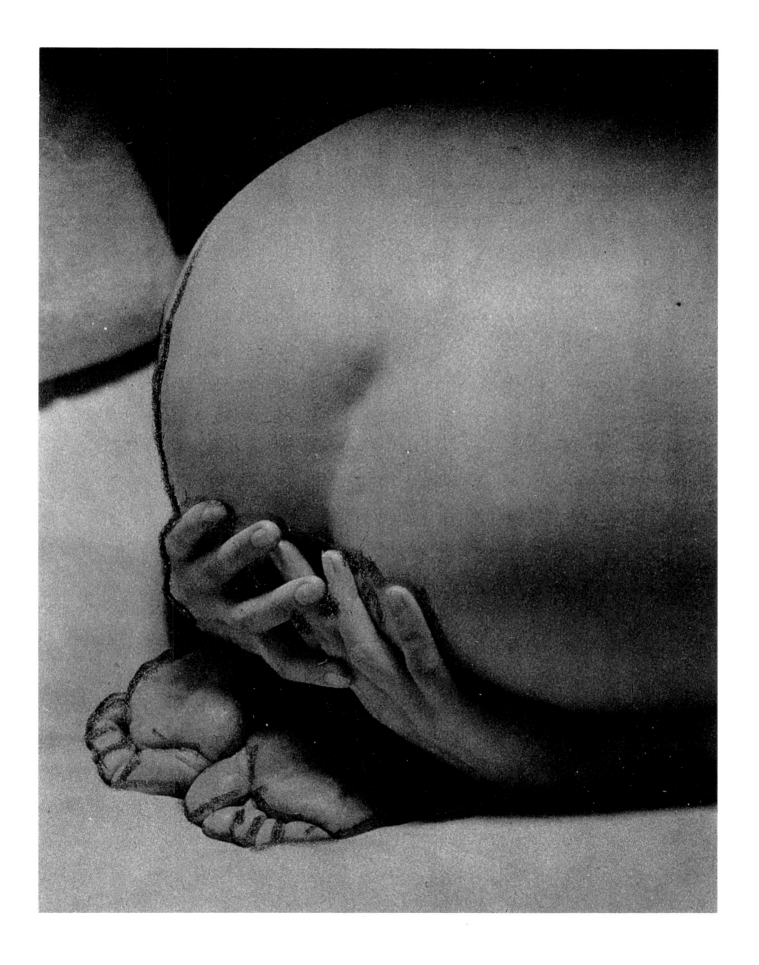

La Prière [Prayer], circa 1930

From the series *La Prière* [Prayer], circa 1930

Self-portrait with "dead" nude, from the series *La Prière* [Prayer], circa 1930

Érotique Voilée, 1933

Érotique Voilée, 1933

Érotique Voilée, 1933

Érotique Voilée, 1933

Érotique Voilée, 1933

Érotique Voilée, 1933

Study for *Noire et Blanche*, 1926

Le Masque [The Mask], 1926

Noire et Blanche, 1926

"Drink to me only with ......", circa 1932

Lydia and wooden figures, 1932

Lydia, study for *Les Larmes* [*Tears*], 1932

Les Larmes [*Tears*], 1932

Study for *L'Aurore des Objets*, 1937

Study for *L'Aurore des Objets*, 1937

L'Aurore des Objets, 1937

Study for *L'Aurore des Objets*, 1937

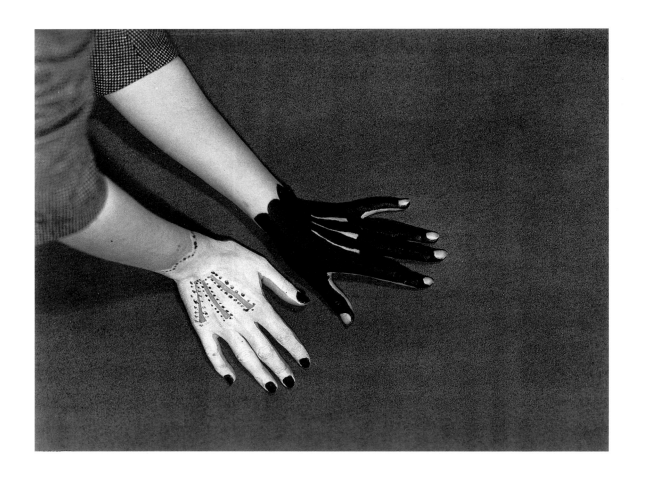

Mains Peintes par Picasso [Hands Painted by Picasso], 1935

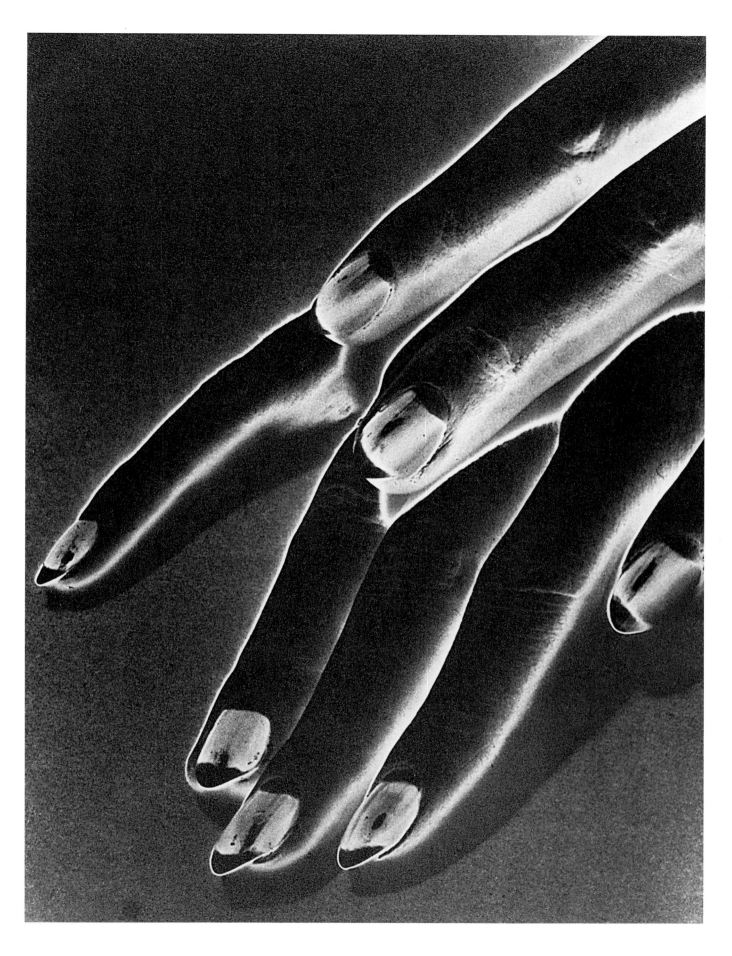

Untitled, 1930

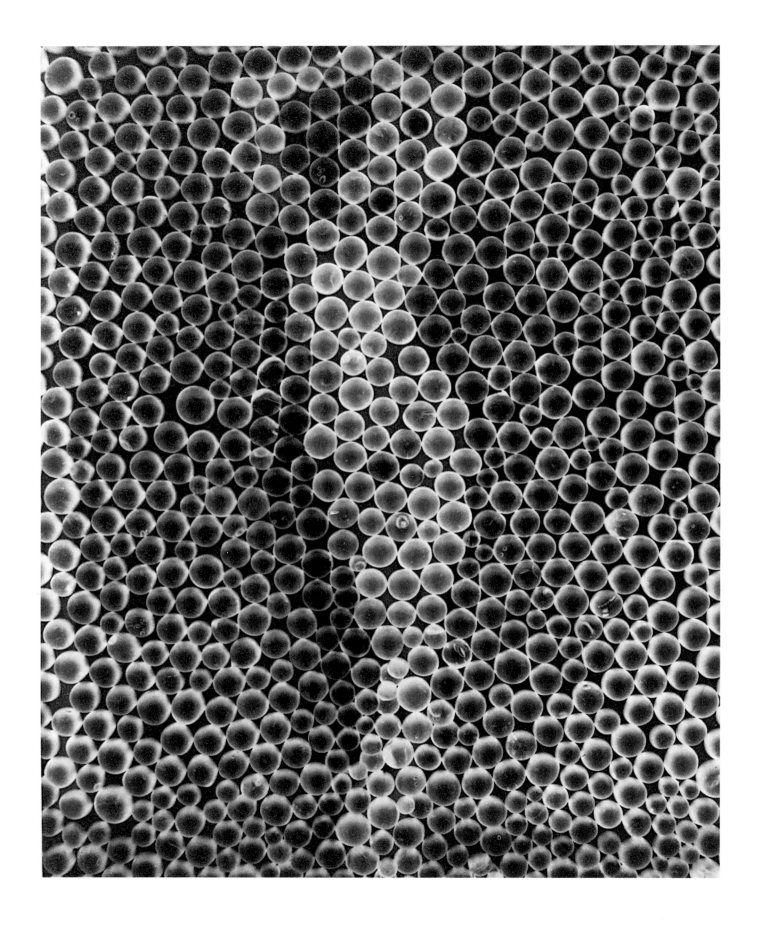

Untitled, 1926

Untitled, 1931

With the rayograph Man Ray created a type of image that made all of his previous works seem like steps along a predetermined path. Even his decision in early youth to discard his family name and call himself Man Ray seems like an act of fate.

Man Ray began his career as an artist. He was exhibited at a number of New York galleries, and although he experienced a degree of success he was never quite satisfied with his painting. He varied his style, his technique, his subjects. It is possible that his encounter with Marcel Duchamp led him to analyze the reasons for this dissatisfaction. It was not a matter of the style of his painting, but of the principle of art conceived as a means to express his feelings. Ultimately, he abandoned this ambition and his painting, and turned to more technical, almost clinical methods of expression. At school his technical drawings had been considered brilliant, and his talent was greatly respected at the map and atlas publishing company where he was employed. He took up the tools he used as a draftsman — drawing pen, T-square, pencil, stencil, French curves, and airbrush — and used them to create art : pseudo-technical drawings of devices which feigned functionality and emanated precision.

Several of these works anticipate aspects that later emerge in his rayographs, e.g., a technical drawing, untitled, from 1915. This drawing features the "three-dimensional model" of the spiral and actually looks like a concept for a rayograph. The spiral reappears a little later in the "Revolving Doors" series of ten individual constructions, in which primary colored stencil-like forms are laid one on top of another to create the impression of shadows cast by different light sources. He used airbrush technique to transform positive and negative stencils into shadowlike images, finally replacing the stencils with objects that he would place directly on paper and spray. The resulting images are clear, interwoven forms surrounded by a soft hue which gives the impression of slight corporeal curves. Man Ray named these pictures "aerographs" and was extremely pleased that he was able to create them without having touched a canvas.

He taught himself photography, and since he had given up his profession as a draftsman, considered becoming a portrait photographer. After all, the camera was also a technical instrument with which one could create pictures. Man Ray collected objects made from all sorts of material and photographed them in various combinations. Following the principle Duchamp had used for his "ready-mades," he gave these works names that were totally unrelated to the subject matter. For example, in 1918 he photographed an object comprised of clothes pegs, glass, and two reflectors and gave it the name "Woman ;" a photograph of an eggbeater with cast shadow he named "Man," although it is interesting to note that in 1917 he had chosen the same subject, busily spinning, for a cliché-verre and had called it simply "Eggbeater." In 1921 he decided that the titles of the images "Man" and "Woman" should be interchanged.

Man Ray had distanced himself from his subjects. He no longer tried to analyze them intellectually and portray them through his perceptions. Presentation was governed by technical means ; his only personal contribution was the title, and this he used to distance himself even further. The visual appearance of his work did

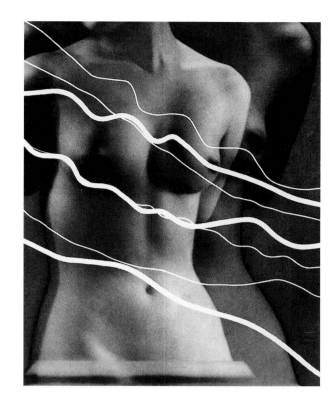

Electricité, 1931

1) This photogram has not been found. In this context, however, a rayograph often mentioned features a black bottle, a black funnel, a black pipe stem, and a white pipe bowl on a gray background. Due to the reversal of tone values this photogram can only be the result of copying from an original. During the copying process the white pipe bowl must have been added, which strongly suggests that this particular photogram stems from a later period.

not serve primarily as an experience for the eye, but rather as a stimulus for the spirit of the viewer.

By then the essential elements that would combine to form the rayographs were to be found in his immediate surroundings : the objects, the photography, the shadows. All that was needed to bring them together was a minor incident in the darkroom. It happened in Paris at the beginning of 1922, when sheer co-incidence brought together object, photosensitive material, and light. Man Ray instantly recognized that in the course of carrying out a routine procedure he had chanced upon a totally new genre of photograph. Working a little absentmindedly in his makeshift laboratory — his hotel room at night actually — he had unintentionally placed some objects on photographic paper and switched on the light. In simple terms that is how his first rayograph came into existence. Because the paper was already lying in developing solution he was able to observe how it turned black everywhere except where he had placed the objects. This thoroughly plausible account of the incident comes from Man Ray's book *Self Portrait*. That night he had been engaged in making prints from photographic plates (then still composed of glass) ; the photos were fashion shots featuring the clothing of Paul Poiret. At the time he did not possess an enlarger so he would place the 18 x 24 cm developed plates directly onto photographic paper to make an exposure. Through the exposure the negative image on the plate was copied onto the paper ; the paper was subsequently placed in developing solution to create a positive. At one point, without noticing, he inadvertently picked up two sheets of photographic paper together. The two sheets separated only after they had been placed in the developer, and because he did not want to throw the unexposed sheet away, he placed a glass funnel, a measuring glass and a thermometer on it and switched on the light. [1]

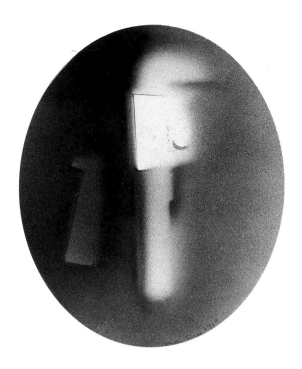

Droller, 1918

The photogram — in the case of Man Ray a rayograph — is therefore a photographic copying process in which flat, three-dimensional, transparent or opaque objects are placed directly onto light-sensitive paper and exposure is executed with an ordinary light bulb. It is usually a dry process and is carried out in darkroom conditions, i.e., almost total darkness. Developing takes place after exposure. Those parts of the paper which are directly exposed to light turn black, those which are covered by an object, or are unexposed, remain white. Other areas, neither covered completely nor exposed to direct light, react to refracted light which is reflected between the object and the white paper, and turn to shades of gray. The photogram, of course, is also a type of silhouette-picture, because those parts of three-dimensional objects which are not directly in contact with the paper, require only the smallest amount of light from the side in order to cast a shadow. Moholy-Nagy employed light in such a way that it governed form and the objects became unrecognizable. In contrast, Man Ray utilized light so that his objects, although slightly distorted, remain identifiable. Photograms are created principally by three effects : in places where the object is in direct contact with, or covers the light-sensitive paper, the area remains white ; the shadow of the object becomes gray ; and, the surrounding area, which is exposed directly to the light, becomes black.

With the photogram technique, Man Ray distanced himself even further from his subjects. He allowed his images to be formed by an invisible agent, light, using a method that was virtually impossible to control. The results were clear, negative forms or non-forms, as it were : although the object appears absent, a fleeting moment of contact captures its presence.

According to an account Man Ray gave in his biography *Self Portrait*, [2] it is evident that the first rayograph came into existence sometime early in 1922. He wrote : "Later that year I conceived the idea of doing an album of some prints, in a limited edition, which I called *Les Champs Délicieux….*" The *Champs Délicieux* album was published in 1922.

Frantically he set about producing rayographs which his dadaist friends received with rapturous enthusiasm. In an open letter to "Man Ray American Photographer," published in the April 1922 issue of *Les Feuilles Libres*, Jean Cocteau mentioned that Man Ray had sent him "some eighty" photograms. In the same month the Dada magazine *Le Coeur à Barbe* [3] announced that "an album of 12 original photographs would be published under the title *Les Champs Délicieux*" (the name finally became *Champs Délicieux* which made it a little less specific).

The title was chosen deliberately. It followed an example set earlier by André Breton and Philippe Soupault, who together had published a collection of "automatic texts" titled *Les Champs magnétiques*. [4] Looking back on his moment of absentmindedness, a moment in which he was carrying out a technical process routinely, Man Ray saw a psychic analogy in the discovery he had made by chance, and the principle of automatic writing.

In November 1922 the American magazine *Vanity Fair* published a one page report titled "A New Method of Realizing the Artistic Possibilities of Photography." It featured four rayographs for which Man Ray wrote the captions, and one of which alluded to his surrealistic practices : "Composition of Objects Selected With

2) Man Ray : *Self Portrait*, Boston 1963.

3) *Le Coeur à Barbe* (Tristan Tzara, editor) Issue No. 1, Paris, April, 1922.

4) André Breton, Philippe Soupault : Les Champs magnétiques, Paris 1920.

5) Laszlo Moholy-Nagy : Painting Photography Film, *Bauhaus book No. 8, Langen 1925.*

6) André Breton : Manifeste du Surréalisme, in : Poisson soluble, *Paris 1924.*

Both Eyes Closed'. This suggests the modern artistic passion for machinery."

The pseudonym Man Ray turned out to be extremely fitting for an artist who became "a man who experimented with rays." The term "rayograph" derives from the pseudonym, but it also relates to the process he used to create these particular images which called for the application of light rays. Man Ray first used the term rayograph for a photogram published in the magazine *The Little Review* Number. 3, autumn issue, 1922.

Schadograph was another name given to photograms in an attempt to reflect both their character and creator. In 1919, under the influence of the Zurich Dadaists, the painter Christian Schad created the very first photograms of the 20th century. Much later, in 1936, at the exhibition "Fantastic Art, Dada, Surrealism" at the Museum of Modern Art in New York, Tristan Tzara (who had published one of Schad's photograms in 1920) christened them Schadographs : therewith blending a fundamental feature of the photogram (the shadow) with the artist's name.

The term "photogram" itself was introduced in 1925 by Laszlo Moholy-Nagy [5] and since that time it has been utilized as a generic term in many languages. Himself a reputed creator of photograms, Moholy-Nagy saw in this term an analogy with the speed of telegraphic transmission.

The very first rayographs, from which Man Ray chose 12 images for the album *Champs Délicieux*, show no identifiable signs of intentional composition. Even the light, the most important creative element of the photogram, was seldom varied. This is not a surprise if one considers that Man Ray probably wanted to follow the recommendations of André Breton in the first *Manifeste du Surréalisme*, [6] for automatic writing. Breton described it :

"Make yourself comfortable in a place where you are best able to concentrate on your inner self, then have someone bring you something to write with. Put yourself in the most passive, most receptive possible state. Forget your genius, your talent, and the talents of everyone else. Bring yourself to understand that although writing is a path that leads to all things, it is one of the most miserable to tread. Write quickly, without a preconceived theme, so quickly that you cannot remember what you have written and are not tempted to reread...."

Speed was an essential element in the production of both automatic texts and rayographs. Breton described the output of the written form thus : "The ease with which it came was self-evident. At the end of the first day we had produced around 50 pages to read to each other...."

Automatic texts produced these sorts of word streams : "I have always felt sympathy for the plants which rest on top of walls. Of all the people who slipped over me, the most beautiful, in disappearing, left me this wisp of hair, these wallflowers, without which I should have been lost to you ...." which constitute in a sense a prefiguration of the rayograph. The encounter of a grater, a scoop, pencils and cotton balls is a step, a "guide to the spirit" which "little by little confirms the supreme reality of these images. Initially, the spirit contents itself simply to tolerate them, but soon it realizes that they support its intelligence and deepen its insight. The spirit becomes aware of infinity, a place where wishes are formed, where pro and contra constantly strive to outdo each other, where its confusion does not betray it. It pursues its path, inspired by these enchanting images, images

Der Sturm, n°3, 1922

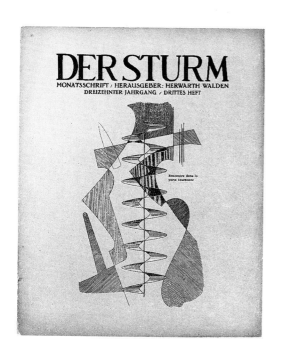

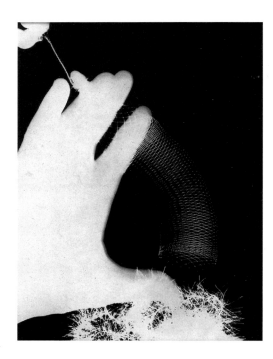

Untitled, 1922

which hardly leave it time to apply a cooling breath to its inflamed fingers. It is the most splendid of nights, the night of lightning storms; compared to such a night, day is night." So wrote Breton in the same 1924 manifesto on the subject of automatic writing.

Marcel Duchamp enjoyed speculation over circumstances which revealed themselves "as soon as the rules of physics and chemistry were relaxed a little."[7] From Henri Poincaré's statement, "That which is not thought is absolutely nothing...."[8] Duchamp reached the converse conclusion that if something could comprise a thought, it could also exist. In one of his mind games he proposed that since it was known that the third dimension could be presented as a projection in the second, it followed that the third dimension is actually a projection of the fourth, the fourth a projection of the fifth, and so on.

To this end he studied projections of all kinds, in theory and in practice. He invited Man Ray into his New York studio to photograph shadows of ready-mades and other objects piled up here and there, and it is likely that this exercise added impetus to Man Ray's own studies of shadow. Duchamp saw in Poincaré's writing a challenge to detach thought from hard fact. His pictures and objects were rough drafts from which logic was suspended and "truth" had no claim. Man Ray adopted this philosophy and endowed it with poetic form in his photograms. He rejected the generally safe methods of photography, which took it for granted that its images were "true." In the photogram he discovered a totally different way of seeing things, one that was ambiguous and multifaceted, one that had nothing in common with the conventional. His rayographs seem to have assumed the idea that visible reality is only a shadow projected by an exterior truth.

In autumn 1922 the forty copies of the album *Champs Délicieux*[9] were ready. Tristan Tzara wrote a foreword which he called "La Photographie à l'envers," which anticipates Man Ray's 1934 description of the proper but disrespectful way an artist deals with his materials. Man Ray would write that the "violation of the medium employed is the most perfect assurance of the author's convictions. A certain amount of contempt for the material employed to express an idea is indispensible to the purest realization of this idea."[10] Photography apparently welcomed such treatment and revealed to Man Ray its most secret and most fertile fields.

Individual photos in the album were not given titles: the photographic medium deals with the concrete in such a way that — once the actors have quit the stage — a title would destroy rather than bolster the impression of strangeness and dream. In this vein yet another parallel can be drawn with *Champs magnétiques*: in Breton's first *Manifeste du Surréalisme*, he "allowed" himself the "slight criticism" of Soupault "for giving titles to certain pages of the book — even if done with the intention of enhancing the mystification."

Almost half of Man Ray's output of rayographs was produced within two to three years of his "discovery." By the end of 1922 he had exhausted all of the formal possibilities that the photogram of objects could offer under the conditions in which he worked. Thus, for example, between exposures he might remove objects or add others; sometimes he held objects or his own hands between the light source and the photographic paper, without letting them come into contact

7) in: Michel Sanouillet: Marcel Duchamp, Duchamp du signe, Paris 1975

8) Henri Poincaré: La Valeur de la science, Paris 1905.

9) Today there are only 20 known copies still in existence.

10) in Man Ray's text: "The Age of Light", in James Thrall Soby, editor, Photographs by Man Ray 1920 Paris 1934 (Hartford, Conn., James Thrall Soby, 1934). The text appeared first in the magazine Minotaure, 1., No. 3/4, Paris, October/December 1933.

Untitled, 1922

with the paper — this produced the effect of a soft, out of focus image, superimposed over the original object. The items he transformed in his rayographs were taken from his immediate surroundings. They were completely normal objects he used in everyday life, most of which fitted into the 18 x 24 cm format: his drawing tools, glasses, light bulbs, photographic and laboratory equipment, an egg, prisms, rolls of film, sand, souvenirs and small fetishes, pieces of jewelry, cooking utensils, cotton wool, flowers, spirals, pubic hair, hands, heads, and also — as was the case with his airbrush work — some of his 'Objects of Affection' (e.g., the "Lampshade"). He did not leave home in search of his material, but instead chose items that were intimately domestic in character.

Of some images two or three variations are known. In retrospect, however, it is clear that they did not result from attempts at systematic improvement. The twelve motifs that appeared in *Champs Délicieux* were all created by following the same method: He used a single light source which always came from the same direction, made only one exposure, and did not move or change the position of the objects because this would have robbed them of their identity. Only the second image remains mysterious, since it features positive and negative forms side by side — an impossibility given the basic photographic process he was using. The reversal of the tone values in this picture resulted neither from solarization nor from some other process of partial inversion, whatever part mirrored reflections may have played. It is important to remember that Man Ray created these images in his hotel room, an environment that was hardly conducive to technical experimentation, even if he had been so inclined.

Perhaps this negative/positive rayograph was the result of an attempt to create the motifs for the album on film (in his case on 18 x 24 cm photographic plates), rather than on the same size photographic paper, since in order to create the 40 copies of *Champs Délicieux*, he had to reproduce each image 40 times without a substantial loss of tonality. For this he used a camera with an 18 x 24 cm glass negative from which the images were copied directly onto paper. It is conceivable that during the process he attempted to create a photogram directly on a glass plate. Copying from this glass plate would of course produce a positive image — black forms on a white background — and would have been completely lacking in the characteristic which made his rayographs so fascinating: namely, a form brilliant in clarity and aura. It was an idea he abandoned rather quickly, allowing it to come to light only in this puzzling image (probably the result of copying a photogram from film and at the same time combining it with other objects, possibly a stencil).

With these photograms Many Ray accomplished a classic work of surrealism, at a time when surrealism was still in its infancy. He recognized that photograms automatically transcended the worldly form of objects by transforming them into "creatures of light." His photograms expose the extraordinary qualities of things ordinary, but each item — pipe, light bulb, funnel — remains identifiable. A contrasting program was that of Moholy-Nagy whose photograms — almost half of his entire oeuvre — were exhibited at the Centre Georges Pompidou in 1995. He allowed the form of his objects, all of which were things he found in his studio, to disappear completely. By multiplying both the sources of light and the exposures, and in moving his objects around, he rendered them unrecognizable. They do not, however, convey the impression of abstract composition. On the contrary, one senses clearly that the objects from which the forms derive were once present, and recognizes that through light they have been transformed. These images beautifully illustrate the remarkable qualities of light and its creative power.

In 1931 Man Ray produced a portfolio of ten photograph/photogram combinations which the Paris Electricity Board(CPDE) published in a limited edition of 500 copies titled *Electricité*. In creating this series he pushed the possibilities of the photogram even further, concentrating on their ability, through light and transparency, to elevate "things" to the level of idol. The resultant images appear to be charged with a universal energy, like stars in a dark universe.

In the foreword to *Electricité*, Pierre Bost contemplated that electricity as a phenomenon is "no more comprehensible to us than a sunrise, a shooting star, a rainbow or a flash of lightning would have been to prehistoric man." Man Ray, in his portrayal of the phenomenon, presents it as a willing servant, albeit one endowed with the fascination of the inexplicable. This servant will undertake any task with which he is confronted, no matter how large or how small ; for example, he is capable of lighting the entire city of Paris, or, admitted to the intimate sphere of the bathroom, will generate warmth and comfort. The photogram effectively communicates the extremely close contact man has with electrical devices, but at the same time renders them invisible, as is the mysterious energy that drives them. Man Ray placed electricity on the same level as the familiar power of eroticism — it functions yet we do not understand how. Through the combination of photography and photogram, the picture — the intimate connection to the inconceivable device — bridges the gap between the idol and its sphere of action.

In the series of ten images published in *Electricité*, Man Ray begins with a portrayal of cosmic energy (also titled "Electricité") ; in the second, "Le Monde," he shows us a darkened Earth, a world that wants to be lit at night — and light, of course, he makes readily available : one simply has to reach out for the switch. On the next leg of the journey he arrives in the sparkling city of Paris, "La Ville," by night, and enters "La Maison ;" in the "Salle de bains" he observes the lady of the house operating curious devices, watching closely as she irons her "Lingerie ;" later he drops into "La Cuisine" and "La Salle à manger ;" finally "Le Souffle" fans him a little air so that at last in the closing picture (also titled "Electricité") he can yield to the electric thrill of eroticism.

With these titles Man Ray places us at varying distances from each image : "Le Monde" presents the light side of the moon seen from the earth by night, and the switch holds the promise that, if turned on, it could be just as light here as it is there. In the "Cuisine" we see the potential consequences of using energy to excess in a roast chicken that appears to be slightly burnt. The title "La Maison" he has given to the photogram of a lampshade : it reminds us of the light it is capable of reflecting (thanks to the Paris Electricity Board), and acts as an ironic symbol for the soft, warm comforts of home. In the final image the cosmic energy of the first picture transforms itself into erotic electricity, and it is at this point at the very latest, that the observer feels the stimulus of cerebral (electric) impulses and a release of spiritual energy.

Untitled, 1923

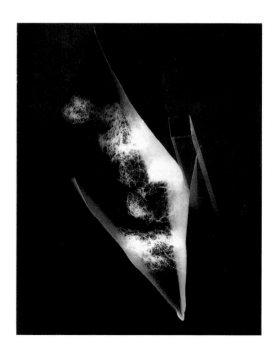

In the 1940s Man Ray decided to give the name "Objects of my Affection" to miscellaneous objects which he had transformed by adding or eliminating some of their parts, together with furniture he made for his own use. In creating a portrait of each object, he subjected it to sympathetic photographic treatment. Clearly his power to imagine the inanimate as animate was so strong that he actually developed true affection for these "things." Man Ray's erotic treatment of certain objects created another avenue of access to his rayographs. If, with a little humor, the eggbeater of 1918 reduced eroticism to basic mechanics, then the rayographs — authentic portrayals of encounters, contact, penetration, superimposition and delicate movements — excited a spiritual form of voyeurism unknown until then. In this type of voyeurism intuitive recognition of the erotic is sublimated by a double irritation : that which is presented is not in itself erotic (only the method of presentation suggests the personal). One does not actually see what is being presented because, to some extent, it is only visible through its absence.

In some rayographs of the *Champs Délicieux* period he abandoned the automatic process in favor of a more deliberate method involving several steps. In the rayograph of 1923 titled "Colifichet" for example, he made a stencil by tearing a rhombus-like shape from the center. For the first exposure he placed the stencil on photographic paper, and placed within the hole a small, upright tube and a dressmaker's pin. After the first exposure, he placed the rhombus-like shape he had removed from the original stencil over the empty space, but slightly lower. During the process one of the upper corners of the rhombus curled up and threw a shadow. He removed the stencil and replaced it with the cake doily and the candle. Then he made the second exposure. (It is also possible that these two steps were undertaken in the reverse order.)

In 1934 a series of 20 rayographs were published in his book titled *Photographs by Man Ray 1920 Paris 1934*. One of these, a theatrical scene, features similar imagery : a rhombus-like form fades upwards in the slot of an opening stage curtain to reveal a delicate cloud of pubic hair. Next to it, waiting, is a square glass rod.

Each chapter of this book contains a brief preface, the texts by Man Ray himself, Paul Eluard, André Breton, Marcel Duchamp, and Tristan Tzara (who had already sung the praises of rayographs in *Champs Délicieux*). The first chapter is devoted to photographs of objects (for example, his home-made furniture), various structures, stones and plants ; the second shows female nudes, and the third "The Visages of Women ;" following the chapter featuring portraits of famous men, the rayographs — the pictures of absent objects — bring the book to a close. Introduced by Tzara's text , "When things dream," the photograms begin with three automatic images from the *Champs Délicieux* period, become progressively more erratic but equally more refined, and conclude with one generally referred to as "Man Ray Kissing Kiki."

His own introduction to the book Man Ray titled "The Age of Light," which was a direct reference to his rayographs. He wrote : "It is in the spirit of an experience and not of experiment that the following autobiographical images are presented. Seized in moments of visual detachment during periods of emotional contact, these images are oxidised residues, fixed by light and chemical elements, of living organisms." [11]

11) in Man Ray's text : "The Age of Light", in James Thrall Soby, editor, Photographs by Man Ray 1920 Paris 1934 (Hartford, Conn., James Thrall Soby, 1934). The text appeared first in the magazine Minotaure, I., No. 3/4, Paris, October/December 1933.

Untitled, 1927

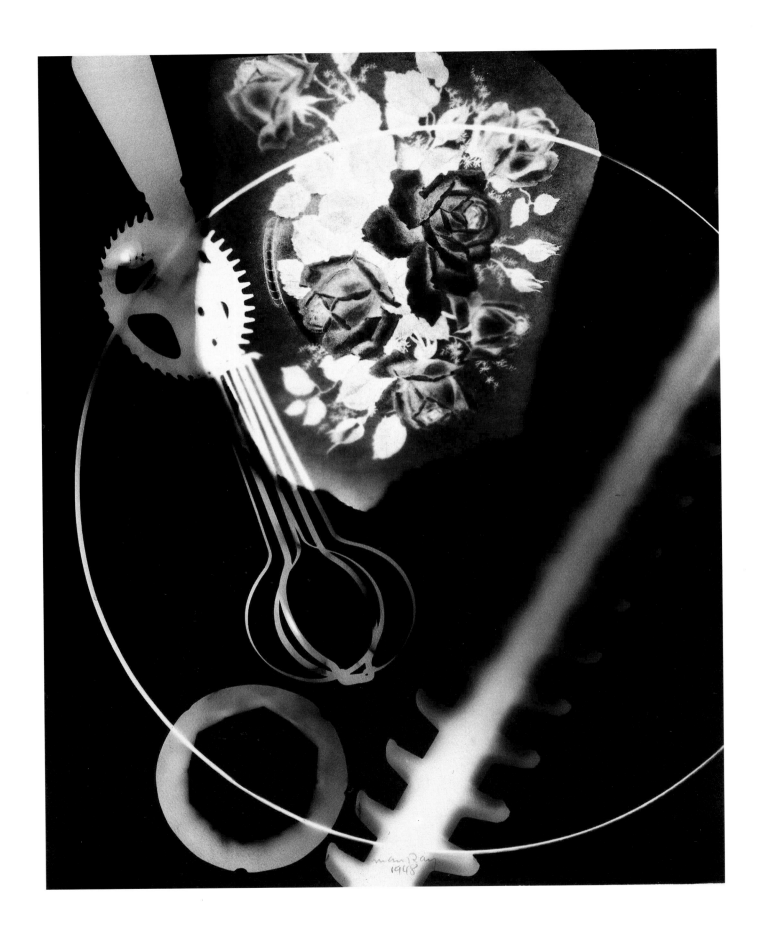

Untitled, 1943

Untitled, 1925

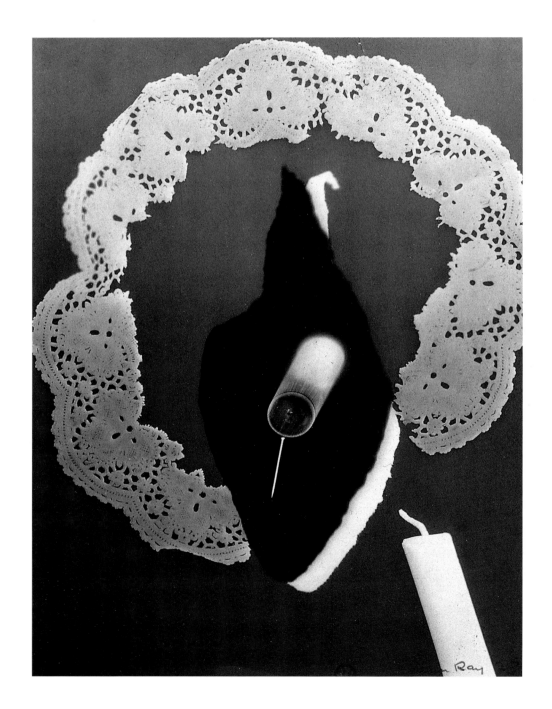

Colifichet [Frippery], 1923

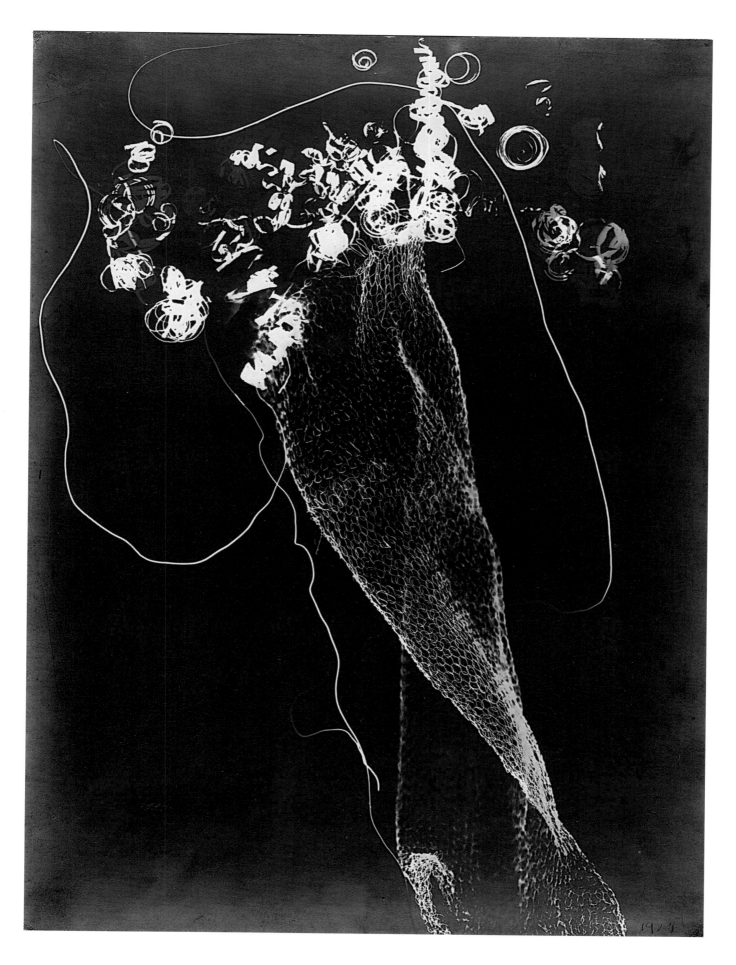

Untitled, 1924

Untitled, 1945

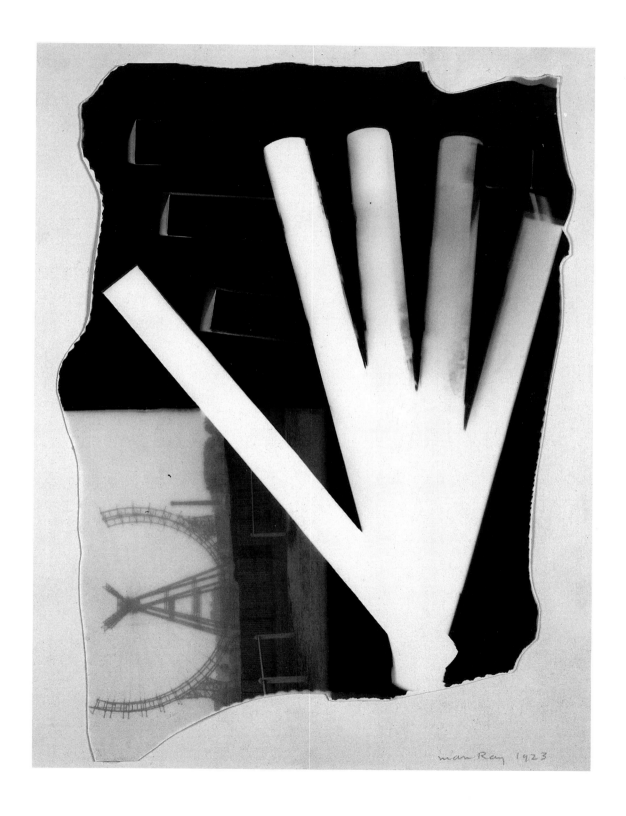

Untitled, 1923

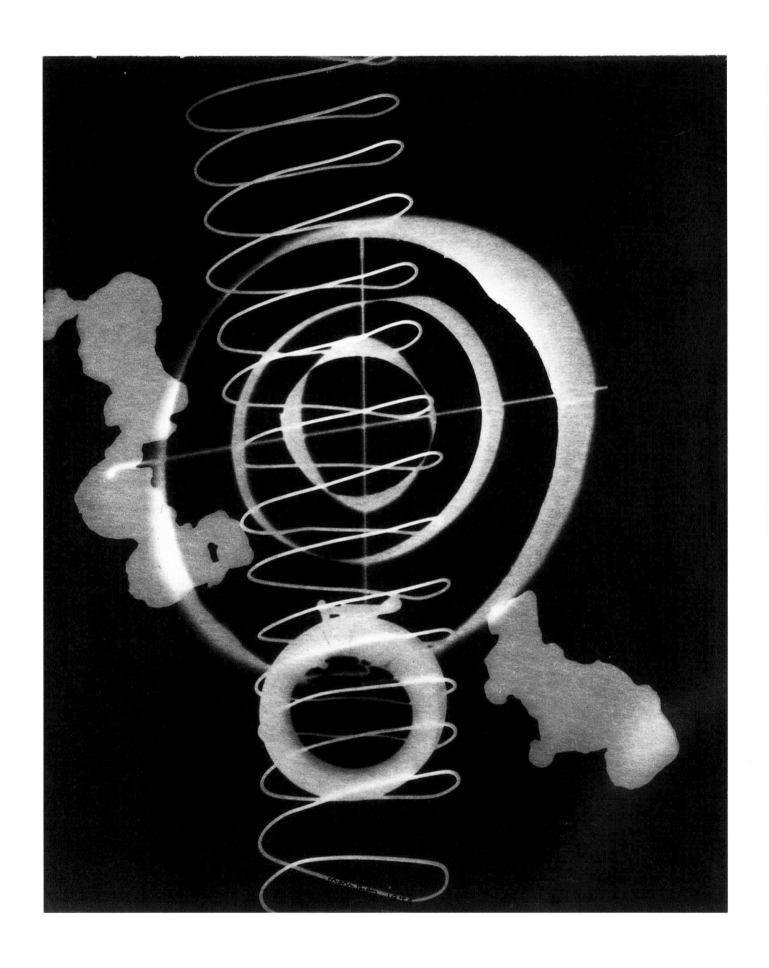

Untitled, 1945

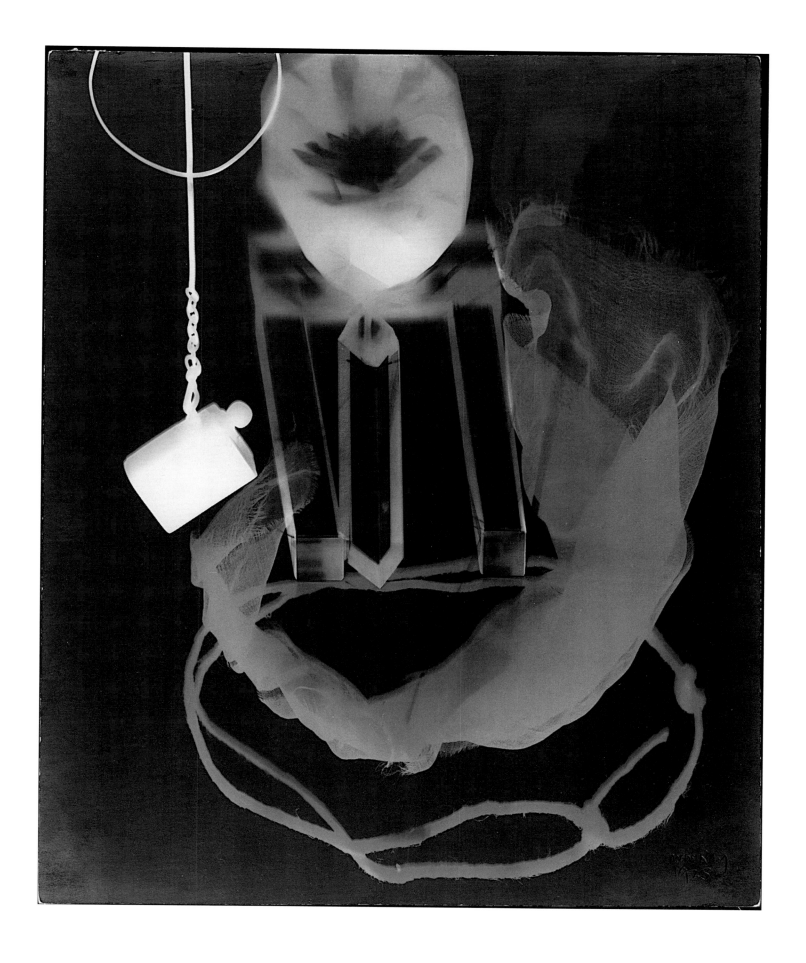

Untitled, 1923

Untitled, 1923

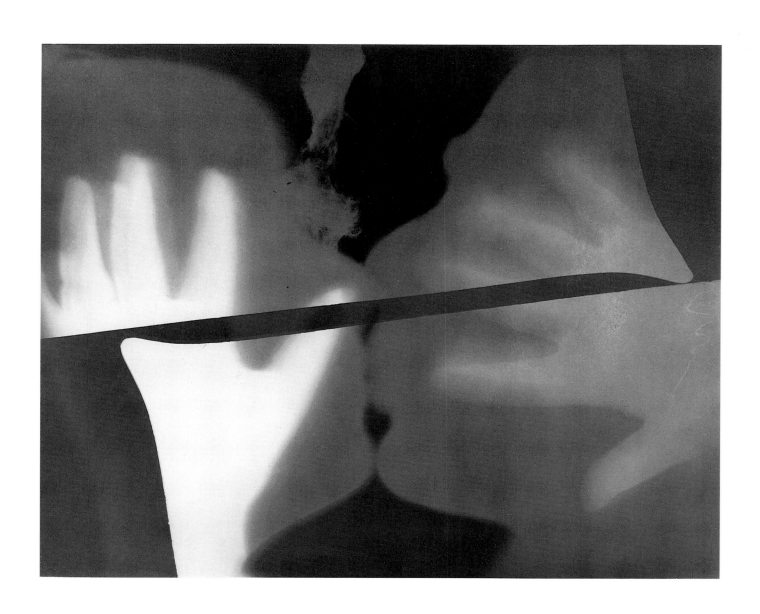

Untitled, 1922

Head, New York, 1920

DENATURING REALITY

Photography as a Depiction of Non-Euclidean Space

In addition to good, routine photography, or the more elaborate work marked by the use of clearly "artistic" effects (solarization, double exposures, rayographs, etc.), Man Ray explored a still narrower path where discoveries were more unpredictable yet more promising.

The camera thereby became a way to shatter the fundamental ambiguity of the world. As early as 1918, Man Ray used it not only to challenge standard conventions of perspective (as modernist photographers would do when they adopted new "angles"), but also to underscore the indeterminate nature of photographed reality. Without wanting to assert a direct correlation between the publication of new scientific theories and the new visual idiom explored by Man Ray, his efforts now appear striking in the way they placed photography at the center of one of the major aesthetic debates of the day.

Integration of Shadows, 1919

L'Homme, 1920

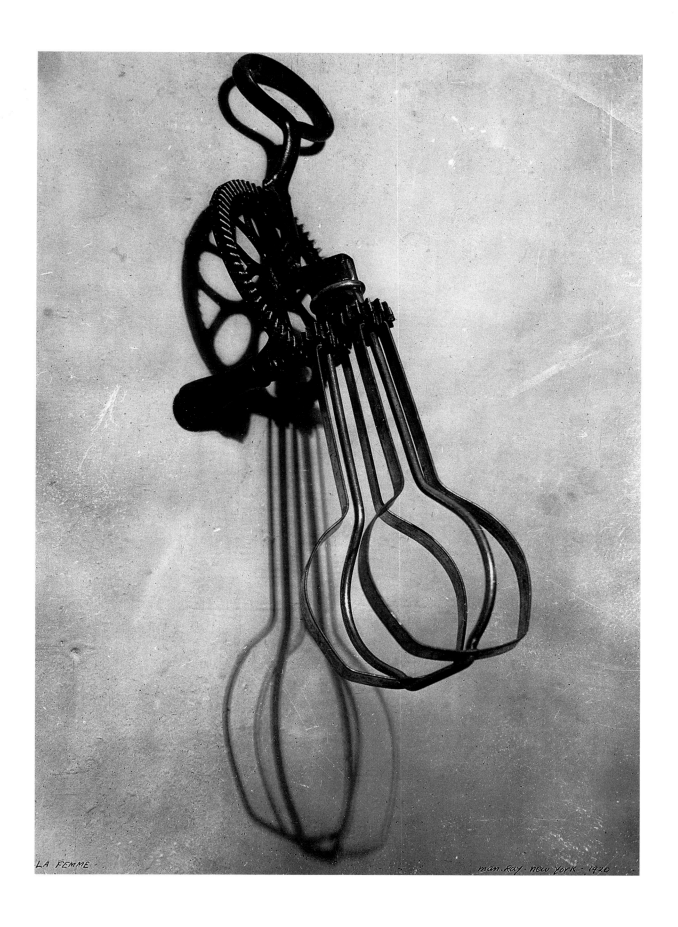

La Femme, 1920

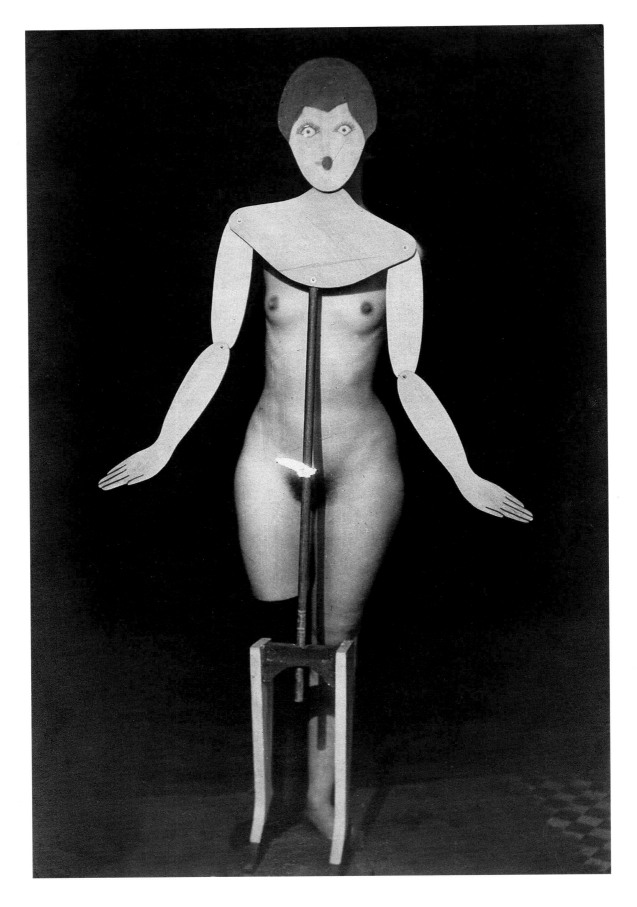

Coat Stand, 1920

Duchamp and Man Ray : Exchanging Glances
Michel Sanouillet

Recent decades have seen a proliferation of studies both of Man Ray and Marcel Duchamp. Light has been shed on practically every aspect of their respective achievements, from different angles and from different parts of the globe. Shadowy areas remain, of course, along with unknown or unused material. In general, however, it can be said that the lives and works of the two men are now as familiar as those of their well-known contemporaries.

More pertinent to this exhibition, the relationship of both artists to photography has been the subject of lengthy and often relevant study, [1] not to mention the exhaustive exhibition catalogues. Man Ray's enormous contribution to modern art was little known, underestimated or misunderstood until recently, yet has now been quantitatively and artistically reassessed in its diversity. Today we realize that he was not only the "twentieth-century Nadar" but that as a painter, filmmaker, and creator of objects as well as photographer, he was able, beginning in his early New York period, to play on all possible combinations; he successively (or simultaneously) employed canvases, pigments, lenses, and "things," assigning them all roles beyond the scope of ordinary usage and effectively scrambling the picture.

Correspondences

It is nevertheless worth dwelling for a moment on the relationship between Man Ray and his friend Marcel Duchamp, attempting to detect points of convergence and divergence, explaining the special status conferred on them by the contemporary art world in both America and Europe.

Comparison of the symmetrical careers of the two artists may well astonish future generations. One was the son of Brooklyn immigrants, the other a young, provincial Frenchmen from an affluent family in Normandy, who would normally have become a local notable like his father — what mischievous sprite could have brokered their encounter and subsequent journey down parallel paths?

Everything, at the outset, should have kept them apart — geography, language, culture, education, history, social status, political tendencies. And yet two lines from Baudelaire come stubbornly to mind whenever I recall their silhouettes:

> *Comme de longs échos qui de loin se répondent*
> *En une ténébreuse et profonde unité ....*
>
> [Like long echoes answering one another from afar
> in deep and somber unison]

Having visited them often in the two decades prior to their deaths, I was frequently able to sense the physical and spiritual brotherhood linking the two men.

As individuals, first: they were approximately the same age (Duchamp was born in 1887, Man Ray in 1890) and, like Picabia, belonged to the older generation of dadaists (Breton, Aragon, Tzara, and Eluard were ten years younger). This spurred a certain complicity born of joint action. Striking similarities also marked their instinctive reactions, their gestures, behavior, attitudes, tastes and

1) Jean Clair, Duchamp et la Photographie, Paris : Le Chêne, 1977.

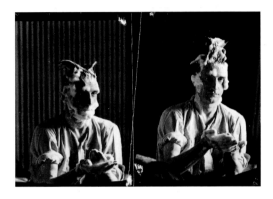

Marcel Duchamp, Bonds for Monte-Carlo roulette, 1924

preferences, their relationships, friendships, character traits, lifestyles. Their general attitude toward existence has been rendered more understandable by Paul Feyerabend's text on the "lightness of dadaist being." [2]

With his inimitable humor, Man Ray recounted his first meeting with Duchamp, who came to visit him in the company of Walter Arensberg in 1915 at the little house in Ridgefield, New Jersey, that he shared with "Donna" (Adon Lacroix). [3] Despite their ignorance of each other's language, they immediately found themselves on the same wavelength. Over the years, a few pithy phrases marked their entente. Duchamp used to say, "Yes, we're very fond of each other — we play chess and we don't have children." To Duchamp's famous statement that "There's no solution, because there's no problem," Man Ray replied, "I have no problems, I only have solutions."

Both of them tried to take their complementary and contradictory experiments to the limit: painting without a brush (air-brushing), then without canvas, then without use of the human hand, letting machines drive the artwork, abandoning plan or goal, taking chances, always going further just to see, to see....

Even without referring to texts or images, it is easy to see that, as their respective oeuvres evolved, innovations came to light almost simultaneously, according to a mode of remote communication that recalls DNA's double helix. It is possible to cite dozens of works that emerged at the same moment from their respective studios, yet accompanied by a silent inflection that saved them from absolute similarity. All along their parallel paths, from the Ridgefield meeting onward, a "mirroring effect" can be observed in their output: one echoed the other, harmonically rather than fundamentally identical. The effect was sometimes the fruit of deliberate collaboration, usually a distant exchange between two symbiotic minds. This type of echoing creativity has been noted between certain dadaists, especially between Picabia and Duchamp during the period of mechanomorphic canvases (New York, 1915–1920), although never so obstinately nor over so long a period.

Man Ray and Duchamp shared a love of experimentation elevated into unwritten dogma — the gift of inventiveness in its natural state. Both of them clearly found it impossible not to create. This led to all those things they did together, pell-mell: optical machines and cinematic experiments, "a-paintings," indulgence in games of chance, chess and chessboards, the New York dada publications, the founding of the Société Anonyme, fascination with magical objects and inventions. The close relationship between Duchamp's "ready-mades" and Man Ray's "objects of my affection" leaps to the eye. No difference of execution or intention can be perceived between the latter's *Gift* and the former's *Trébuchet*. Puns, mockery, sophisticated enigmas: *L'Enigme d'Isidore Ducasse* [*The Riddle*] is echoed by *Ready-Made à Bruit Secret* [*Ready-Made with Secret Sound*]. To hark back to Baudelaire once again, forms, ideas, and sounds echo one another.

One might establish, for example, an interesting parallel between research into the photographic handling of the image, notably Man Ray's solarizations, and certain works by Duchamp such as the *Portrait du Dr. Dumouchel* (April 1910) where the doctor's body is bathed in a halo or "miraculous aura" (Duchamp *scripsit*). Forty years later, the Soviet engineer Semen Kirlian would discover the aural doubling or "Kirlian effect," an electroluminescent phenomenon specific to living structures, characterized by a coronal image around the photographic plate of the subject.

2) Paul Feyerabend, Contre la Méthode, Paris : Le Seuil, 1979.

3) Man Ray, Self Portrait, Boston : Little, Brown, 1988, p. 56.

Divergences

And yet, the oneness of tone and meaning in the works and lives of the two friends cannot mask the differences that guarantee the originality of each man. Study of these disparities should not be limited, however, to a superficial list of points of dissimilarity. An heuristic tool is required to develop a global and exhaustive explanation of the feeling that Marcel Duchamp and Man Ray were each stamped with a fundamental originality that brooked neither copy nor replica.

The most convenient, if not the newest, tool is supplied by the typology elaborated by Pierre Bourdieu in his writings on the sociology of art. In his best known volume, *La Distinction, Critique Sociale du Jugement*, he showed how social background influences individual and collective behavior toward the products of artistic activity. [4] On one hand there is what he calls "legitimate" art, produced by and aimed at the "bourgeois" classes, developed and disseminated through traditional channels of cultural transmission, namely family school, college, church, army, and all establishment organizations whose goal is to elaborate and perpetuate tradition, that is to say develop a tree of cultural heritage for the dominant classes.

Each class has its own cultural domain. At the top are those who, although ignorant of much specialized knowledge, are able to locate it on a given branch of the tree of acquired information and therefore give the impression of having genetically received, so to speak, culture without having made an effort to acquire it. This is the realm of bourgeois aestheticism and eclecticism.

In counterpoint, "working-class aesthetics" is a *dominated* aesthetic which must constantly define itself in relation to dominant aestheticisms. [5] Each of the dominated classes is called upon to imitate, to the extent of its possibilities, artistic fields circumscribed by the upper class, considered to be the sole heir to artistic legitimacy. Having neither the financial resources nor the essential cultural institutions, a dominated class invents impoverished substitutes inspired by the legitimate cultural property it covets : thus operetta emerges in counterpoint to opera, movies to theater, records to concerts, collections of key-rings to collections of pre-Columbian statuettes.

Two methods of acquiring culture are therefore presented :

"Total, precocious, and painless learning, practiced from early childhood within the family, extended by academic learning which presupposes and completes it, as distinguished from later, methodical, accelerated learning not so much by the depth and durability of its effect — as the ideology of cultural 'polish' would have it — as by the modality of the language and culture that it furthermore tends to inculcate. It confers the self assurance that goes with the certainty of possessing the cultural legitimacy and ease identified with excellence ; it produces a paradoxical relationship, displayed by the old bourgeoisie, of confidence in (relative) ignorance and casual familiarity with culture, perceived as a kind of family property that has been legitimately inherited." [6]

Duchamp : eclectic, legitimate art

This latter picture seems to apply to Duchamp rather well. Raised in a close-knit,

4) Pierre Bourdieu, La distinction, Critique Sociale du Jugement, *Paris : Editions de Minuit, 1979, passim. The following quotations are translated directly from the French. (Cf. English translation by Richard Nice under the title of* Distinction, *Cambridge, Mass : Harvard University Press, 1984.)*

5) Bourdieu, p. 42, fn.

6) Bourdieu, p. 71.

affluent milieu, he received a classical education at the primary and secondary level, and passed his "baccalauréat" (a highly valued diploma at the time) at the Lycée Corneille in Rouen. Despite his intellectual bent, he did not shrink from technical training as a print-making "artisan," having inherited etching genes from his grandfather Emile Nicolle a well-known engraver. Strongly rooted in Normandy, and imbued with a sharp sense of family, Duchamp often returned to Rouen for reunions with his five brothers and sisters.

Thus he never had to worry about making a name (already taken, for that matter, by his two elder brothers, Raymond and Jacques); at the most, he would have to make his first name. He failed to get into the Ecole des Beaux-Arts in Paris, but attended, with no illusions, a private art studio called Académie Julian. Although on his own financially, he had enough elbow room to give free rein to his independent — indeed, libertarian — tendencies. He was neither ambitious nor concerned with success. His capital was composed not of money but of the symbolic property inherited from the family.

He therefore remained largely untroubled by financial problems throughout his life. He survived one way or another on minor jobs (librarian, French teacher, art adviser and broker, etc.). Later, he married Alexina Sattler, Pierre Matisse's first wife, reestablishing contact between himself and the art world.

He was a true dilettante, his life based on an innate sense of his own legitimacy, a source of security and confidence in a future guided by a strong if invisible thread. Although he went through difficult times just as everyone else did (notably during the two world wars), he did not show it.

Duchamp felt no need to tell his own story. Unlike Man Ray, he did not publish a biography or memoirs. Duchamp never indulged in that type of confession. He deliberately let silence reign over everything that concerned him personally, the events and incidents of his private or social life. It took the recollections of a few friends, plus the perseverance of Jacques Caumont, to assemble the scrupulous ephemerides that constitute the almanac of his existence. [7]

Duchamp's correspondence was often swift and superficial. He displayed sovereign haughtiness and affable serenity in the face of everyday incidents. He projected the outward appearance of a deliberately hieratic sphinx, with an enigmatic, Mona Lisa smile.

The term that might describe Duchamp's demeanor at any given moment is the sense of being *at ease*. As Bourdieu wrote, "Material or symbolic consumption of the art work constitutes a supreme sign of ease (with which excellence is identified) in the simultaneous meanings of condition and attitude that ordinary language gives to that word." [8]

Appearances were misleading. From those still waters would surge an intellectual rebellion, the most insidious of the twentieth century insofar as it sought to smash mental structures with powerful social roots.

His was a rebellion, not a revolution — and a solo rebellion at that. As Yeats pointed out, art is a social act by a lone individual. Indeed, it took a person sufficiently strong and undeniably legitimate to *validate aesthetically* ordinary or even "uncouth" objects (those aesthetically appropriated — or not — by the "uncouth," as in the ready-mades, for instance). [9]

7) See Jacques Caumont and Jennifer Gough-Cooper, Ephemerides On and About Marcel Duchamp and Rrose Sélavy, *Cambridge, Mass: MIT Press, 1993.*

8) Pierre Bourdieu, "*Anatomie du Goût*," Actes de la Recherche en Sciences Sociales, *no. 5, October 1976, Paris, p. 21.*

9) *Bourdieu,* La Distinction*..., p. 41.*

Joseph Stella and Marcel Duchamp

Man Ray : indiscriminate, illegitimate art

The other part of Bourdieu's picture would seem to cover Man Ray's particular case. Born into a poor Jewish immigrant family of Russian extraction, he spent his childhood in the "difficult" borough of Brooklyn, New York. He did well at elementary school and high school, was highly gifted in mechanical drawing, considered and then rejected a career as architect. He was curious about everything, and gifted in everything, yet seemed to have difficulty finding a direction in life. He frequented the anarchistic Francisco Ferrer art center as well as, from 1905 onward, Alfred Stieglitz's Photo-Secession Gallery, known as 291. He thereby closely linked painting and photography with an atmosphere of libertarian effervescence. He acquired the rudiments of literary culture through his first wife, the Belgian-born poet Adon Lacroix.

The social milieu in which Man Ray took root fully corresponds to Bourdieu's "illegitimate" category. Born on American soil, he was brought up on that country's founding values : Weber's redeeming ethic of work and money, the capitalist myth of the self-made man who starts with nothing but who owes everything to hard work and determination. Under these conditions, as a man of acquired culture, he could not entertain the casual relationship with culture that permitted the freedom and boldness displayed by those who possessed it by birthright, that is to say by nature and essence.

Throughout his *Self Portrait*, Man Ray recounts the ins and outs of his everyday adventures in an anecdotal style. As delightful and appealing as it is, this picaresque novel — highly lucid, disarmingly frank, alternately warm and vindictive — paints the uncompromising picture of a man caught in the storm of events, grumbling (sometimes brooding) about men (and women). His attractive character seems much more human, moving, freer and easier to grasp than Duchamp's. Although mystery remains, neither the life nor works of Man Ray are shrouded in darkness.

It was only in the occasional foreword to exhibition catalogues that Man Ray indulged in considerations of a more general order, suggesting that he had indeed thought deeply about major human issues. He followed an uncertain path governed by life's vicissitudes, chance encounters, and a feeling of financial insecurity. He was often anxious, uncomfortable, and linguistically tongue-tied in good (and critical) French circles, despite having many friends and "rubbing elbows" with high society.

Photography as a middling — but not minor — art

Frequently penniless, unsure of the future, not having Duchamp's naturally carefree attitude, Man Ray felt a need for recognition and social status. Simultaneously he feared being stuck in the role of art photographer (like Karsh or Harcourt) or darkroom wizard, as this would undermine his status as painter, or legitimate artist.

Indeed, the legitimate castes of the 1930s still considered photographic technique to be a derivative art. Because it was more accessible than painting, it was reserved for people "devoted to motley fields and middle arts, among which were recruited most of the fervent photographers, jazz and film specialists, or operetta lovers."[10]

10) Bourdieu, "Anatomie du Goût," p. 37. See also Pierre Bourdieu et al., Un Art Moyen, les Usages Socieaux de la Photographie, Paris : Editions de Minuit, 1965, passim.

As an intrinsically utilitarian medium, photography was granted aesthetic validity only for the information it conveyed and for the legibility of that information, which led to Man Ray's feeling of awkwardness during the period of his society portraits.

What truly interested Man Ray were precisely the impoverished substitutes for "chic" objects and practices — objects yanked out of context, incongruous and provocative paintings, photographs whose meaning was found only in the images themselves. Yet his public was probably disoriented by the variety of subjects and techniques he employed, making it hard to judge or distinguish between what was legitimate and what was crudely indiscriminate. As Man Ray himself pointed out, he was disturbed by the idea of having to stick with fixed, recognizable style, for it would turn painting into a colossal bore. He was an artist seeking an identity, without managing to find one.

Convergences

According to Bourdieu's typology, Man Ray and Duchamp were predestined to "go with the grain" of their social categories, Duchamp in the cosy realm of the cream of bourgeois society, Man Ray within the disjointed culture of America's *uomo qualunque* ("man in the street"). Yet it so happened that both found themselves, at the end of a long and chaotic road, liberated or excluded from their respective classes. They reconciled illegitimacy with eclecticism, legitimacy with disorder. This was something not anticipated by Bourdieu, himself a prisoner of Marxian analysis in which social environment inescapably and inexorably seals the fate of individuals and societies.

The fact is that the indiscriminate has become legitimate in today's artistic context. Industrial objects, diverted from their original purpose, now hold pride of place alongside Rembrandts in the most famous collections. If Duchamp's original urinal were to turn up, the most glamorous galleries in the world would shamelessly offer extravagant bids at Christie's. During the 1988 Man Ray exhibition in Washington, monumental reproductions of his *Object to Be Destroyed* (metronome) swept their inquisitorial, mocking eyes over the steps of official buildings in the U.S. capital, even as the nation's Smithsonian Institute elevated little Emmanuel Radnitsky to the rank of "An American Master."

The approach followed by both men, totally spontaneous and unconscious at first, slowly took the form of a unified set of theoretical concepts over the years, which appears to us today to represent a new socio-artistic model. It is safe to say that it will survive over and above national and linguistic cultures, racial and geographic borders, and that as the century draws to a close it will thrive thanks to numerous imitators — indeed forgers — as well as authentic heirs.

We are witnessing the rehabilitation of the indiscriminate at the expense of eclecticism and salonesque aestheticism. Dada in general — and Man Ray and Duchamp in particular — overturned the establishment's tendency to impose order. They granted titles of nobility, so to speak, to middling art forms once consigned to daily consumption by the proletarian classes. For Man Ray, this meant abandoning the constraining Graflex of his early days for rayographs, and later for the rediscovery of chromatic emulsions that had so delighted nineteenth-century pictorialists.

Transatlantic, 1921

Duchamp's personal path, modus operandi, and implementation were identical. They ultimately convey extreme coherence when considered with enough distance and height so that every calculated gesture, every thought, every idea, every work (thing done), every word and text (things said) takes its place, like so many dots in a pointillist painting that requires a certain density of points before it suddenly congeals meaningfully.

The intention to invert or transgress limits, as constantly manifested by Duchamp's oeuvre, ultimately obliges the legitimate intelligentsia to recognize this very transgression of limits as an *aesthetic*.

The concomitance of the two men's approaches was patent even prior to their encounter, and it could be said that intellectually they were fated to meet despite an unfavorable historical and geographic conjuncture. They shared the same purpose, same process, same result — abolishing the distinction made by Bourdieu (who, moreover, remains superbly ignorant of dada, Duchamp, and Man Ray). One of them — Duchamp — started from a covert conceptualization of how to execute a fundamental challenge to bourgeois aestheticism, while the other — Man Ray — began empirically, from the outside, by turning products of lower-class aesthetics against that aesthetic, until everything resulted in a new, original cultural product accessible to all, transcending both proletarian color prints and aristocratic old masters.

One might legitimately wonder why it took so long for the general public to appreciate the true value of work of Man Ray and Marcel Duchamp. I remember having questioned Duchamp on this point. He told me that it was only natural, since no art dealer could have backed and defended someone like himself, who had produced so few saleable objects, or like Man Ray who created so many diverse pieces with no apparent link between them. "We were both stricken with a crippling vice — we couldn't repeat ourselves."

A reading of the books now available, covering the quasi-totality of the works of Man Ray and Marcel Duchamp, indeed gives this impression of an inextricable jumble. Nothing fulfills our insatiable appetite for order and logic. Yet beneath this apparently heterogeneous clutter lies the hint of a source of endless, unknown riches.

Collection d'Hiver [Winter Collection], 1936

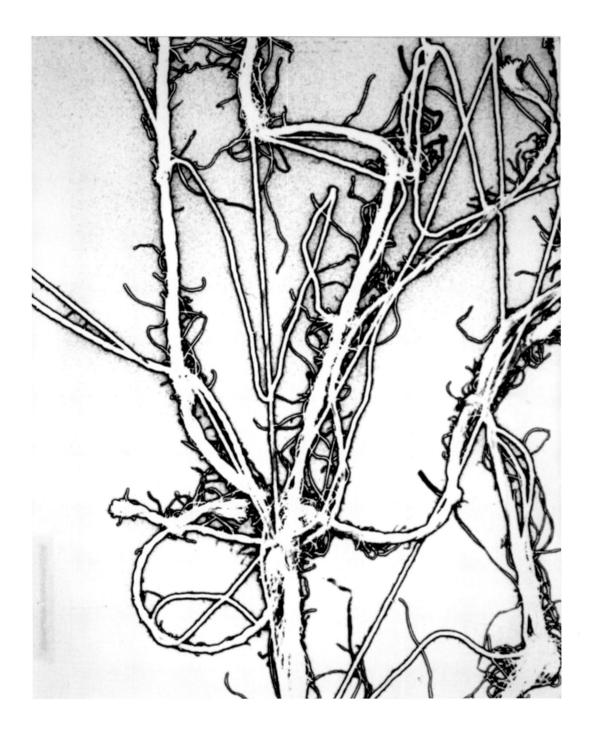

Enough Rope, 1944

Le Bouquet, 1935

Feu d'Artifice [Fireworks], 1934

Lee Miller, circa 1930

Silhouette, 1930

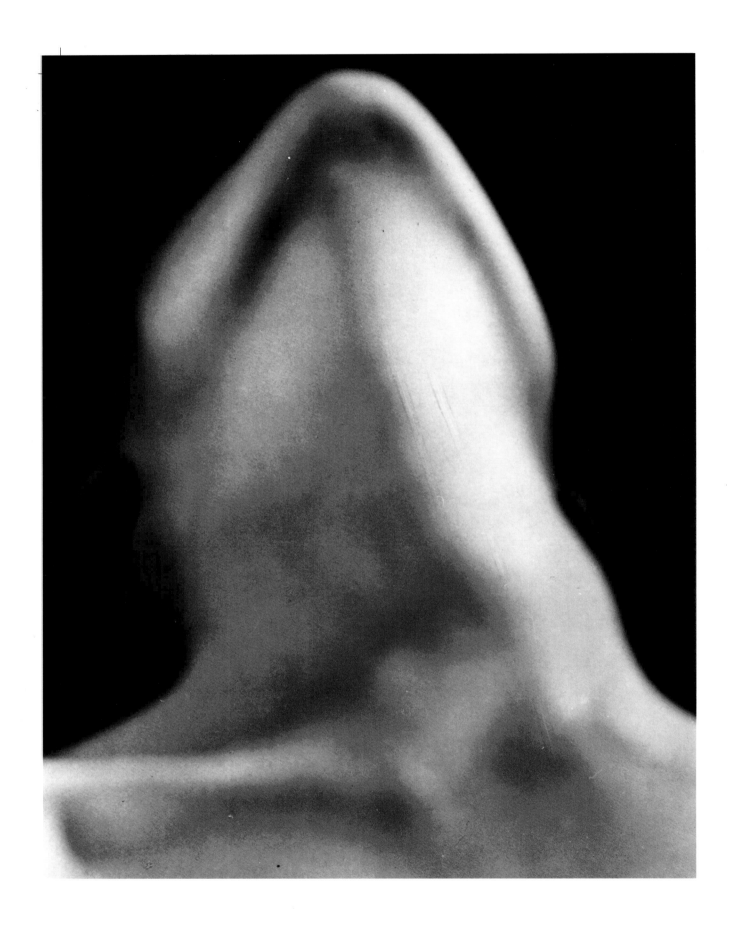

Anatomies, 1929

Untitled, 1933

Minotaure, 1933

Explosante-fixe, 1934

Prou del Pilar, study for *Explosante-fixe*, 1934

Prou del Pilar, study for *Explosante-fixe*, 1934

1) Man Ray, Self Portrait, Boston : Little Brown, 1988, 97.

2) Man Ray, Self Portrait (1988), p.135.

3) Man Ray, Self Portrait (1988), p. 206

4) Paul Hill and Thomas Cooper, Dialog with Photography, Thames & Hudson, 1979, p.9. Reprinted in Camera and in Philippe Sers, Man Ray Photographe, Paris, 1981, withut crediting the interviewers.

5) Rene Crevel, "Le Miroir aux Objets," L'Art Vivant, no 14-15, July 1925, p.24.

Untitled, 1924

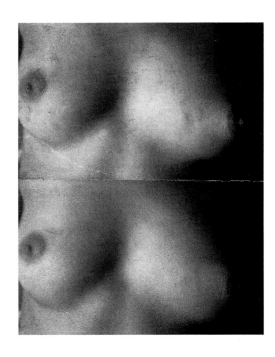

What is so original about Man Ray's oeuvre ? What makes it unique among the particularly worthy output of photographers in Paris between 1922 and 1936 ?

Perhaps the source of his originality lay, as suggested by Herbert Moderings and Michel Sanouillet, in his enduring relationship with Marcel Duchamp and in his poorly understood determination to show us another way of grasping the sensible world. Man Ray, who was no theorist, allegedly used the means at his disposal — most notably photography — to attempt to convey this new experience.

Although he practiced the trade of photographer on a daily basis, providing magazines and other clients with competent "hackwork", [1] he strove to distinguish it from what he called his "creative productions," which he felt demanded "the same deference accorded to a work of art." [2] He noted that certain ideas "demanded a more flexible medium for their expression than the rigidity of the camera," which he had taken "to the limits of [his] inventive capacities," and that only painting enabled him to avoid "daily routine". [3] Yet he immediately added that if he had had access to the technical means to make a huge enlargement of Lee Miller's lips, which he placed in the sky above the landscape of A l'Heure de l'Observatoire — Les Amoureux [Observatory Time — The Lovers], he would have willingly abandoned the boring, repetitive manual chore that occupied him almost every morning for nearly two years, in favor of another, more efficient and less painstaking method, such as photography. And although he added that he painted only what he could not photograph — things that sprang from the imagination, dreams, or a "subconscious impulse," [4] he did not intend to establish an opposition between what he painted and what he photographed.

It would therefore be misleading, within Man Ray's work, to set photography and painting against one another. As René Crevel pointed out, "photography is not painting..., yet [Man Ray's] photography is not photography, that is to say not just a copy. He knows how to raise the key issues — the ones that arise from the spectacle of the world. So when it comes to a corkscrew, the legs of the Eiffel Tower, or a piece of sugar, [he] forces us to ask whether the corkscrews, Eiffel Tower legs and pieces of sugar that uncork, kick, or feed our dreams are in fact less questionable than the everyday corkscrews, Eiffel Tower legs, and pieces of sugar which are so familiar that they become invisible and therefore non-existent." [5] There indeed lies the essence, the ease with which Man Ray transformed the most banal image or modest visual record into a source of "mystery."

This was the direction in which Breton attempted to prod Jacques-André Boiffard when he asked him to provide photographic illustrations for Nadja in 1928. The results are well known : Boiffard's pictures — perhaps hamstrung by overly strict instructions — remain uninterestingly banal. Man Ray, meanwhile, knew how to "paint" with the most modest photo ; it might even be said without exaggeration that this was all he could do, given that his strictly painterly creativity was almost always destroyed by dismayingly impoverished technique.

An example can be found in his "mathematical equations," which yielded a series of photographs between 1934 and 1936 and a series of paintings some ten years

Élevage de Poussière [Dust Breeding], 1920

6) Christian Zervos, "*Mathématiques et Art Abstrait,*" Cahiers d'Art, *1936, p.10.*

later. There is no trace of his visit to the Institut Poincaré (leading to the suggestion that his interest was the result of a chance encounter with these physical models of mathematical formulas, rather than the encouragement of Duchamp or Max Ernst), but his interest is incontrovertible since, if Lucien Treillard is to be believed, he photographed them on various occasions between 1934 and 1936. Above all, he allowed the photos to be published in 1936 as illustration to a long article by Christian Zervos criticizing abstract art which "reduces art to the positioning of several squares and circles, [to] decorativeness in its lowliest form." [6]

Unfortunately, a small album of contact prints titled Contacts for *Shakespearian Equations*, acquired by the Musée National d'Art Moderne in 1994, sheds little light on the issue. Dated 1935-1948 on the back cover, it contains 31 contacts, many of which bear cropping indications as well as annotations such as a mathematical description by Michel Colinet, a title from Shakespeare, the letter "T" in red pencil (referring to a potential *tirage*, or print?), or occasional indications of dimensions. Sometimes the letter "C" is added in blue pencil, the meaning of which is obscure. Nothing indicates the purpose of this album: was it a series of "photographic notes" for a set of paintings, or a dummy of a small book of photographs? What is revealing, however, is Man Ray's own discussion of the objects, for he indicates what it was that sparked his interest. It was not just the fantastic nature of these three-dimensional transcriptions of highly precise mathematical

7) *Man Ray, Self Portrait (1988), p. 291.*

8) *Man Ray, Self Portrait (1988), p. 291.*

9) *Zervos, p. 6.*

10) *Umberto Eco, L'Oeuvre Ouverte, Paris : Le Seuil, 1965, p. 123.*

11) *Eco, p. 123.*

12) *See Emmanuelle de l'Ecotais, Le Fonds Photographique de la Dation Man Ray, étude et inventaire, PhD dissertation, Université de Paris IV (Sorbonne), 1997, pp. 170-171.*

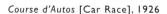

Course d'Autos [Car Race], 1926

equations (which would earn them a place in the Museum of Modern Art's 1934 Fantastic Art Show), but "the fact that they were man-made."[7] This meant the pictures he produced were not abstract, as Breton feared, because "all abstract art appeared to [Man Ray] as fragments : enlargements of details in nature and art, whereas these objects were complete microcosms."[8] Their shapes "are undeniably beautiful, often unpredictable, sometimes haunting, which draws them close to the shapes of art. But when they revert to their true nature ... these objects have absolutely no relationship to the irrational [element] inherent in art."[9] What pushes them into the artistic sphere, then, is the photographic image Man Ray produced, representing an approach that establishes these images as an extension of the photographs he did from 1918 onwards, such as *Man* and *Woman*, where photography was already being used as a tool for generating ambiguity, for revealing the fundamentally indeterminate nature of photographic reality. Man Ray enabled photography to participate in art's new-found freedom, namely the infinite power of unconscious, proliferating projections, spurring him to follow a path where discoveries were always highly unpredictable. In theory, then — as Umberto Eco has suggested — there might be a parallel between the development of non-Euclidean geometries and the abandonment of classical geometrical forms by fauvist and cubist artists, between the advent of abstract painting and the emergence in mathematics of imaginary numbers, transfinite numbers, and set theory."[10] As Eco notes, of course, one should be wary of the perils of a determinism which is now tending to replace the Marxist vulgate with a causality as absurd as it is illusory. Yet it remains true that "values once thought to be absolute, thought to constitute the metaphysical framework of the world" now appear, in the light of new scientific concepts, to be a question of convention. They are "no longer indispensable for explaining the world or for creating another one." When it comes to art, however, "it is less a question of finding rigorous formal equivalents for these new concepts than of negating old concepts. Here again one finds, alongside a science which promises nothing more than a supposed structure of things, an effort by art to give this new world an image that is at least plausible, an image that general sensibility — always lagging behind intellect — has not yet adopted."[11]

By overturning the conventions of perspective deemed intrinsic to the photo-graphic process, beginning with his earliest "autonomous" experiments in the medium, Man Ray placed photography at the heart of the artistic debate of the day. Thanks to him, photography — an instantaneous and mechanical appropriation of reality — even became the ideal medium of surrealism. A photograph like the 1920 *Moving Sculpture*, for instance, does not seem like a simple depiction of sheets on a clothesline, but appears instead to answer Leonardo's question : how can the wind be painted?[12] This materialization of a "breath of air" tells us more about Man Ray's desire to free sculpture from materiality than it does about the primitive state of French society which willingly aired its laundry in public (as suggested by the caption "France" when this picture was published in the sixth issue of *La Révolution Surréaliste*, March 1, 1926).

Contrary to what might be thought, however, the dematerialization of photography was not linked to the use of new photographic processes. Attentive study of MNAM's Man Ray archives shows that special technical effects

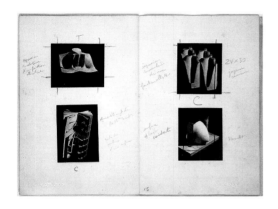

Contacts For Shakespearian [Sic],Equations, 1935-1948

(superimposition of negatives or screens, inversion, solarization, etc.), were more likely to be used in pictures of a professional nature, indicating their "artistic" status. Cropping was the only artifice that Man Ray employed consistently. Whether indicated in pencil, pen, or by folding the contact print, he constantly "de-realized his images" by cropping them.[13] What at first was probably a technical constraint dictated by his lack of adequate lighting and lenses, soon became a strength. "Some of the most effective photographs ... were magnifications of a detail of the face and body. .... I carried this idea further by giving such details a texture inherent in the medium itself, coarse grain, partial reversal of the negative and other technical variations; all frowned upon by straight photographers."[14]

Yet while it is true that several of his major images combined all these methods, their use was in no way mandatory in obtaining an effect of unreality. An example of this is his 1920 photograph of the "Large Glass" in Duchamp's New York studio. The feeble light level that forced him to open the aperture wide and make a long exposure, the apparent change in scale, and the tilting of the picture plane turned what could have been a banal reproduction of work-in-progress into a strange landscape in which the eye contrives to see dust and tufts of cotton either as a vast, cloudy expanse partly obscuring traces of unintelligible architecture, or as a sandy desert dotted with rocks and enigmatic ruins.

For Man Ray, photography freed painting from its role of anecdotal depiction. But painters still had to free photography from its strictly utilitarian role. With photography, he claimed, "we merely enlarged our scope, our vocabulary."[15]

Fifty years later, the lesson taught by Man Ray is still valid. Although one needs "a mirror and larks to hunt larks, mirroring the object alone will not suffice to charm. That is why photographers, like painters and poets, cannot be content with a meticulous account."

13) Of the 5,004 contact prints in the MNAM archives, 1,120 bear cropping indications, which corresponds fairly closely to the number of pictures actually used. Emmanuelle de l'Ecotais's analysis of the archives show that not a single negative was printed "full frame."

14) Man Ray, Self Portrait (1988), p. 206.

15) Man Ray, La Photographie Peut Etre de l'Art

Objet Mathématique [Mathematical Object], 1934-1936

Objet Mathématique [Mathematical Object], 1934-1936

 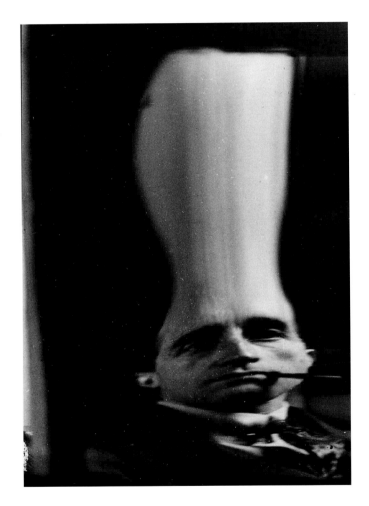

Marcel Duchamp, Distorsion [Marcel Duchamp Distorted], 1925

Moving Sculpture or *La France*, 1920

Portrait, circa 1930

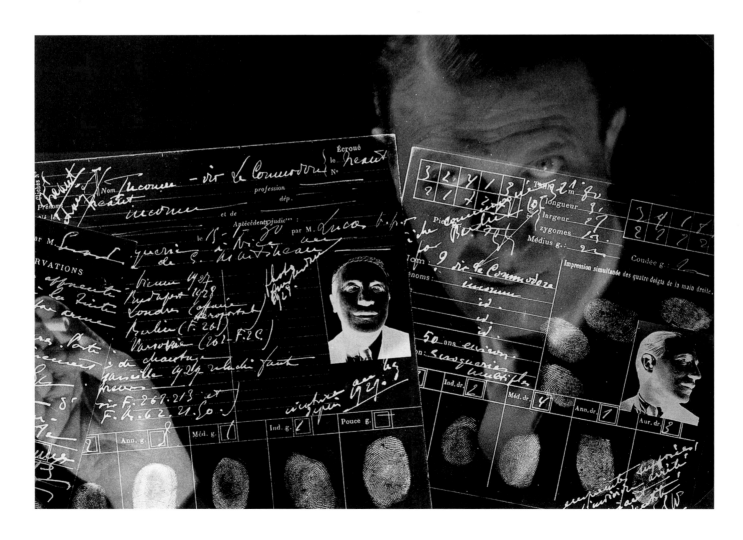

Untitled, circa 1930

Marcel Duchamp, circa 1920

Interview with Lucien Treillard

Musée National d'Art Moderne (MNAM) : *When did you meet Man Ray?*

Lucien Treillard (L.T.) : At the time I was working for Georges Visat, who published editions of Max Ernst, Matta, etc. He sent me to see Man Ray because he wanted to do prints and books with him. So I went to Rue Férou and knocked on the door. That was in the early 1960s. Man Ray's dealer was Petithory. Man Ray received me cordially, and I went back more and more often, because he needed help — he was beginning to get old. There was a lot of physical handling in his studio : you had to climb up to the loft to get paintings, bring them down, hunt for negatives, and so on. I began working one hour a day, then two, then nine — it happened little by little.

At the time, Petithory was a bookseller and publisher — he was the one who published the treatise on *Mannequins*. When preparing his catalogues, he would delve into Man Ray's library, since he had saved nearly all his documents. He also took [Man Ray] on vacation, to the south of France and more or less everywhere.

Man Ray asked me to help him with editions of lithographs and engravings. Things were beginning to pick up, and it was more than he could handle. A Man Ray wasn't expensive — he was paid 3,000 francs for an edition of an object, it was pathetic. Arturo Schwarz manufactured the objects in Paris, and had Man Ray sign them before leaving for Italy again. Man Ray wasn't very satisfied; he wanted to monitor the execution. He was demanding. I remember that he made me redo *N for Nothing*, a pretty simple object, five or six times, because the sandpaper was never glued just right. The simpler the object seemed, the trickier the execution turned out to be.

MNAM : *Was he demanding in terms of the technique required for an idea he had in mind, or in terms of an earlier version?*

L.T. : In terms of the idea as it had been originally materialized. He felt, for example, that Schwarz's executions were inadequate. When Zerbib and Marconi wanted to issue objects in silver, he thought it would betray the original works, which were in wood most of the time.

MNAM : *It was always in terms of the original work?*

L.T. : Or the photo of the original work, since very often the original work had been lost or destroyed. A lot were lost during the war, in particular at Rue du Val-de-Grâce, where Ady had remained long after Man Ray left for the United States.

An absolutely charming man, who had come back from Germany, moved in with her. She cared for him, fed him, and so on. Obviously, they had no source of income. The day they couldn't meet the rent, they simply walked out, taking everything in the studio, but not in the maid's room. The things in the cellar, two Mirós and Duchamp's *Bottle Rack*, were never found — which is understandable, since the Mirós were in wood and were probably used for firewood during the war, whereas Duchamp's *Bottle Rack* probably reverted to its original use.

Part of the collection of 1,500 negatives I have given to the museum comes directly from Man Ray ; the rest I bought from Ady's friend. He's still alive, although Ady herself died several years ago. When he wanted to sell his house on Rue Pascal, he sent me a note asking me to come over, and he showed me what he had saved. I acquired it all, except for the birds used for props in fashion photos, birds executed by J.-M. Frank, probably after a model by Giacometti.

MNAM : *And yet many negatives have been lost.*

L.T. : All the negatives were kept in the maid's room on Rue du Val-de-Grâce. Two people went into that room during the war : Eluard, who had the right to take works and sell them, in agreement with Man Ray, and Ady Fidelin's brother, who did not have the same respect for Man Ray's oeuvre and probably destroyed or sold the photos.

MNAM : *But he didn't sell negatives.*

L.T. : No, they were unsalable. But negatives are fragile — they were easily dispersed or broken. Man Ray told me that when he returned, a lot of them were in pieces on the floor.

MNAM : *When we made an inventory of the collection, we were amazed by the almost total absence of negatives of rayographs. No more than thirty exist, which is relatively few in terms of the two-hundred-odd that are listed. Yet a certain number of rayographs were re-photographed, notably for* Les Champs Délicieux.

L.T. : That's not all — there are many items for which the negatives have disappeared, like *Mannequins*, which Man Ray never found again. You only needed to have a box on a ledge of the maid's room, it could fall to the floor and get smashed.

MNAM : *So you think the destruction was random, rather than systematic?*

L.T. : Completely random. The only destruction intended by Man Ray concerned negatives of "clients." He broke a certain number of them himself, then one day he gave me an enormous box and a hammer, and he said, "Take that home and bust it up, there'll be too much broken glass, I don't want to see it around here." But now you have them [in the archives], and I think they have a certain interest.

MNAM : *What do you mean by "clients?"*

L.T. : People who came to his studio to be photographed, with their wives, children, and dogs. You have a whole stack of them, but he probably did ten times as many. Man Ray was a highly popular photographer. All the Americans who came to Paris wanted to sit for him.

When I first arrived at Rue Férou, the negatives were all filed in a back room, with names on the boxes. But some boxes were already ruined, because dampness had seeped under the emulsion. I remember a box of portraits of Kiki and another of Duchamp, which he had me print contacts from. Duchamp's face can barely be made out.

MNAM : *What's surprising is that, in the end, there are relatively few major pictures among the contact prints. There are stacks of portraits, but Man Ray's really important pictures don't exist in contacts, as though he worked directly on them. For instance, with an image like* Tears, *we have a full-frame contact of the entire head, but we don't have the cropping indications, which we know thanks to various vintage prints — one of just the two eyes, and one of a single, upside-down eye.*

L.T. : Pictures like those were largely composed in the darkroom, based on trial-and-error. It should be added that composition was often ignored when the photo was taken. There's a strong link between photographers' visual defects and what they produce.

MNAM : *What do you mean by that?*

L.T. : A photographer might be near-sighted or astigmatic, and Man Ray claimed that you could see it on the print.

In his case, since he didn't plan the final composition during the session, his subsequent work was one of cropping — cropping in pen or pencil as you have on the contacts, or cropping by cutting the negative, you have that too, and sometimes by taking the contact print and folding it. Those are basically the three

techniques he used. At that point, a difficulty arose when making the print : if you want a print of very fine quality — something that Gassman fully understood — you have to develop a system of masks because you can't use the standard system. You're obliged to do the masking by hand, which means that to get a high quality photo, a positive print, you have to produce ten that go straight into the garbage can. For a certain number of pictures, Gassman was very successful. Man Ray showed him how to proceed.

He wanted to reproduce the original framing and the atmosphere of the photograph as it had been at the outset. That's why I say that the contact prints are crucial, since they're the prints he made to have a quick view of what he'd shot, in order to choose the final image.

MNAM : *He nevertheless did a lot of work in the darkroom to produce his key images. If we take other examples, like the 1923* Nude Kiki, *it's an image that matured through darkroom work, work at the printing stage. He was not as lazy as he made out, that was just a pose he adopted.*

L.T. : He didn't function like the other artists he knew, like Braque and Picasso, who entered their studios at 8 a.m., left at noon, and started again at 2 p.m. He created when the spirit moved him, when he felt like it ; even when he had a commission, he had to be prodded to get it done. But when I accompanied him during shooting sessions, for photos of mannequins in front of the television, for instance, or the final De Sade portraits, which are his last photos, the composition required a great deal of preparation time — the lights were all carefully calculated, he was constantly intervening. Taking the photo was really work.

MNAM : *And when he was doing a portrait?*

L.T. : I think there were two different cases. I'll exclude the family portraits because, when he came to my place on Sundays — I'd bought him a Polaroid — he'd take portraits at great speed, just for fun. But getting a portrait just right was extremely tricky. When he left for vacation on the Basque coast, Boiffard would stay at his studio, where [Man Ray] had set up spot lights, the camera, all the equipment, and people had to sit at a precise spot. He gave Boiffard full instructions, as their letters confirm.

MNAM : *But Boiffard wasn't his assistant for very long.*

L.T. : After [Boiffard] left, he hired another assistant — he always had one. He hated carrying the plates and box cameras, which were very heavy. Even the Graflex was relatively heavy. Boiffard was useful, being very strong.

MNAM : *Even for his early exhibitions, Man Ray had someone do the printing?*

L.T. : Yes, he didn't print much. Jacqueline Goddard told me she'd seen him print two or three times, that's all. He made the contact prints, and on back of the contacts you have instructions for the assistant. He didn't touch a thing after that, he knew exactly what he wanted, all the technical information — format, paper, full instructions — were given to the assistant. He wanted to be as free as possible. He couldn't do everything, couldn't paint, build his objects, take care of his friends, go to surrealist meetings, do fashion photos. So it was his assistant who worked in the photo studio. That's why he always had a studio.

MNAM : *He did a lot of fashion work, but didn't do advertising, for example.*

L.T. : He did a few ad photos for jewelry, for necklaces, rings — fashion-related advertising. There were a few photos done for industrial furnaces and steel mills, there was *Electricité*, but it was on the fringe of commission work; he didn't need to do it to survive. At that time, he was the only one who was comfortably off — all the people I've met who knew him in the 1920s and '30s have told me that he was the only one who was financially secure. I forget who told me — Meret, maybe, or Jacqueline — that they all ran up bills at the cafés, whereas he always had the wherewithal to pay for his meals and drinks. It should be mentioned that he began doing fashion photography very early thanks to Yvonne Chastel and Elsa Schiaparelli, whom he met in New York in 1919. It's important since fashion paid best at the time.

MNAM : *It's true that there are fashion photographs published in 1924–1925. The oldest examples are the Poiret photos from 1922, but only two are known to exist. Above all, one gets the impression that the fashion business really took off with* Harper's Bazaar, *beginning only in 1934–1935.*

L.T. : That's because of economic conditions : France was in a crisis, whereas he was working for the American market, which was

picking up again. He benefited from an advantageous situation. In the 1930s, America was in depression, but he was living in France. He was also able to build up a special clientele, and I think that special clientele continued to grow. Rich Americans began to visit France, and they all wanted to be photographed by Man Ray.

MNAM : *Strangely, he no longer profited from that situation in the 1950s.*

L.T. : He was no longer interested in photography at that point. He did a little in the United States, especially portraits of Juliet, as well as a few reproductions of paintings. But it was no longer his source of income. During the war, in the United States, he'd tried to sell his art work through exhibitions. When he returned to Paris, he wanted to come across as a painter, or a sculptor, or anything you like, but not a photographer ; so he didn't do any more photography. He was interested in being recognized as an artist, not as a photographer. He wanted to forget that label.

At one point, he wanted to sell all his photographic material, the negatives along with the prints and the cameras. I think it was in 1961 when he made the first move. An American university was interested, but when he told them the price — he wanted $50,000 — they thought it was too much. He didn't pursue it, he thought it was unsalable.

MNAM : *Why did Man Ray begin re-printing photographs after the war?*

L.T. : The reprints from old negatives were the result of exhibition requests, which were increasing at that time, whereas he didn't have any old prints. In 1962, when the Bibliothèque Nationale gave him a retrospective, he had to ask Pierre Gassman to do the prints. He didn't have enough old prints, especially not of the major pictures that would give a true idea of his work.

MNAM : *Or the idea he wanted to give. . . .*

L.T. : Or the idea he wanted to give of his work. Because when the negatives where chosen, he eliminated some things and selected others that he wanted reproduced. Moreover, like Duchamp, he wanted to see the same works reproduced over and over, which he thought was the best form of publicity. He was an American — pragmatic and efficient.

MNAM : *But how could he agree to release such mediocre prints, especially for exhibitions? Why didn't he print them himself?*

L.T. : In fact, Man Ray only printed his contacts. He always had an assistant. He couldn't have cared less about the quality of the final print, it didn't interest him — he was very pleased with the show at the BN in 1962.

MNAM : *He didn't like to print?*

L.T. : He always told me that when he found an assistant able to do things as well as he could, or better, he'd let him get on with it.

MNAM : *And yet you get the impression that he liked technical manipulations a lot, that there was a "craft" side to him.*

L.T. : There was a manual side to him, but it was for innovating, for installing a canopy in the studio, or inventing a swinging table so that he could have tea or read in bed. Whereas printing was always more or less the same thing.

MNAM : *Did he place more importance on old prints than on modern prints?*

L.T. : At first he was shocked that people only wanted old prints — at the time they were called "vintage." People always wanted vintage prints, without knowing exactly what the term covered; it might be a 1922 negative printed in 1938. This vagueness still exists today, for that matter, nurtured by dealers.

MNAM : *And what do you think? These days, people tend to think that Man Ray's original production is limited to the vintage prints, and that the modern versions, such as the prints done for Photokina in 1960, are only an approximation of the original work.*

L.T. : I find that modern prints lack the presence found in the old prints. Especially the contacts, which have a kind of aura.

MNAM : *Don't you think it's something we project onto those works — which are theoretically reproducible works — a mind-set which is always the same, related to the idea of a relic?*

L.T. : I don't think so. There's a quality to the image, there is also a deepness to the blacks, an aging, which is very lovely. The papers are different. Man Ray placed great importance on the paper for certain images. He conducted trials with Guilleminot, Kodak, Léonard and Agfa papers, and he used nearly transparent paper for certain portraits, rayographs, and *Noire et Blanche*. His papers were very handsome, often buff-colored, slightly tinted, and produced a richness, substance, that has been lost with modern papers, which are much too white.

MNAM : *So, according to you, the real difference between a print done in the 1960s and a vintage print is not whether Man Ray printed it himself or not, since clearly he didn't even do his own printing in the 1920s, instead it's the paper....*

L.T. : It's the object. The object isn't the same. When you hang them on the wall, there's not a moment's hesitation. I find the contact prints even richer. Man Ray made lots of small prints, for economic reasons — between 1920 and 1940 paper was expensive, as were darkroom materials, which explains the number of post cards he had in the studio, I'm convinced there were at least a thousand. Postcards were done on very handsome heavy paper or card, and he loved his prints on postcards, which he often did himself.

MNAM : *Postcards were also a good way of disseminating his images.*

L.T. : That's right. It should be said that at the time, between 1920 and 1940, the dissemination of his works was totally amazing. Publications in every European country made it possible to know what photographers were producing — his work was seen even in Japan and the United States. And Man Ray's prints are small format — although you have a large format rayograph in your collection, there are not many of them, because it's simpler to produce a rayograph by direct contact than by enlarging with a lateral light source.

MNAM : *Rayographs are another matter. It's true that there are few large-sized exhibition prints. Except for later shows like the ones at the BN and Photokina—and in the latter case it was at Grüber's request.*

L.T. : The pictures he exhibited, and which I know, are mostly rather small, glued to cardboard or to heavy large-format paper, as was fashionable at the time.

MNAM : *Because, unlike the Russians and Moholy-Nagy, he refused to make photography the equivalent of painting.*

L.T. : For him, photography was another medium which, like painting, allowed him to create art works. He was aware of this right from the early 1920s.

MNAM : *So he returned to photography only in the context of the exhibitions in the 1960s, and only in terms of his personal development.*

L.T.: He only took up photography again because the dealers encouraged him to. Photos were beginning to reach a public, to sell. The first pictures I saw bought by [Arnold] Crane went for $40, I think. Later, prices went up a little, going to $50, $60, $70. But Crane made purchases in installments. I remember that Man Ray had me stamp them [with one of the various studio stamps] and would say, "It's for Crane, just put any old stamp on it; don't bother asking me — whichever one you like." He enjoyed earning money, but he hated people who came solely for that. He dictated which pictures he'd sell, and slipped modern prints in. He jumbled up the prints, just like in the BN show.

MNAM: *So the conclusion is that dating cannot be reliably deduced from the studio stamp?*

L.T.: It's often very tricky. The problem of dating Man Ray's prints, as with almost every photographer, is highly complicated. The same goes for the dates written next to his signature. When he wrote "Man Ray Paris 1928," 1928 was often the date the photo was taken, not when the print was made. He did that often, though not systematically.

MNAM: *So you think that if he returned extensively to the field of photography in the 1960s, it was due to pressure from the context, from dealers?*

L.T.: When Crane arrived — who deserves credit for being one of the first American collectors after the war — he bought a lot from Man Ray, who said to himself that he could profit from it. Even at a modest price, the money added up. He also saw the attraction of working with Petithory: the *Traité des Mannequins* sold well. The same thing held for the Italians. So why not redo the photographs?

MNAM: *Especially when you have them redone by others, which is even easier.*

L.T.: When he produced the book *Voies Lactées* [*Milky Ways*], it was still photographic work even if it appeared in book form. He was highly interested in the problem of grays at the time. He was shocked by the photos he received, which were always in black and white. There was a point when it was totally black and white, which he found shocking. At that point, he wanted to do the white book on milky ways, therefore completely white,

since the typeface was white and white dominated in the photos, white and values of gray; he even did the three photos of Julie Lawson which are studies in gray. He really wanted to have gray images, with various values of gray. It was total experimentation.

MNAM: *Why wasn't he more interested in color?*

L.T.: He patented a color process, but it didn't have much success. He nevertheless used this transparent process to photograph all the celebrities of the day — Greco, Montand, Dominguez. The drawback was that it produced a unique work, painstakingly. Very few photographers of his generation were interested in color. Man Ray himself began with autochromes at an early date, in 1925; he also used a three-color system for the 1934 album. But reproducing colors was extremely difficult at the time. He also did some color photographs in California with the first Kodacolor film, which are rather successful. They're portraits of Juliet.

MNAM: *Let's talk about the rayographs. Tristan Tzara was known to have a collection of schadographs, and Tzara and Man Ray were pretty close.*

L.T.: Man Ray must have seen them. He didn't discover rayographs by chance. Schad's work was published in *Dadaphone*, he saw it, everyone saw it at the time. And then there was an explosion of photograms, everyone was doing them — they existed in Poland, Russia, in practically every country. So it is probable that he was aware of Schad's work. It's also significant that Tzara, who owned some schadographs, wrote the preface to *Champs Délicieux* and helped launched rayographs. But [Man Ray] always denied it, because he wanted to present a certain image of his oeuvre. There's an enormous difference between rayographs and schadographs. They don't occupy the same universe, they don't use the technique in the same way — Man Ray worked in the darkroom, which was not the case with Schad.

MNAM: *The same problem arises with solarization, because there are two stories: in the first, Man Ray says that the door to the studio opened accidentally, while in the second Lee Miller says that a mouse ran under her feet, startling her, and that she turned on the light. Which version is true?*

L.T.: I haven't a clue. Lee always told me that she was the one who turned on the light, and that she showed the outcome to

Man Ray, who found it very beautiful and began to systematize it.

MNAM: *So she really stuck to her version?*

L.T.: Don't forget that Lee Miller, often presented as a complete beginner, was the daughter of a photographer and was already familiar with the technique; she came to Paris to perfect her skills with Man Ray. They worked together on many pictures — there's perhaps a topic of research on what is due to one and what is due to the other, if it can be done.

MNAM: *Is it conceivable that unknown photographic works by Man Ray still exist, or do you think it's totally impossible?*

L.T.: When I was working with him, I'd find boxes of negatives and he'd say, "I never printed that one; do it, and let's see what turns up." And some pictures appeared that way, which are not without interest, but for which he had never made a contact print. It's possible you'll find things that have never been printed in the collection now in your hands. Even I didn't do it systematically. But remember that in most cases, he would have cropped the image.

MNAM: *Not because he thought the images were uninteresting, but simply because circumstances led him to overlook them?*

L.T.: He just took a look at them against the light, and since they didn't interest him at that very moment....

MNAM: *And when he went back to his photogrphy in the 1960s....*

L.T.: He made a very precise selection of images that he thought were important and that he wanted to show. It was at that point that he set aside the things he wanted me to reproduce, and which appeared in his exhibitions.

MNAM: *But that was in terms of an image of the published work, not in terms of his collection of negatives.*

L.T.: A more complete image could perhaps be given, which would not be his personal selection. There are interesting images that you have in the archive of negatives, which he put aside, neglected, and which were never reproduced.

MNAM: *Wasn't his selection ultimately highly subjective? When you see, for example, the number of post-war pictures of Juliet, doesn't it ultimately skew the image of his overall production?*

L.T..: Absolutely, but that corresponds to his output in America, where he only took pictures of Juliet. There are at least 200 of them. She was his only model. He also photographed the Heytum family. But he met lots of other people he didn't photograph — Calder, Richter, and so on.

MNAM: *He didn't take pictures of them the way he had of the surrealists.*

L.T.: That's right. He photographed Copley, took pictures of Arthur Miller, and Charlotte Heytum and her husband, but it was highly limited. In California, he no longer wanted to take photographs, he wanted to draw and paint. He took photos almost by chance; on the other hand, he produced rayographs — you now have one — that I find very interesting.

MNAM: *But he didn't do many.*

L.T.: No, maybe ten or so. Not all of them have been catalogued, for that matter. Remember that he no longer had a studio in California — he was forced to go to an outside darkroom to work. And back in Paris, he practically never used the darkroom on Rue Férou. He no longer had an assistant, and would constantly call on outside labs — Pierre Gassman, Serge Beguier when he lived on Rue de la Chaise, and that's all. The darkroom at Rue Férou went unused — the rain came in, he tried to protect the premises so that things wouldn't be ruined, but photography no longer interested him after he returned to Paris. He wanted to be recognized as an artist at last, not as a photographer.

1890   Born in Philadelphia, Pennsylvania, on August 20.

1911   Lived in New York, frequented Alfred Stieglitz's Gallery 291.

1912   Moved to Ridgefield, New Jersey.

1913   Discovered Marcel Duchamp's work at the Armory Show. Met the Belgian-born poetess Adon Lacroix, whom he married in May.

1915   Published *The Ridgefield Gazook*, a four-page pamphlet in the Dada spirit. Met Marcel Duchamp. Executed his first photographic reproductions for the catalogue of his show at the Daniel Gallery (October-November). Moved back to New York.

1916   First portrait photos.

1917   First airbrush work. First cliché-verre.

1918   *Man* and *Woman*.

1920   Founded the Société Anonyme with Marcel Duchamp and Katherine Dreier. Photographed part of Duchamp's "Large Glass," a photo that Duchamp later titled *Élevage de Poussière* [Dust Breeding].

1921   First work exhibited at a photography show, the 15th Annual Exhibition of Photographs, in Philadelphia (March 7–26). Published the sole issue of *New York Dada* (April) with Duchamp. Sent two photographs, *L'Homme* and *La Femme*, to the Paris show called *Salon Dada : Exposition Internationale* (June 6–30). Arrived in Paris on July 22. First stayed in the same hotel as Tristan Tzara, Hôtel de Boulainvilliers, then moved in August to a room in the apartment of Yvonne Chastel and Marcel Duchamp at 22 Rue de la Condamine. Began to photograph reproductions of paintings for artists, finishing the sessions by doing a portrait. Met Adrienne Monnier, who had him do portraits of the writers she published. In December, took a room at the Grand Hôtel des Ecoles on Rue Delambre, which he turned into a small photographic studio. Met Alice Prin, known as Kiki of Montparnasse. The *Exposition Dada Man Ray* show was held at Librarie Six (December 3-31).

1922   Jean Cocteau published an "Open Letter to Monsieur Man Ray, American Photographer," concerning the rayographs, in *Les Feuilles Libres* (April–May). Man Ray's portraits of artists and writers were published in *Vanity Fair* (June). Success as a portrait photographer enabled him to move to a veritable studio at 31 bis, Rue Campagne-Première, in July. The October issue of *Littérature* published *Dust Breeding* (under the title, *Voici le domaine de Rrose Sélavy – Comme il est aride – Comme il est fertile – Comme il est joyeux – Comme il est triste*). Published his album *Champs Délicieux* in December, with a preface by Tristan Tzara.

1923   Hired Berenice Abbott as his assistant, which she would remain until 1926. Made his first film, *The Return to Reason*, first shown on July 6 during a Dada performance called *Le Coeur à Barbe* at the Théâtre Michel. In December, moved to the Hôtel Istria at 29 Rue Campagne-Première, the studio at number 31 bis being henceforth devoted exclusively to his photography.

1924   The June issue (no. 13) of *Littérature* published his *Violon d'Ingres*. Began to work for *Vogue* (English, French and American editions) in July. Article on Man Ray by Robert Desnos in *Paris-Journal* on December 14.

1925   Georges Ribemont-Dessaignes published an article on "Man Ray" in *Les Feuilles Libres* (no. 40, May/June). Photographed the "Pavillon de l'Élégance" for *Vogue* (published in the French and English editions in August, in the American edition in September).

1926   The Galerie Surréaliste opened with *Tableaux de Man Ray et Objets des Iles* (March 26-April 10). Published *Noire et Blanche* in *Vogue* (French edition, May). Made the film *Emak Bakia* (first shown at the Théâtre du Vieux Colombier on November 23). Presented his rayographs at the *International Exhibition of Modern Art Assembled by the Société Anonyme* at the Brooklyn Museum (November 19, 1926 – January 1, 1927).

1927   Voyage to New York for his *Recent Painting and Photographic Compositions* show at the Daniel Gallery (February – April).

1928   Worked for the magazine *Vu*, only occasionally for *Vogue*. Participated in the *Exposition Surréaliste* at the Sacre du Printemps gallery (April 2 – 15) and in the Salon des Indépendants de la Photographie (called the Salon de l'Escalier) at the Théâtre des Champs-Élysées. Made the film *Étoile de Mer*, which premiered at the Studio des Ursulines on May 13.

1929   In January, filmed *Les Mystères du Château de Dé* in the villa of the count and countess de Noailles in Hyères. The Arts Club of Chicago hosted *Photographic Compositions by Man Ray* (February 5–19). Participated in the Stuttgart show, *Internationale Ausstellung des Deutschen Werkbunds, Film und Foto* (May 18 – July 7). Met Lee Miller, who worked as his assistant until 1932. Took a studio at 8 Rue du Val-de-Grâce. Discovered solarization. Show of *Tableaux and Derniers Rayogrammes* at the Galerie des Quatre-Chemins (November 2–14).

1930   The first monograph on Man Ray was written by Georges Ribemont-Dessaignes and published by Gallimard.

1931   Produced an advertising booklet for the Paris Electricity Board, *Electricité*, with a preface by Pierre Bost. The Galerie Alexandre III in Cannes hosted *Photographies de Man Ray* (April 13–19), with a catalogue preface by Francis Picabia. The October issue of *Art et Médicine* published his photographs of Paris.

1932   Participated in the *Surrealist Exhibition* at the Julien Levy Gallery in New York. Photographed the French can-can dancer Lydia, whose make-up inspired his photograph, *Tears*.

1933   Worked for the magazine *Minotaure*,

which published his text "L'Age de la Lumière" (*Minotaure*, no. 3/4). During the summer, joined Duchamp, Gala, and Dalí in Cadaquès, and photographed Gaudí's architecture in Barcelona.

1934 James Thrall Soby published *Photographs by Man Ray 1920 – Paris 1934*, with texts by Tristan Tzara, Paul Eluard, André Breton, and Rrose Sélavy (Marcel Duchamp). Participated in the *Minotaure* show at the Palais des Beaux-Arts in Brussels (May 12 – June 3).

1934-1936 Discovered and photographed mathematical objects at the Institut Poincaré.

1935 Published "On Photography" in *Commercial Art and Industry* (vol. XVII, no. 104, February). First fashion photographs published in *Harper's Bazaar* in March. Produced the images for Paul Eluard's *Facile*. Published "Sur le Réalisme Photographique" in *Cahiers d'Art* (no. 5/6, text translated from English by Eluard).

1936 Met Adrienne Fidelin (known as Ady). Participated in the *Cubism and Abstract Art* show at the Museum of Modern Art in New York (March 2– April 19).

Moved to Rue Denfert-Rochereau. Bought a house in Saint-Germain-en-Laye. Spent the summer in Mougins with Picasso, Dora Maar, Nusch and Paul Eluard, Roland and Valentine Penrose. Showed his photographs of *Mathematical Objects* and his rayographs at the exhibition of *Fantastic Art, Dada, Surrealism* at the Museum of Modern Art in New York (December 7, 1936 – January 17, 1937).

1937 Rented an apartment in Antibes, and devoted himself entirely to painting. Published *La Photographie n'est pas l'Art* (Paris : GLM).

1938 Participated in the *Exposition Internationale du Surréalisme* at the Galerie des Beaux-Arts in Paris, photographing all the dummies on display.

1940 During the summer, left Paris for Lisbon, where he sailed for New York. Moved to Hollywood, California in July. Met Juliet Browner.

1944 Last pictures published by *Harper's Bazaar*. Took few photographs, except for portraits of Juliet and friends. The Pasadena Art Institute presented

Man Ray : Retrospective Exhibition, 1913 to 1944 (September 19 – October 29).

1946 Married Juliet. Met Bill Copley.

1948 Painted the *Shakespearian Equations* series, based on his photographs of mathematical objects.

1951 Returned permanently to Paris with Juliet in March. First lived at 5 Rue Jules-Chaplain, then moved in September to 2 bis Rue Férou (official declaration of change of residence dated September 7), where he remained until his death.

1961 Awarded Gold Medal for Photography at the Venice Biennial.

1962 The Bibliothèque Nationale in Paris organized *Man Ray, l'Oeuvre Photographique*, comprising 76 items, including four clichés-verre, 55 photographs, and two albums (*Champs Délicieux* and *Electricité*).

1963 Published his autobiography, *Self Portrait* (Boston : Little, Brown).

1966 *Man Ray* exhibition at the Los Angeles County Museum of Art.

1976 Died in Paris on November 18.

Solo Exhibitions which Included Photographs

1921 *Exposition Dada Man Ray*, Librarie Six, Paris, December 3–31 (2 photographs).

1926 *Tableaux de Man Ray et Objets des Iles*, Galerie Surréaliste, March 26 – April 10 (4 photographs).

1927 *Recent Painting and Photographic Compositions by Man Ray*, Daniel Gallery, New York, February – April.

1929 *Photographic Compositions by Man Ray*, The Arts Club of Chicago, Chicago, February 5–19.

Tableaux et Derniers Rayogrammes, Galerie des Quatre-Chemins, November 2–14.

1931 *Exposition de Photographies par Man Ray*,

Galerie Alexandre III, April 13–19.

1932 *Photographs by Man Ray*, Julien Levy Gallery, New York, April 9–30.

L'Exposition Man Ray, Oeuvres 1919–1932, Chez Dacharry, Paris, began November 25.

Oeuvres Récentes de Man Ray, Galerie Vignon, Paris, December 2–15.

1934 *An Exhibition of Photography by Man Ray*, Lund Humphries & Co., London, November 22 – December 8.

1935 *Man Ray Photographs*, Lund Humphries & Co., London, December 5–15.

Photographs and rayographs, Wadsworth Atheneum, Hartford, Conn.

Photographs and drawings, The Art Center School, Los Angeles, Ca.

1936 Valentine Dudensing Galleries, New York.

1937 *Les Dessins de Man Ray*, Galerie Jeanne-Bucher, Paris, November 5–20 (photographic enlargement of details of drawings).

1938 *Drawings and Photographs by Man Ray*, The Art Center School, Los Angeles, Ca.

1941 *Man Ray : Exhibition of Paintings, Watercolors, Drawings, Photographic Compositions*, Frank Perls Gallery, Hollywood, Ca., March 1–26.

1944 *Man Ray : Retrospective Exhibition 1913 to 1944*, The Pasadena Art Institute,

Pasadena, Ca., September 19 – October 29.

1948   *Man Ray*, Copley Galleries, Beverly Hills, Ca., December 14 – January 9.

1962   *Man Ray : l'Oeuvre Photographique*, Bibliothèque Nationale, Paris, May 22 – July 13.

1963   *Man Ray : Paintings, Drawings, Watercolors, Etcetera*, Cordier & Ekstrom, Inc., New York, April 30 – May 18.

1964   *Man Ray : Oggetti del mio Affetto*, Galleria Schwarz, Milan, March 14 – April 3 (one photograph).

1966   *Man Ray : Retrospective Exhibition 1908 –1965.* Los Angeles County Museum of Art, Los Angeles, Ca. (8 photographs).

1969   *Man Ray*, Studio Marconi, Milan, April – May (5 photographs).

      Man Ray, Galleria Il Fauno, Turin, October 13 – November 3.

1970   *Man Ray, A Selection of Paintings*, Cordier & Ekstrom, Inc., New York, January 14 – February 7 (one photograph).

      Man Ray, Photographs & Rayographs, Noah Goldowsky Gallery, New York, November 21 – December 21.

1971   *Man Ray, Photographs & Rayographs, Retrospective Exhibition*, Harry Lunn Gallery, Washington, D.C., October 16 – November 8.

      Man Ray : Duecentoventi Opere 1912–1971, Galleria Milano, Milan, June – September.

      Man Ray, Boymans–Van Beuningen Museum, Rotterdam, September 24 – November 7, 1971 ; Musée National d'Art Moderne, Paris, January 7 – February 28, 1972 ; Louisiana Museum, Humblebaek, Denmark, March – April 1972.

1972   *Man Ray : 40 Rayographies*, Galerie des Quatre-Movements, February 25 – March 25.

      Man Ray, Gissi Galleria d'Arte, Turin ; Galerie Françoise-Tournie, Paris, November 7 – December 15 ; Galleria dell'Arte Libreria Pictogramma, Rome.

1973   *Man Ray Opera Grafica*, Galleria Il

Collezionista d'Arte Contemporanea, Rome, October 24 – December 8.

Man Ray Photo Graphics from the Collection of Arnold H. Crane, Milwaukee Art Center, Wisc., February 10 – March 11.

1974   *Man Ray*, The Mayor Gallery, London.

      Man Ray, l'Intervenzione Fotografica, Galleria Il Fauno, Turin, April.

      Man Ray, Iolas Gallery, New York, May – June.

      Man Ray, Galerie Alexander Iolas, Paris, October.

      Man Ray, Galeria Iolas-Velasco, Madrid (9 photographs).

      Man Ray, Exposition Rétrospective 1913– 1973, Galerie Alexandra-Monett, Brussels, October – November.

1975   *Man Ray*, Der Spiegel Gallerie, Cologne, January.

      Man Ray, L'Occhio e il suo Doppio, Palazzo delle Esposizioni, Rome, July – September.

      Man Ray, Designi, Tempere, Fotografie e Oggetti, Galleria Dell'Oca, Rome, July 16 – October 10.

1976   *Man Ray*, Artcurial–Centre d'Art Plastique Contemporain, Paris, May 8 – July 19.

      Man Ray, l'Immagine Fotografica, Venice Biennial, San Giorgio, Venice, July 18 – October 10.

1977   *Man Ray, Photographies des Années 20 et 30*, American Cultural Center, Paris, May 17 – June 30.

1979   *Man Ray, Inventionen und Interpretationen*, Steinernes Haus am Romberge, Frankfurter Kunstverein, Frankfurt, October 14 – December 23, 1979 ; Kunsthalle, Basel, January 20 – February 24, 1980.

1980   *Man Ray, Photographs and Objects*, Birmingham Museum of Art, Alabama, February 1 – March 9 ; Columbia Museum of Art, South Carolina, April 13 – May 25 ; Columbus Museum of Art, Ohio, June 22 – August 3 ; Hunter Museum of Art, Chattanooga, Tennessee, September 7 – October 19.

1981   *Man Ray*, Knoedler Gallery, London, December.

      Man Ray, Musée National d'Art Moderne, Centre Georges Pompidou, Paris, December 10, 1981 – April 12, 1982.

      Man Ray, Objects and Photographs, Seibu Museum of Modern Art, Takanawa, November 9, 1981 – March 11, 1982.

1982   *Man Ray, Publications & Transformations*, Zabriskie Gallery, New York, February 10 – March 13 ; Meredith Long & Co., Texas, April 6 – May 1.

      Man Ray et ses Amis, Galerie Marion-Meyer, Paris, February 23 – April 3.

      Man Ray, Assemblages, Dipinti, Fotografie, Disegni dal 1912 al 1972, Galleria d'Arte Niccoli, Parma.

      Man Ray Foto's 1916 – 1975, Boymans-Van Beuningen Museum, Rotterdam, May 22 – July 5.

      Atelier Man Ray, Musée National d'Art Moderne, Centre Georges Pompidou, December 2, 1982 – January 23, 1983.

1983   *Man Ray*, Centre d'Art Contemporain, Rouen, March 4 – 26.

      Man Ray, Mathematical Objects, Still Life Photographs from 1936, Robert Miller Gallery, New York, May 3 – June 30.

      Man Ray Photografies, Galeria Eude, Barcelona, May.

      Man Ray, Care Varie e Variabili, Padiglione d'Arte Contemporanea, Milan, December 1, 1983 – January 9, 1984.

      Man Ray Photographe, Maison des Jeunes et de la Culture, Dole, December 10, 1983 – February 28, 1984.

1984   *Man Ray*, Odakyu Gallery, Tokyo, August 10–22, 1984 ; Museum of Modern Art, Kamakura, January 26 – February 24, 1985 ; Regional Art Museum, Shiga, March 2 – April 7, 1985 ; Regional Art Museum, Mië, April 13 – May 12, 1985 ; Navio Museum, Osaka, May 24 – June 18, 1985.

1985   *Man Ray, Objects of My Affection*, Zabriskie Gallery, New York January 23 – February 23.

Man Ray Fotograf, Centar Za Fotografiju, Film i Televisiju, Zagreb, February 7–27; Musej Savremene Umetnosti, Belgrade, March 3 – 28.

Man Ray Photographien, Wolfgang Gurlitt Museum, Linz, February 21 – April 8.

Uit het Atelier van Man Ray, Gemmentelijk van Reekum-museum, Apeldorn, Holland, June 22 – August 18.

Man Ray Designi, Museo Regionale di Palazzo Bellomo, Syracuse, Sicily, June 29 – July 28 (6 photographs).

Man Ray, Light Gallery, New York, October – November.

1986   *Cafe Man Ray*, G. Ray Hawkins Gallery, Los Angeles, Ca., January.

Man Ray : Fotografi, Rayogram, Tecniga, Objekt, Grafic, Kontshall, Lunds, June 7 – August 31.

Man Ray, Centre d'Action Culturelle, Saint-Brieuc, July 2 – August 29.

Man Ray, Nus, Galerie Octant, Paris, November 19 – December 19.

Man Ray, Galleria Vivita, Florence, December 13, 1986 – February 28, 1987 (2 photographs).

1987   *Man Ray*, Levy Gallerie, Hamburg, September 21 – October 30.

Man Ray, Seoul Gallery, Seoul, December 5, 1987 – January 1, 1988.

1988   *Man Ray : Photographien, Filme, frühe Objekte*, Schweizerische Stiftung für die Photographie, Kunsthaus, Zurich, March 12 – May 23.

Man Ray, Musée Municipal, Saint-Dié, March 12 – April 10.

Perpetual Motif, The Art of Man Ray, National Museum of American Art, Washington, D.C., December 2, 1988 – February 20, 1989; The Museum of Contemporary Art, Los Angeles, Ca., March 17 – May 28, 1989; The Menil Collection, Houston, Tx., June 30 – September 17, 1989; Museum of Contemporary Art, Philadelphia, Pa., October 14, 1989 – January 7, 1990.

1989   *Man Ray's Paris Portraits : 1921 – 1939*, Middendorf Gallery, Washington, D.C.

Man Ray Portraits, Zeit-Foto Salon, Tokyo, March 10 – 31.

Man Ray "360 Degrés de Liberté," Trianon de Bagatelle, Paris, March 28 – June 5.

Man Ray, l'Età delle Luci, Galleria Civica, Modena, October 29, 1989 – January 7, 1990.

1990   *Cent Ans de Man Ray*, Musée de l'Elysée, Lausanne, February 15 – April 1.

Man Ray, "Cent Anni de Libertà," Palazzo Fortuny, Venice, July 7 – August 26.

Man Ray, Derrière la Façade, Rencontres Internationales de la Photographie, Arles, August.

Man Ray, Bazaar Years : A Fashion Retrospective, International Center of Photography Midtown, New York, September 7 – November 25; Sala de Exposiciones del Circulo de Bellas Artes, Madrid, April 29 – June 23, 1991; Musée des Arts de la Mode et du Textile, Paris, October 14, 1992 – January 31, 1993.

Man Ray, Galerie Sona Zanettacci, Geneva, September 13 – October 16.

Man Ray 1890 – 1976, Sezon Museum of Art, Tokyo, September 29 – November 4, 1990; Tsukashin Hall, Amagasaki, November 10 – December 16, 1990; Tenjin Daimaru, Fukuoka, March 14–26, 1991; Museum of Art, Yokohama, April 6 – May 8, 1991; Daimaru Museum, Kyoto, August 15–20, 1991; Gobankan Seibu Akarenga Hall, Sapporo, August 31 – September 23, 1991.

1992   *Portraits Photographiques de Man Ray*, Musée Municipal, Orange, May 27 – June 30.

1993   *Man Ray et les Femmes*, Galerie 15, Paris, February 4 – March 27.

Cinéma, Exposition et Projection des Films de Man Ray, Festival du Cinéma Américain, Deauville, September 2–14 (2 photographs).

1994   *Man Ray 1890 – 1976*, Ronny Van de Velde Gallery, Antwerp, September 18 – December 18.

Man Ray Neues wie Vertrautes, Fotografien 1919–1949, Kunst Museum, Wolfsburg, October 8, 1994 – January 15, 1995.

1995   *Man Ray*, Serpentine Gallery, London, January 18 – March 12.

Man Ray Fotografia, Instituto Leones de Cultura, León, September 6 – October 1.

Man Ray, Sala de Exposiciones de la Diputación de Huesca, Huesca, December.

Man Ray, La Construzione dei Sensi, Galleria d'Arte Moderna e Contemporanea, Turin, October 5 1995 – January 7, 1996.

1996   *Man Ray*, Centre Photographique d'Ile-de-France, Pontault-Combault, June 12 – July 28.

Man Ray Fotografias, Museo Rufino Tamayo, Mexico, September.

Man Ray, Kunsthaus Wien, Vienna, September 19, 1996 – January 26, 1997.

Man Ray : Paris–LA, Robert Berman Gallery, Santa Monica, Ca., September 21, 1996 – January 31, 1997.

Man Ray : Photographic Retrospective 1917–1975, Station Gallery, Tokyo, October 20; Umeda Daimaru Museum, Osaka, October 29 – November 11; Daimaru Museum, Kyoto, April 3–15, 1997.

Man Ray at Rue Férou 1951–1997, Zabriskie Gallery, New York, October 29, 1996 – January 4, 1997.

Man Ray of My Affection (Teruo Ishihara Collection), City Art Museum, Nagoya, December 1–25.

1997   *Man Ray, Rétrospective 1912–1976*, Musée d'Art Moderne et d'Art Contemporain, Nice, February 22 – June 9.

List of Illustrations

Page 77 *Kiki*, circa 1924
Gelatin silver print
9 × 6 cm — 3 1/2" × 2 1/4"
Man Ray Estate Settlement, 1994
Mnam/Cci, Centre Georges Pompidou
AM 1994-394/2168

Kiki, circa 1924
Gelatin silver print
9 × 6.5 cm — 3 1/2" × 2 1/2"
Man Ray Estate Settlement, 1994
Mnam/Cci, Centre Georges Pompidou
AM 1994-394/2169

Kiki, circa 1924
Gelatin silver print
9.1 × 6 cm — 3 1/2" × 2 1/4"
Man Ray Estate Settlement, 1994
Mnam/Cci, Centre Georges Pompidou
AM 1994-394/2164

Kiki, circa 1924
Gelatin silver print
9 × 6 cm — 3 1/2" × 2 1/4"
Man Ray Estate Settlement, 1994
Mnam/Cci, Centre Georges Pompidou
AM 1994-394/2163

Page 78 *Étienne de Beaumont*, 1925
Gelatin silver print
12 × 6.9 cm — 4 3/4" × 3"
Man Ray Estate Settlement, 1994
Mnam/Cci, Centre Georges Pompidou
AM 1994-394/3850

Page 79 *Étienne de Beaumont*, 1925
Gelatin silver print
29.1 × 23 cm — 11 1/2" × 9"
Man Ray Estate Settlement, 1994
Mnam/Cci, Centre Georges Pompidou
AM 1994-360

Étienne de Beaumont, 1925
Gelatin silver print
8.8 × 6.1 cm — 3 1/2" × 2 1/2"
Man Ray Estate Settlement, 1994
Mnam/Cci, Centre Georges Pompidou
AM 1994-394/3849

Page 80 *Jacqueline Goddard*, 1932
Gelatin silver print
29.5 × 23 cm — 11 3/4" × 9"
Man Ray Estate Settlement, 1994
Mnam/Cci, Centre Georges Pompidou
AM 1994-370

Jacqueline Goddard, 1932
Gelatin silver print
8.2 × 5.5 cm — 3 1/4" × 2 1/4"
Man Ray Estate Settlement, 1994
Mnam/Cci, Centre Georges Pompidou
AM 1994-39 /3175

Page 81 *Jacqueline Goddard*, 1932
Gelatin silver print
8.2 × 5.5 cm — 3 1/4" × 2 1/2"
Man Ray Estate Settlement, 1994
Mnam/Cci, Centre Georges Pompidou
AM 1994-394/3829

Jacqueline Goddard, 1932
Gelatin silver print
23 × 29.3 cm — 9" × 11 1/2"
Mnam/Cci, Centre Georges Pompidou
AM 1987-889 ph

Page 82 *Yves Tanguy*, 1936
Gelatin silver print
8.2 × 5.7 cm — 3 1/4" × 2 1/4"
Private collection, Paris

Yves Tanguy, 1936
Gelatin silver contact print made from the
original negative by
Jacques Faujour and Daniel Valet in 1998
Man Ray Estate Settlement, 1994
Mnam/Cci, Centre Georges Pompidou

Page 83 *Yves Tanguy*, 1936
Gelatin silver print
8.2 × 6.2 cm — 3 1/4" × 2 1/2"
Private collection, Paris

Page 84 *Nancy Cunard*, 1926
Gelatin silver print
28.2 × 22.5 cm — 11" × 8 3/4"
Manfred Heiting Collection, Amsterdam

Study for the portrait of *Nancy Cunard*, 1926
Gelatin silver contact print made from the
original negative by
Jacques Faujour and Daniel Valet in 1998
Man Ray Estate Settlement, 1994
Mnam/Cci, Centre Georges Pompidou

Page 85 *Nancy Cunard*, 1926
Gelatin silver print
8.3 × 9.3 cm — 3 1/4" × 3 3/4"
Private collection, Paris

Study for the portrait of *Nancy Cunard*, 1926
Gelatin silver contact print made from the
original negative by
Jacques Faujour and Daniel Valet in 1998
Man Ray Estate Settlement, 1994
Mnam/Cci, Centre Georges Pompidou

Study for the portrait of *Nancy Cunard*, 1926
Gelatin silver contact print made from the
original negative by
Jacques Faujour and Daniel Valet in 1998
Man Ray Estate Settlement, 1994
Mnam/Cci, Centre Georges Pompidou

Page 86 *Jacqueline Goddard*, 1932
Gelatin silver print
8.3 × 5.7 cm — 3 1/4" × 2 1/4"
Man Ray Estate Settlement, 1994
Mnam/Cci, Centre Georges Pompidou
AM 1994-394/2704

Page 87 *Jacqueline Goddard*, 1932
Gelatin silver print
8.1 × 5.6 cm — 3 1/4" × 2 1/4"
Man Ray Estate Settlement, 1994
Mnam/Cci, Centre Georges Pompidou
AM 1994-394/3166

Page 88 *Salvador Dalí*, 1929
Gelatin silver print
5.6 × 7.8 cm — 2 1/4" × 3"
Private collection, Paris

Salvador Dalí, 1929
Gelatin silver print
8.9 × 6.1 cm — 3 1/2" × 2 1/2"
Private collection, Paris

Page 89 *Salvador Dalí*, 1929
Gelatin silver print
9 × 5.7 cm — 3 1/2" × 2 1/4"
Private collection, Paris
3239

Page 90 Portrait of a woman with *La Lune Brille sur
l'île de Nias*, circa 1924
Gelatin silver print
12 × 9 cm — 4 3/4" × 3 1/2"
Man Ray Estate Settlement, 1994
Mnam/Cci, Centre Georges Pompidou
AM 1994-394/3245

Page 91 *La Lune Brille sur l'île de Nias*, circa 1924
Gelatin silver print
14 × 9 cm — 5 1/2" × 3 1/2"
Mnam/Cci, Centre Georges Pompidou
AM 1987-887

Portrait of a woman with *La Lune Brille sur
l'île de Nias*, circa 1924
Gelatin silver print
9.1 × 7.4 cm — 3 1/2" × 3"
Man Ray Estate Settlement, 1994
Mnam/Cci, Centre Georges Pompidou
AM 1994-394/3244

Portrait of a Woman with *La Lune Brille sur
l'île de Nias*, circa 1924
Gelatin silver print
10.2 × 7.8 cm — 4" × 3"
Man Ray Estate Settlement, 1994
Mnam/Cci, Centre Georges Pompidou
AM 1994-394/3239

Page 92 *Jean-Charles Worth*, circa 1925
Gelatin silver print
12 × 9 cm — 4 3/4" × 3 1/2"
Man Ray Estate Settlement, 1994
Mnam/Cci, Centre Georges Pompidou
AM 1994-394/2839

Jean-Charles Worth, circa 1925
Gelatin silver print
12 × 9 cm — 4 3/4" × 3 1/2"
Man Ray Estate Settlement, 1994
Mnam/Cci, Centre Georges Pompidou
AM 1994-394/2816

Page 93 *Untitled*, circa 1935
Gelatin silver print
10.7 × 7.8 cm — 4 1/4" × 3"
Man Ray Estate Settlement, 1994
Mnam/Cci, Centre Georges Pompidou
AM 1994-394/2357

Page 94 *Blanc et Noir* [White and Black], circa 1929
Gelatin silver print
11.1 × 8 cm — 4 1/2" × 3 1/4"
Man Ray Estate Settlement, 1994
Mnam/Cci, Centre Georges Pompidou
AM 1994-394/2342

Blanc et Noir [White and Black], circa 1929
Gelatin silver print
11.2 × 8.1 cm — 4 1/2" × 3 1/4"
Man Ray Estate Settlement, 1994
Mnam/Cci, Centre Georges Pompidou
1994-394/2341

Blanc et Noir [White and Black], circa 1929
Gelatin silver print
11.1 × 7.2 cm — 4 1/2" × 2 3/4"
Man Ray Estate Settlement, 1994
Mnam/Cci, Centre Georges Pompidou
AM 1994-394/2344

Page 119 *Tristan Tzara*, 1921
Superimposition, gelatin silver print
10.7 x 7.8 cm — 4 1/4" x 3"
Man Ray Estate Settlement, 1994
Mnam/Cci, Centre Georges Pompidou
AM 1994-394/4246

Page 120 *André Breton*, circa 1930
Solarized gelatin silver print
9 x 6.2 cm — 3 1/2" x 2 1/2"
Private collection, Paris

Page 121 *André Breton*, circa 1930
Solarized gelatin silver print
9 x 6.1 cm — 3 1/2" x 2 1/2"
Private collection, Paris

Page 122 *Nusch and Sonia*, 1935
Gelatin silver print
13.3 x 9.3 cm — 5 1/4" x 3 3/4"
Man Ray Estate Settlement, 1994
Mnam/Cci, Centre Georges Pompidou
AM 1994-394/4246

Page 123 *Nusch and Sonia*, 1935
Gelatin silver print
5.3 x 9 cm — 2" x 3 1/2"
Man Ray Estate Settlement, 1994
Mnam/Cci, Centre Georges Pompidou
AM 1994-394/4226

Nusch and Sonia, 1935
Gelatin silver print
5.7 x 8.9 cm — 2 1/4" x 3 1/2"
Man Ray Estate Settlement, 1994
Mnam/Cci, Centre Georges Pompidou
AM 1994-394/4227

Page 124 *André Breton*, circa 1930
Gelatin silver print
29.6 x 23.6 cm — 11" x 9 1/4"
Private collection, Morges

Page 126 *Lee Miller*, 1929
Solarized gelatin silver print
19.2 x 24.7 cm — 7 1/2" x 9 3/4"
Lee Miller Archives, Great Britain

Page 127 Untitled, 1929
Solarized gelatin silver print
29.7 x 22.8 cm — 11" x 9"
The Museum of Modern Art, New York
Gift of James Thrall Soby

Tanya Ramm, circa 1929
Solarized gelatin silver print
21.9 x 16.8 cm — 8 3/4" x 6 3/4"
The Art Institute of Chicago, Julien Levy
Collection
Special Photography Acquisitions Fund,
1979.95

Page 128 *Dora Maar*, 1936
Gelatin silver print
6.5 x 5.3 cm — 2 1/2" x 2"
Private collection, Paris

Page 129 *Dora Maar*, 1936
Solarized gelatin silver print
6.5 x 5.3 cm — 2 1/2" x 2"
Private collection, Paris

Page 130 *Lee Miller*, 1929
Gelatin silver print
28.9 x 22.2 cm — 11 1/2" x 8 3/4"
Ludwig Museum, Cologne

Page 131 *Lee Miller*, circa 1930
Gelatin silver print
5.3 x 4.3 cm — 2" x 1 1/4"
Man Ray Estate Settlement, 1994
Mnam/Cci, Centre Georges Pompidou
AM 1994-394/2022

Page 132 *Meret Oppenheim*, 1932
Gelatin silver print
10.4 x 7.9 cm — 4" x 3"
Private collection, Paris

Page 133 *Meret Oppenheim*, 1932
Gelatin silver print
11 x 7.9 cm — 4 1/4" x 3"
Manfred Heiting Collection, Amsterdam

Meret Oppenheim, 1932
Gelatin silver print
11 x 7.6 cm — 4 1/4" x 3"
Private collection, Paris

Meret Oppenheim, 1932
Gelatin silver print
11 x 8 cm — 4 1/4" x 3 1/4"
Private collection, Paris

Page 134 *Lee Miller*, circa 1930
Gelatin silver print
29.6 x 22.5 cm — 11 3/4" x 8 3/4"
Lee Miller Archives, Great Britain

Page 135 *Retour à la raison* [Return to Reason], 1923
Gelatin silver print, frame enlargement from
the film, Return to Reason
18.7 x 13.9 cm — 7 1/4" x 5 1/2"
The Art Institute of Chicago, Julien Levy
Collection
Special Photography Acquisitions Fund,
1979.96

Page 136 Study for *Le Violon d'Ingres*, 1924
Gelatin silver print
8.1 x 5.5 cm — 3 1/4" x 2 1/4"
Man Ray Estate Settlement, 1994
Mnam/Cci, Centre Georges Pompidou
AM 1994-394/3825

Page 137 *Le Violon d'Ingres*, 1924
Gelatin silver print
28.2 x 22.5 cm — 11" x 8 3/4"
Mnam/Cci, Centre Georges Pompidou
AM 1993-117

Page 138 Untitled, 1927
Gelatin silver print
29.3 x 22.5 cm — 11 1/2" x 8 3/4"
The Museum of Modern Art, New York
Gift of James Thrall Soby

Page 139 Untitled, 1927
Gelatin silver contact print made from the
original negative by
Jacques Faujour and Daniel Valet in 1998
Man Ray Estate Settlement, 1994
Mnam/Cci, Centre Georges Pompidou

Page 140 *Kiki*, 1923
Gelatin silver contact print made from the
original negative by
Jacques Faujour and Daniel Valet in 1998
Man Ray Estate Settlement, 1994
Mnam/Cci, Centre Georges Pompidou

Page 141 *Kiki*, 1923
Gelatin silver print
22.1 x 16.7 cm — 8 3/4" x 6 1/2"
Private collection, Paris

Untitled, 1926
Gelatin silver print
28.2 x 18.1 cm — 11" x 7 1/4"
Roger Therond Collection, Paris

Page 142 Untitled [Natasha], 1931
Solarized gelatin silver print
28 x 21 cm — 11" x 8 1/4"
The Museum of Modern Art, New york.
Gift of James Thrall Soby

Page 143 Untitled [Natasha], 1931
Gelatin silver contact print made from the
original negative by
Jacques Faujour and Daniel Valet in 1998
Man Ray Estate Settlement, 1994
Mnam/Cci, Centre Georges Pompidou

Page 144 *Jacqueline*, 1930
Solarized gelatin silver print
29.2 x 22.7 cm — 11 1/2" x 9"
The Museum of Modern Art, New York
Gift of James Thrall Soby

Page 145 *Primat de la matière sur la pensée*
[The Primacy of Matter over Mind], 1932
Solarized gelatin silver print
21.5 x 27.2 cm — 8 1/2" x 10 3/4"
Arturo Schwarz, Milan

Primat de la matière sur la pensée
[The Primacy of Matter over Mind], 1932
Gelatin silver contact print made from the
original negative by
Jacques Faujour and Daniel Valet in 1998
Man Ray Estate Settlement, 1994
Mnam/Cci, Centre Georges Pompidou

Page 146 Lee Miller in Cocteau's film, *The Blood of a
Poet*, 1930
Gelatin silver print
9.8 x 6.2 cm — 3 3/4" x 2 1/2"
Private collection, Paris

Page 147 Nude, circa 1930
Gelatin silver contact print made from the
original negative by
Jacques Faujour and Daniel Valet in 1998
Man Ray Estate Settlement, 1994
Mnam/Cci, Centre Georges Pompidou

Page 148 Nude female torso, circa 1930
Gelatin silver print
9 x 6.4 cm — 3 1/2" x 2 1/2"
Private collection, Paris

Nude female torso, circa 1930
Gelatin silver print
9 x 6.4 cm — 3 1/2" x 2 1/2"
Private collection, Paris

Nude female torso, circa 1930
Gelatin silver contact print made from the
original negative by
Jacques Faujour and Daniel Valet in 1998
Man Ray Estate Settlement, 1994
Mnam/Cci, Centre Georges Pompidou

Page 210 *Coat Stand*, 1920
Gelatin silver print
41 x 28.6 cm — 16 1/4" x 11 1/4"
Mnam/Cci, Centre Georges Pompidou
AM 1996-217

Page 212 Marcel Duchamp, Bonds for Monte-Carlo
roulette, 1924
Gelatin silver print
8.9 x 11.9 cm — 3 1/2" x 4 3/4"
Man Ray Estate Settlement, 1994
Mnam/Cci, Centre Georges Pompidou
AM 1994-394/2319

Marcel Duchamp, Bonds for Monte-Carlo
roulette, 1924
Gelatin silver print
9 x 11.9 cm — 3 1/2" x 4 3/4"
Man Ray Estate Settlement, 1994
Mnam/Cci, Centre Georges Pompidou
AM 1994-394/2318

Page 215 *Joseph Stella and Marcel Duchamp*
Gelatin silver print
20.5 x 15.6 cm — 8" x 6 1/4"
The J. Paul Getty Museum, Los Angeles

Page 217 *Transatlantic*, 1921
Gelatin silver print, collage, paint on wood
36.7 x 24.8 cm — 14 1/2" x 13 3/4"
Jedermann Collection N.A., New York

Page 218 *Collection d'Hiver* [Winter Collection], 1936
Gelatin silver print
35 x 24.1 cm — 13 3/4" x 9 1/2"
Private collection, Paris

Page 219 *Enough Rope*, 1944
Gelatin silver print
25.8 x 20 cm — 10 1/4" x 8"
Private collection, Paris

Page 220 *Le Bouquet*, 1935
Gelatin silver print
28.9 x 23 cm — 11 1/2" x 9"
Private collection, Morges

Page 221 *Feu d'Artifice* [Fireworks], 1934
Gelatin silver print
29.2 x 22.5 cm — 11 1/2" x 8 3/4"
Mnam/Cci, Centre Georges Pompidou
AM 1982-169

Page 222 *Lee Miller*, circa 1930
Gelatin silver print
22.9 x 17.7 cm — 9" x 7"
Lee Miller Archives, Great Britain

Page 223 *Silhouette*, 1930
Gelatin silver print
29.3 x 22.5 cm — 11 1/2" x 8 3/4"
The Museum of Modern Art, New York
Gift of James Thrall Soby

Page 224 *Anatomies*, 1929
Gelatin silver print
22.6 x 17.2 cm — 9" x 6 3/4"
The Museum of Modern Art, New York
Gift of James Thrall Soby

Page 225 Untitled, 1933
Gelatin silver print
17.9 x 21.3 cm — 7" x 8 1/2"
Private collection, Geneva

Untitled, 1933
Gelatin silver print
17.2 x 13.4 cm — 6 3/4" x 5 1/4"
Private collection, Geneva

226 / 227 *Minotaure*, 1933
Gelatin silver print
15 x 23.3 cm — 6" x 9 1/4"
Michael Senft, Jack Banning, New York

Page 228 *Explosante-fixe*, 1934
Gelatin silver print
22.8 x 17.8 cm — 9" x 7"
Private collection, Paris. Courtesy Galerie
1900*2000

Page 229 Prou del Pilar, study for *Explosante-fixe*, 1934
Gelatin silver print
10.7 x 7.8 cm — 6 3/4" x 3"
Man Ray Estate Settlement, 1994
Mnam/Cci, Centre Georges Pompidou
AM 1994-394/883

Prou del Pilar, study for *Explosante-fixe*, 1934
Gelatin silver print
10.7 x 7.8 cm — 4 1/4" x 3"
Man Ray Estate Settlement, 1994
Mnam/Cci, Centre Georges Pompidou
AM 1994-394/882

Page 230 Untitled, 1924
Gelatin silver print
16 x 11.5 cm — 6 1/4" x 4 1/2"
Courtesy Alain Paviot, Paris

Page 231 *Élevage de Poussière* [Dust Breeding], 1920
Gelatin silver print
11.4 x 17.2 cm — 4 1/2" x 6 3/4"
Manfred Heiting, Amsterdam

Page 232 *Course d'Autos* [Car Race], 1926
Gelatin silver print
8.9 x 11.9 cm — 3 1/2" x 4 3/4"
Timothy Baum Collection, New York

Page 233 *Contacts For Shakespearian [Sic], Equations*,
1935-1948
Album (10 pages), 31 contact prints glued to
paper
21.6 x 14.1 cm — 8 1/2" x 5 1/2"
Man Ray Estate Settlement, 1994
Mnam/Cci, Centre Georges Pompidou
AM 1994-392

Page 234 *Objet Mathématique* [Mathematical Object],
1934-1936
Gelatin silver print
24 x 30 cm — 8 1/2" x 11 3/4"
Man Ray Estate Settlement, 1994
Mnam/Cci, Centre Georges Pompidou
AM 1994-391 (3)

Page 235 *Objet Mathématique* [Mathematical Object],
1934-1936
Gelatin silver print
24 x 30 cm — 9 1/2" x 11 3/4"
Man Ray Estate Settlement, 1994
Mnam/Cci, Centre Georges Pompidou
AM 1994-391 (2)

Page 236 *Marcel Duchamp, Distorsion* [Marcel
Duchamp Distorted], 1925
Gelatin silver print
12.6 x 8.8 cm — 5" x 3 1/2"
Private collection, Paris

Page 237 *Moving Sculpture* or *La France*, 1920
Gelatin silver print
7.5 x 12 cm — 3" x 4 3/4"
Jedermann Collection N.A., New York

Page 238 Portrait, circa 1930
Gelatin silver print
12.2 x 17.2 cm — 4 3/4" x 6 3/4"
Man Ray Estate Settlement, 1994
Mnam/Cci, Centre Georges Pompidou
AM 1994-394/547

Untitled, circa 1930
Superimposition, gelatin silver print
13 x 17.8 cm — 5 1/4" x 7"
Private collection, Paris

Page 239 *Marcel Duchamp*, circa 1920
Superimposition, gelatin silver print
17.9 x 12.8 cm — 7" x 5"
Private collection, Paris

Page 258 *Homme d'Affaires* [Businessman], 1926
Gelatin silver print
4.4 x 5.7 cm — 1 3/4" x 2 1/4"
Man Ray Estate Settlement, 1994
Mnam/Cci, Centre Georges Pompidou
1994-394/1002

Homme d'Affaires [Businessman], 1926
Gelatin silver print
4.4 x 5.6 cm — 1 3/4" x 2 1/4"
Man Ray Estate Settlement, 1994
Mnam/Cci, Centre Georges Pompidou
AM 1994-394/1003

Homme d'Affaires [Businessman], 1926
Gelatin silver print
4.4 x 5.8 cm — 1 3/4" x 2 1/4"
Man Ray Estate Settlement, 1994
Mnam/Cci, Centre Georges Pompidou
1994-394/1005

Page 259 *Homme d'Affaires* [Businessman], 1926
Gelatin silver print
4.4 x 5.8 cm — 1 3/4" x 2 1/4"
Man Ray Estate Settlement, 1994
Mnam/Cci, Centre Georges Pompidou
1994-394/1007

Homme d'Affaires [Businessman], 1926
Gelatin silver print
4.4 x 5.9 cm — 1 3/4" x 2 1/4"
Man Ray Estate Settlement, 1994
Mnam/Cci, Centre Georges Pompidou
1994-394/997

Homme d'Affaires [Businessman], 1926
Gelatin silver print
4.4 x 5.9 cm — 1 3/4" x 2 1/4"
Man Ray Estate Settlement, 1994
Mnam/Cci, Centre Georges Pompidou
1994-394/1000

Note on titles :

"Official" titles, whether assigned by Man Ray himself
or acquired by tradition, are given here in italics,
whereas unofficial titles remain in roman typeface.
The same distinction holds for the English versions
of French titles, given in brackets. By convention,
certain French titles are generally employed in English
rather than translated
(*Noire et Blanche, Violon d'Ingres*).

Homme d'Affaires [Businessman], 1926

Photograph Credits

Photograph courtesy of the Art Institute of Chicago
pages 127 (right), 135, 201, 202

Bibliothèque nationale de France, Paris
pages 158, 179 (top), 185

Centre Georges Pompidou, Paris
pages 4, 15, 16, 18, 19, 20, 21, 25, 26, 27, 28, 29, 30, 31, 32, 33, 34, 35, 41, 42, 43, 44, 45, 46, 47, 48, 49, 50, 51, 52, 53, 54, 55 (bottom), 57, 58, 60 (right), 61, 63, 66 (bottom), 67, 72, 73 (bottom), 76, 77, 78, 79, 80, 81, 83, 85, 86, 87, 89, 90, 91, 92, 93, 94, 95, 96, 97, 98, 99, 100, 101 (bottom, top right), 102, 103, 104 (bottom), 105, 106, 108, 111, 114, 115, 117, 118, 119, 121, 122, 123, 128, 129, 131, 132, 133 (bottom), 136, 137, 139, 141 (left), 143, 145 (bottom), 146, 147, 148, 149, 150, 151, 153, 154, 155, 156, 157, 159, 160, 161, 162, 163, 164 (left), 165, 166, 167, 168, 169, 170, 171, 172, 173, 174 (left), 175, 176, 177, 178, 180, 181, 182, 190, 191, 196, 208 (left), 209, 210, 212, 218, 219, 221, 228, 229, 233, 234, 235, 236, 238, 239, 258, 259.
Prints made from the original negatives by Pierre-Henri Carteron, Jacques Faujour, Jean-Claude Planchet, Bertrand Prévost, Daniel Valet
pages 68, 69, 70, 71, 74, 75, 82, 84 (right), 88, 120, 140, 230

Courtesy of Timothy Baum, New York
pages 73 (top), 232

Collection Ken Browar, Paris
page 174 (right)

Jane Corkin Gallery, Toronto
page 113

Harry and Ann Malcolmson Collection, Toronto
page 116

Fondazione Marguerite Arp, Locarno
page 208 (right)

Jedermann Collection N.A., New York
pages 217, 237

The J. Paul Getty Museum, Los Angeles
pages 60 (left), 62, 179 (bottom), 199, 203, 206, 215

Courtesy of Lee Miller Archives, Great Britain
pages 126, 134, 164 (right), 222

The Museum of Modern Art, New York
pages 12, 66 (top), 104 (top right), 112, 127 (left), 138, 142, 144, 152, 183, 184, 192, 204, 205, 223, 224

Collection Sylvio Perlstein, Antwerp
pages 110, 198, 200

Rheinisches Bildarchiv, Cologne
pages 109, 130

Collection Arturo Schwarz. Foto Archivio S.A.D.E., Milan
pages 55 (top), 101 (top left), 145 (top)

All rights reserved
pages 22, 23, 24, 37, pages 84 (left), 124, 133 (top), 141 (right), 187, 188, 189, 195, 197, 220, 225, 226-227, 231

© Man Ray Trust/Adagp, Paris 1998

The Art of
GROUND
FIGHTING

The Art of
GROUND
FIGHTING

PRINCIPLES & TECHNIQUES

MARC TEDESCHI

Weatherhill

The Art of Ground Fighting:
Principles & Techniques

Copyright © 2002 by Marc Tedeschi

Published by Weatherhill Inc., 41 Monroe Turnpike,
Trumbull, CT 06611 USA. Protected by copyright
under the terms of the International Copyright
Union; all rights reserved. Except for fair use in
book reviews, no part of this book may be used or
reproduced for any reason by any means, including
any method of photographic or electronic reproduction, without permission. Printed in China on
acid-free paper meeting the ANSI Z39.48 Standard.

FIRST EDITION, 2002
Second Printing, 2003

Book and cover design: Marc Tedeschi
Photography: Shelley Firth, Frank Deras
Creative consultant: Michele Wetherbee
Editorial supervision: Ray Furse, Thomas Tedeschi
Printing and binding: Oceanic Graphic Printing
and C&C Offset Printing in China
Typeset in Helvetica Neue, Univers, Sabon,
Adobe Garamond, Weiss, and Times.

Library of Congress Cataloging-in-Publication Data
Tedeschi, Marc.
    The art of ground fighting: principles &
    techniques / Marc Tedeschi. —1st ed.
        p. cm.
    Includes bibliographical references.
    ISBN 0-8348-0496-4
    1. Martial arts. 2. Self-defense. I. Title
GV1112 .T38 2002
796.8—dc21   2001045532

Notice of Liability

Trademarks:
Kuk Sool Won™ and Hwa Rang Do® are claimed
as trademarks of their respective owners.

*For all those who
unselfishly share their
wisdom and experiences,
without thought of
their own profit.*

CONTENTS

Editorial Notes
The information in this book is a
reorganized and expanded version
of material found in the author's
1136-page *Hapkido*, and employs
similar editorial conventions:
To avoid sexist grammar, *they*,
them, *their*, and *themselves*
are used in place of the singular
pronouns *he*, *she*, *him*, *her*,
his, *hers*, *himself*, and *herself*.
To avoid wordiness, articles may
be omitted, and abbreviations are
employed: (R) for right, (L) for left.

This book outlines the essential principles and techniques that define the art of ground fighting in most martial arts. The technical differences between most martial styles are defined by the unique ways in which they use and combine skills. This is largely determined by philosophical ideas, as the techniques themselves are often very similar. The reasons for this are not difficult to grasp: since all martial techniques seek to capitalize on the strengths and limitations of the human form, they by necessity come to similar conclusions

OVERVIEW

and embody similar technical principles. While these principles may be expressed differently in different styles, they usually reflect the same basic concepts. The techniques in this book come from Hapkido, a varied and practical martial art that shares historical and technical similarities with many other arts, including Jujutsu, Judo, Chinese wrestling, and Korean styles. It is hoped this book will enrich your practice, regardless of style, and help you to recognize your style's place within the larger culture of martial arts.

Introduction

Not all confrontations can be resolved from a standing position. You may be forced to the ground, or you may already be there. Consequently, your ability to attack or defend from the ground is as important as your ability to fight while standing. Today, this reality is widely acknowledged in numerous styles. Many martial arts systems which did not originally include ground techniques are currently incorporating them into their repertories to remain vital and practical.

Ground-fighting techniques typically consist of strikes, blocks, holds, and throws, which are executed while you are on the ground, or as you drop to a ground position. Ground fighting can involve standing, kneeling, sitting, or reclining postures against opponents operating from any position, including airborne, standing, kneeling, sitting, or reclining. Ground-fighting techniques are based on the same principles as standing techniques; they have merely been modified to compensate for differences in body position and distance. As with standing techniques, specific methods of locomotion are used to facilitate execution of offensive or defensive techniques, or to remove oneself from the area of confrontation. Ground fighting could become necessary for any of the following reasons:

- You have been thrown
- You have tripped or fallen
- You are executing a sacrifice technique
- You are surprised while seated or resting
- You cannot stand due to leg damage
- You cannot stand due to restricted space
- You need to remain low to avoid hazards (e.g., gunfire, explosions, machinery)
- You have been restrained or tied up
- You prefer to fight on the ground

The material in this book will cover basic principles, fundamental skills, common ground techniques, ground defenses, and sacrifice techniques—all of the categories that typically define the art of ground fighting. Most of the techniques in this book are shown in the context of self-defense; however, sport-oriented martial arts will often embody similar principles. In eclectic martial arts, such as Hapkido, *ground fighting* is never thought of as an isolated body of techniques, but rather as an integral part of a larger system embracing a broad range of standing martial skills (strikes, blocks, holds, throws, etc.). Those martial artists seeking an eclectic, comprehensive approach to self-defense, should obtain the author's 1136-page book, *Hapkido: Traditions, Philosophy, Technique.*

Different Approaches

There are many different approaches to ground fighting. Some martial arts are sport-oriented; others focus on self-defense and combat. There are also styles which attempt to blend both approaches. When evaluating the appropriateness of specific ground-fighting skills, it is important to consider the context in which the technique will be used. For example, many holds used in sport situations, which are very effective in that context, are not prudent in self-defense situations. Competition holds often restrain the body while leaving the hands free to strike extremely vital targets. Recognize that one good poke to the eyes can completely turn the tables. In competition, this response is not permitted, and hence not a concern.

Although strength, leverage, and body position are important in any grappling situation, some martial arts, such as Hapkido and Chinese fast-wrestling, tend to place a greater emphasis on speed, unbalancing, and returning to your feet. Ground kicks are used extensively in Korean arts, but are not much in evidence in Japanese systems. In combat and self-defense arts, strikes are usually directed to pressure points or vital targets, such as the eyes, throat, and groin. In sport arts, such as Freestyle Wrestling and Judo, these blows are prohibited. In many grappling arts, such as Judo and Jujutsu, one opponent will attempt to straddle the other, in an effort to choke, restrain, or knock them out. Generally, this tactic is less emphasized in self-defense arts, where the preference is usually to strike from a standing or kneeling posture, so that you can immediately move away to address other attackers, or abandon a situation when you are losing control. Also, rolling around on gravel or other hazardous surfaces can be far more destructive than rolling around on a padded mat.

The differences previously discussed between various grappling arts are not meant to imply that one style is superior to another, only that they are different. In fact, a grappler skilled in any comprehensive ground-fighting art is a formidable opponent. When comparing the ground techniques of different martial arts, you will find that there are a great many similarities in technique and principles, although the manner in which skills are organized and practiced may be quite different. Many masters have also trained extensively in different grappling styles, and have integrated other elements into their own systems. This strengthens a martial art, keeping it contemporary and practical.

Cross-Training

Cross-training in different grappling arts can be of enormous benefit in learning a range of grappling principles, and also leads one to a deeper understanding of the strengths and limitations of their own art. Although sport competition does encourage techniques that are inherently risky when used for self-defense, it also provides you with a safe forum for becoming familiar with aggressive, violent body contact. If you expect to maintain your composure in a real fight, this type of experience is essential. For this reason, many contemporary martial arts schools combine training in both self-defense and sport-oriented martial arts. For example, Hapkido and Judo, or Jujutsu and Judo.

Types of Techniques

The material presented in this book will outline typical ground-fighting techniques, and specific defenses to common ground situations. There are many different ways to organize this type of material. For example, in Judo, ground skills are usually organized into three categories: joint locks, chokes, and pins. In Korean self-defense arts, such as Hapkido, Kuk Sool Won, and Hwa Rang Do, ground skills are organized into defense systems based on body position (for instance, reclining defenses or seated defenses). In this book, ground techniques are classified using a combination of both approaches, and are organized into seven chapters:

• Chokes + Head Locks
• Pinning Holds
• Ground Kicks
• Seated Defenses
• Reclining Defenses
• Kneeling Defenses
• Sacrifice Techniques

The first three chapters summarize techniques that are applied from a broad range of ground positions. The remaining four chapters outline specific defenses employed from specific standing or ground positions. A brief description of these seven categories follows:

Chokes + Head Locks
Chokes and head locks are specific types of holds applied to the neck and head. They are typically used to control or restrain a person, and work in one or more of three ways: by reducing the flow of blood or air to the brain via strangulation, by applying painful pressure to nerves and pressure points, or by twisting the head to stress the cervical spine. Ground chokes can be applied from most positions, even to an opponent straddling your chest.

Pinning Holds
Pinning holds are used to restrain movement by pinning an opponent to the ground, or against a wall or other obstacle. Pinning holds can consist of joint holds or chokes, or may simply involve the use of your body weight.

Ground Kicks
Ground kicks are very similar to standing kicks, except they are delivered from a kneeling, seated, or reclining position. Kicks are usually directed to standing opponents; however, kneeling or reclining targets are also possible. There are two types of ground kicks: *drop kicks* and *seated kicks.* Drop kicks are executed while making a transition from standing to ground positions, often returning to standing postures at the completion of the kick. Seated kicks are executed from a kneeling, seated, or reclining position.

Seated Defenses
Seated defenses are techniques employed when you are sitting on the ground and must engage a standing opponent.

Reclining Defenses
Reclining defenses are techniques employed when you are reclining against standing, kneeling, or reclining opponents.

Kneeling Defenses
Kneeling defenses are techniques employed when you are kneeling in a variety of positions against a reclining opponent.

Sacrifice Techniques
Sacrifice techniques are strikes, holds, or throws in which you will drop to the ground as you execute the technique. In most cases, the technique is a hold or throw that also forces your opponent to the ground. The force of your dropping body-weight is often an essential ingredient powering these techniques.

Responsible Use of Force
Martial techniques such as ground-fighting skills should only be used for self-defense, the protection of others, physical exercise, or in organized sport competition between consenting individuals. The use of force to resolve a situation carries with it a social and moral responsibility to apply force in an appropriate and sensible manner. When we attempt to control another person by striking, holding, or throwing, our expertise in martial arts and our knowledge of the human body allows us not only to attack with increased efficiency, but with greater compassion. By manipulating the body's weak points and using skillful, efficient techniques, it becomes possible to immobilize or restrain an attacker without causing serious or permanent injury. Our degree of skill directly influences our ability to do this safely, without endangering ourselves. To seriously injure or kill someone is not very difficult. It requires no special knowledge, and often occurs unintentionally. For the skilled martial artist, the *excessive use of force* is an inexcusable and morally reprehensible act, deserving condemnation.

Types of Techniques

Chokes + Head Locks

Pinning Holds

Ground Kicks

Seated Defenses

Reclining Defenses

Kneeling Defenses

Sacrifice Techniques

Comparing Martial Arts
The photos on the following four pages show examples of similar ground techniques from different martial arts, as they are applied by notable masters. In some cases, the differences are obvious; others require a more educated eye or prior experience with specific styles to be able to perceive the subtleties that distinguish one art from another.

The purpose of these photos is not to make any particular point, but to invite the reader to look outside of their own art. Understanding how other martial arts interpret similar techniques can lead one to a deeper understanding of their own art, and its place in the larger culture of martial arts. Please recognize that these photos have been selected for their similarities. Each of these martial

arts also possess numerous qualities and techniques that are relatively unique unto themselves. Please do not assume that by looking at these photos you understand these arts. To make in-depth comparisons and draw intelligent conclusions would require the examination of hundreds of techniques, decades of training, and a great deal of familiarity with specific martial arts.

Hapkido: *Reclining Arm Bar as demonstrated by the author in his book* Hapkido: Traditions, Philosophy, Technique

Judo: *Juji Gatame (Cross Arm-Lock) as demonstrated in the book* Best Judo *by Isao Inokuma and Nobuyuki Sato, 1979*

Jujutsu: *Arm bar as demonstrated in the book* Brazilian Jiu-Jitsu: Theory and Technique *by Renzo and Royler Gracie, 2001*

Hapkido: Circle Throw as demonstrated by the author in his book Hapkido: Traditions, Philosophy, Technique

Hwa Rang Do: Over-Flip Throw as demonstrated by Hwa Rang Do founder Lee-Joo Bang in his book The Ancient Martial Art of Hwa Rang Do: Vol. 2, 1979

Aiki-Jujutsu: Karyu Happo (Fire-Dragon Eight-Direction Throw) as demonstrated by Shiro Omiya in his book The Hidden Roots of Aikido: Aiki Jujutsu Daitoryu, 1992

Aikido: Kokyu Nage (Breath Throw) as demonstrated by Aikido founder Morihei Ueshiba in his book Budo, 1938

Hapkido: Drop Side Kick as demonstrated by the author in his book Hapkido: Traditions, Philosophy, Technique

Taekwondo: Drop Side Thrust Kick as demonstrated by Hee Il Cho in his book The Complete Martial Artist: Volume 2, *1981*

Hwa Rang Do: Drop Side Kick as demonstrated by Hwa Rang Do founder Lee-Joo Bang in his book The Ancient Martial Art of Hwa Rang Do: Vol. 2, *1979*

Kuk Sool Won: Reclining side kick as demonstrated by He-Young Kimm in his book Kuk Sool: Korean Martial Arts, *1985*

Hapkido: *Scissor Throw as demonstrated by the author in his book* Hapkido: Traditions, Philosophy, Technique

Judo: *Kani Basami (Scissor Throw) as demonstrated in the book* Kodokan Judo *by Judo founder Jigoro Kano, 1956/1986*

Jujutsu: *Flying Scissor Throw as demonstrated by Grandmaster Wally Jay in his book* Small Circle Jujutsu, *1989*

Chinese wrestling: *Zhuan Shen Gao Fu Tui Wu Long Jiao Zhu (Drop-Turn Body, Twist Legs) from the book* Chinese Fast Wrestling for Fighting *by Shou-Yu Liang and Tai Ngo, 1997*

When building a house, one begins with the foundation. If the foundation is strong, the building's structure will be able to withstand the trials of nature and time. If the foundation is weak, the entire structure will be undermined, and its life span more limited. Before learning and practicing specific ground skills, it is important to first understand the basic principles that govern the execution of virtually all ground techniques. A proper grasp of fundamentals and basic skills will allow practitioners to learn more quickly, refine their

FUNDAMENTALS

skills to a higher degree, enjoy their training, and avoid the unnecessary injuries commonly resulting from improperly applied techniques. The process of learning ground-fighting skills, should not be painful or injurious, but rather a physically robust, confidence-building experience that leaves one exhilarated and looking forward to more training. This chapter will outline basic principles and techniques, all of which must be learned from a qualified instructor to ensure that your martial arts training is safe and rewarding.

Ki

The word *Ki* (also written as *Qi, Chi,* or *Gi*) is essentially untranslatable, although it is often described as the "vital energy" or "life force" that permeates the universe, flowing through and animating all things. It has been the basis of Oriental medicine for thousands of years.

In martial arts, the combative use of Ki usually involves blending and harmonizing your own Ki (internal energy) with that of your opponent and the greater universe. This is done to assist the application of a technique, such as a strike, hold, throw, or escape. Although skillful technique does not require Ki manipulation to be highly effective, focusing Ki will increase a technique's efficiency. When fighting a highly skilled or overpowering opponent, harmonized Ki may be the difference between a technique that works and one that fails. In energy-oriented martial arts, such as Hapkido, Aikido, and Tai Chi Chuan, one's ability to strengthen and control Ki is developed through exercises and meditation. For serious practitioners trying to develop their Ki, a variety of factors must be in balance—diet, air quality, emotional state, sleep, sexual activity, and the level of stress in your life all affect the levels of Ki in your body.

Live-Hand

The term *Live-Hand* refers to specific hand formations which are used in the martial art Hapkido to increase the flow of Ki into the hands and arms. This increases arm strength and power when most needed, such as during a wrist escape or the execution of a strike.

Live-Hand techniques involve visualization, breath control, and tensing of the fingers, hands, and arms. Concentration and focus are very important, as is practice. The use of a Live-Hand is typically characterized by extending one or more fingers and breathing out as a specific technique is applied.

As previously stated, the techniques in this book come from Hapkido; thus, one will notice the use of Live-Hands in many techniques. If you practice a martial art that does not use Live-Hands, merely ignore that portion of the technique. Live-Hands are not a crucial component of the techniques shown, but rather one of the useful additions that can create greater efficiency.

In recent years, the use of extended fingers in combat has fallen into disfavor among some practitioners due to their increased vulnerability to attack or damage. Today many stylists restrict Live-Hand use in fighting to wrist escapes, well-controlled breaking blocks, or holds in which the extra power is often needed and the fingers are well-protected from being grabbed or broken.

Typical Live-Hand Formations

The photographs shown below illustrate two typical Live-Hand formations. In the lower-left photographs, a basic Live-Hand is formed by spreading all five fingers very wide, with the thumb slightly bent. This hand formation expands and hardens the wrist and forearm, concentrating Ki in the hand and fingertips.

It is often used to apply wrist escapes, blocks, arm strikes, and joint locks. In the lower-right photos, a Live-Hand is formed by closing the hand, with only the forefinger extended (in some techniques, the thumb is also extended). This formation is often used when gripping an attacker's limbs or fingers.

Breath Control

Proper breathing when executing techniques is essential. Do not hold your breath. During training or combat, try to breathe deeply and rhythmically. This calms the mind, oxygenates the blood, and maximizes the flow of Ki throughout the body, encouraging peak performance. In most martial arts, you will exhale as a technique is applied. This helps coordinate physical actions, increases physical strength, and channels Ki to the extremities; it is is often referred to as *breath power* or *extending one's Ki*. Conceptually, three actions (breathing, physical action, and the flow of Ki from one's center to the limbs) become one coordinated, powerful response. When these actions are intimately linked to an opponent's energies and actions, technique becomes effortless.

The Energy-Shout

The distinct shout many martial artists emit when executing techniques is essentially breathing meditation converted to dynamic action. In Korean, this energy harmonizing shout is referred to as a *Kihap*. In the Japanese language it is called a *Kiai*. Most Chinese arts do not use an audible shout.

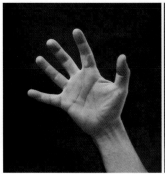

Live-Hand with five fingers spread (pressing the knee to throw attacker backward)

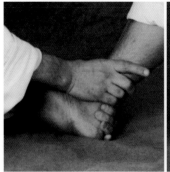

Live-Hand with forefinger extended (gripping the ankle for a pressure point throw)

The word *Ki* is defined as the universal energy or dynamic force that animates all things. *Hap* or *Ai* is the root form for words which connote harmonizing, coming together, or coordinating. Thus the concept of *Kihap* or *Kiai* literally means to harmonize with the dynamic universal life force. The "energy-harmonizing shout" is a means, then, of coordinating our actions with the flow of energies and events of which we are part. All individual actions and events merge into a single flow. This is what is meant by "being at one with the universe."

The Dynamic Release of Energy
When you execute a punch, kick, hold, or throw, or block a strike, energy is released—typically as a rush of air from the lungs. This exhalation of air, coordinated with muscular tension in the body and throat, creates the deep, roaring growl of the true energy-shout. When you are first learning martial arts, the energy-shout will mostly be an artificial adornment, merely accompanying physical actions. However, if you train in an uninhibited way, focusing on the purpose of the shout, you will eventually develop a shout that is natural, spontaneous, and uninhibited. It will become a reflection of your dynamic emotional state, and an expression of the harmonized, total commitment of your body, mind, and spirit to the techniques you are executing. The true energy-shout is often characterized as a low, deep, harsh roar that emerges from the diaphragm, instead of the throat. It should be an expression of indomitable spirit, not fright.

The Silent Shout
The silent shout is not an audible shout, but rather a total commitment of body, mind, emotions, and spirit into the events of the moment. There is no thought of the outcome, only the now. You are completely in tune with your opponent's actions. The silent shout is considered to be the highest level of energy-harmonizing. If there is any sound at all, it might be characterized as a low humming "ohmm" sound, which is a reflection of your own breathing in unison with the events transpiring before you. Remember, the ultimate objective is not to make noise, but to develop a natural and effortless unification of body, mind, and spirit.

Leading and Blending
Leading refers to the act of directing your opponent into a strike, hold, or throw by using their own energy against them. This may involve redirecting a strike or charge, or creating an initially deceptive movement that causes your opponent to react by moving in a direction that assists the execution of your technique. Leading movements can be short or long depending on circumstances, and are often executed in the opposite direction in which you intend your opponent to move. For example, if you pull an opponent's arm toward your right, they will usually react by pulling to your left. This sets up specific techniques.

Blending refers to the act of uniting with your opponent's force. This reduces your chances of injury and increases the efficiency of your techniques, by avoiding a direct confrontation with your opponent's forces. Blending can be thought of metaphorically, as occupying the calm space within a tornado, or joining with the force of the tornado by matching its speed and motion. This is accomplished by knowing when to give way and when to attack. Blending is particularly important when countering with holds or throws, or facing an overpowering opponent. In practical terms, leading and blending require good footwork, timing, speed, power, and versatility, as demonstrated in the photo sequence below.

Pressure Point Attacks
Some martial arts, such as Hapkido, make extensive use of pressure points (also called *acupoints*) to assist the application of techniques. These are the same points commonly used in Eastern medicine to heal the human body. Manipulating pressure points alters the body's energetic state by affecting Ki-flow and neurological functions. In martial arts, specific pressure points may be struck or pressed to cause pain; reduce physical strength; cause involuntary muscle responses; limit motor functions; cause loss of consciousness; or damage neurological, respiratory, or circulatory functions. In ground fighting, pressure point attacks are mostly used to assist your entry, escape from holds, reduce an opponent's strength, or increase the efficiency of strikes. In this book, pressure points are cited using their standard alpha-numeric name (e.g., TW-11). Common points are shown at the end of this chapter.

Leading, blending, breath control, and complete harmony with an attacker's energy are demonstrated in a reversal technique and arm lock, used against a dropping opponent.

Basic Body Positions

Most ground-fighting techniques are selected and employed based on your orientation relative to your opponent. This relationship between your bodies largely determines which techniques are practical and which are not. Although a multitude of body positions are possible, ground positions can generally be simplified into six basic categories. These are usually the positions from which you will be operating:

- Relaxed Seated
- Seated Guard
- Leg-Wrap Guard
- Supine Straddle Position
- Prone Straddle Position
- Side Position

Relaxed Seated

This is a relaxed posture used to camouflage intent. It could also be a resting posture. Your legs are crossed with the hands resting lightly on the thighs. Do not make any gestures that signal your intent to attack or defend. Stay relaxed as the attacker approaches. When you move to defend, act suddenly and swiftly.

Seated Guard

This is a basic defensive posture used against a variety of attacks, coming from one or more standing attackers. Your legs and hands are used for blocking, striking, and holding, and to initiate ground movement. Generally, you should try to keep your legs between you and the attacker. When defending against someone trying to grab or climb on top of you (called mounting or straddling), use your feet to block an attacker's legs, preventing them from stepping in closer. Press with your soles against the ankles or knees. Keep moving your legs so they can't be grabbed and controlled. Spin on your buttock to prevent an attacker from running around to your side. Many forms of ground movement, such as the Buttock Pivot, Crab Walk, Back Roll, Side Roll, and Side Crawl can be used from this position (see *Ground Movement* later in this chapter). You can also execute numerous kicks (see *Seated Kicks* in the *Ground Kicks* chapter).

Leg-Wrap Guard

This is a defensive position. The defender wraps their legs tightly around an opponent's waist, with the ankles crossed. This prevents an opponent on top from moving around to the side or straddling your chest. This is a good controlling position and can be used to rest or catch your breath. When you sense an opportunity, attempt to escape or reverse positions, as part of a counter.

Generally, the person on top is at an advantage when punching, since they can use their body for power and turn their shoulders for extra reach. If the top person punches your face, try to pull their head down by grabbing their arms, collar, or hair; or by chopping into their inner elbow and hugging it to your body. Pulling an attacker close will take away their punching power and set up many counters, such as chokes. Against attackers with short reaches, you can also avoid punches by using your leg-wrap, to push their hips farther away. This keeps your head out of reach.

Although the bottom position appears to be disadvantaged, a skillful grappler can remain in this position and neutralize an attacker by striking, choking, or locking joints. In Jujutsu styles, the bottom person will often choke-out the top person with a clamping hold to the carotid artery, particularly if the top person is inexperienced. When two skilled fighters are engaged in the *Leg-Wrap Guard,* they will often stalemate. The top person will be unable to finish off their opponent; the bottom person will be unable to escape.

Supine Straddle Position

This is a very strong ground position and can be used to execute strikes, chokes, or joint locks. Concentrate your weight on the chest to restrict breathing and movement. Squeeze your knees tight to an opponent's sides. Brace with your arms if an opponent attempts to unbalance you sideways or buck you forward. You can also hook your heels against the back of your opponent's thighs to help stabilize your balance. This can be quite helpful if your hands are otherwise occupied or restrained.

If an opponent tries to turn onto their stomach, let them. They will be very vulnerable to devastating rear chokes or strikes. To return to a standing position when you are in the Supine Straddle Position, shoulder roll forward. Do not stand straight up, since you are more vulnerable to counters. If you are caught in the bottom position by an experienced grappler, counters are very difficult and you will probably be punched out. The *Leg-Wrap Guard* described previously is commonly used to prevent an attacker from gaining a straddle position.

Prone Straddle Position

Lying beneath an opponent, on your belly, is perhaps the worst position you can find yourself in. If you are on top, it is the best. *Never* turn onto your belly with the attacker on top, unless you really know what you are doing. Although this is a basic instinct (you are trying get to your feet) and standard procedure in competitive arts in which you must avoid a pin, it is just about the worst possible thing you can do in a real fight. The back of your head and spine are exposed to devastating hand and elbow strikes, which you have no ability to block. You are also wide open to rear chokes, twisting neck locks, and bent-leg pins. If you are thrown forward or turned over onto your belly, immediately roll to your side or back, into a Seated Guard or a Leg-Wrap Guard, or attempt to stand up.

Side Position

This refers to any position where one person is supine or prone, and the other is attacking from either side, or from above the head. This position is usually used to apply joint locks, chokes, or restraining holds. Strikes are also possible. When using restraining holds (without the aid of joint locks), an opponent can usually be held down by controlling two or three points on an imaginary triangle formed by an opponent's shoulders and head Normally, if you can control two points (using your body weight), you can maintain a pin. This principle becomes very important in sport martial arts in which strikes, chokes, and joint locks are not permitted.

Relaxed Seated

Seated Guard

Leg-Wrap Guard

Supine Straddle Position

Prone Straddle Position

Side Position

The stances you will use depend upon the techniques you are executing, the martial art you are practicing, personal preference, and a variety of other factors. It is not possible to cover all of the stances used when executing martial techniques, as there are simply too many variables. Nonetheless, there are a few fundamental stances that are found in many practical or self-defense oriented martial arts. They are shown opposite. Generally speaking, it is better to think of stances as the links in a series of continuous movements, rather than as precisely defined foot placements. A rigid approach only limits your technique and your ability to adapt and improvise based on the constantly changing dynamics of combat. Most stances fall into two basic categories: relaxed stances and fighting stances.

Relaxed Stances
Relaxed stances resemble everyday standing or sitting postures. Since one never knows when they might be attacked, reacting and applying self-defense techniques from relaxed stances is an important skill for students to learn. Self-defense oriented martial arts, such as Hapkido, also make significant use of relaxed stances to camouflage tactics and lure an opponent into a false sense of security. Attacking and defending from relaxed stances is also useful when one wishes to maintain a low profile or minimize disturbance to people nearby.

Fighting Stances
In fighting stances, the position of the hands, feet, and body is optimized to facilitate execution of techniques. There are many different types of fighting stances. Stances 3–10 are found in many practical martial arts. These stances can be used in a wide variety of circumstances to launch a broad range of techniques, such as strikes, kicks, joint locks, chokes, and throws.

1. Relaxed Standing Stance
Weight Distribution: Equal between both feet. This basic ready stance is often used to disguise tactics and intent. Place your feet shoulder-width apart with the knees slightly bent. Hands are open and hanging loosely at side. The entire body should be relaxed, ready to quickly respond. Do not adopt any hand or foot positions that could be construed as a preparation to attack. Face is expressionless. This stance is also called a *Natural Stance.*

2. Relaxed Walking Stance
Weight Distribution: Constantly changing. This posture is actually a form of offensive movement as well as a stance. It is used to disguise tactics and intent while being constantly mobile. Adopt a normal walk with relaxed arms and legs swinging freely and naturally. The flowing continuous movement of the hands, arms, and feet make this an excellent posture for launching disguised strikes, blocks, holds, or throws.

3. Front Stance

Weight Distribution: 50–60% front foot.
This basic fighting stance is highly mobile, and good for fast footwork and entering. It is excellent for launching strikes, holds, or throws, but lacks stability if you are grappling at close range. Position the feet about 1 to 1.5 times your shoulder-width apart. The back foot may be flat or raised on the ball. This stance is commonly seen in a variety of styles, from boxing to Olympic Taekwondo.

4. Side Stance

Weight Distribution: Equal between both feet.
This is a good stance for executing side kicks, back kicks, and turning kicks—or for fighting two opposing opponents 180° apart. This stance has poor lateral mobility, but is good for moving forward or backward. Position the feet about 1.5 times your shoulder-width, with the legs equally bent. Align the shoulders and hips with the feet. To face an opponent behind you, simply turn your head and shift the arms.

5. Back Stance

Weight Distribution: 50–75% back foot.
This basic defensive stance possesses a good balance between stability and mobility. More weight on the back foot favors defense and use of the front leg for countering and blocking. Position the feet about 1.5 times your shoulder-width, with both legs bent. The front foot points straight forward, the rear foot points sideways (slightly less than 90°), the heels align. Shoulders and hips align with feet.

6. Grappling Stance

Weight Distribution: Equal between both feet. This basic defensive stance is used when grappling, holding, or throwing. It can be very stable, but possesses low mobility. Position the feet about 1.5 times your shoulder-width, with the toes turned outward and legs equally bent. Align the shoulders and hips with the feet. Center of gravity and hip placement are fairly low, to prevent being unbalanced or thrown by a grappling opponent.

7. Two Knee Stance

Weight Distribution: Equal, 3-point balance. This stance is used during grappling or ground fighting. Position the knees about shoulder-width apart, with the feet barely touching, legs equally bent. The feet are under the hips with the bottom of the toes curled under, resting on the ground. Center the hips over the feet; vary the height based on stability desired. From this position it is easy to move to a Seated Guard, or rise to one knee or a standing posture.

8. One Knee Stance

Weight Distribution: Equal, 3-point balance. This stance is used during grappling or ground fighting, and is frequently adopted when entering or exiting a shoulder roll. Position the knee and foot about shoulder-width apart, with the knees bent at about a 90° angle. Bent-knee toes are curled under, resting on the ground. From this position it is easy to transition to a Two-Knee Stance, Seated Guard, or rise to a standing stance.

9. Relaxed Seated Stance

Weight Distribution: Equal.

This defensive stance is used with seated techniques. Sit upright with the legs crossed, back straight, and open hands resting on the thighs, with entire body relaxed and ready. This posture frees the legs more quickly than seated positions with the legs folded under the hips. From this posture, one often moves to a Seated Guard, or directly into ground kicks, leg throws, or takedowns.

10. Seated Guard Stance

Weight Distribution: Equal along backside.

This is a defensive posture used for ground fighting against one or more standing opponents. It is used with strikes, blocks, holds, or throws. Lie on the lower back, curl the spine, tuck the chin, and place the hands forward in a guard position. Bend the knees, placing both feet in a staggered guard aligned with the center of your body, protecting the groin. Curl the feet inward forming Knife-Foot formations.

Note:

Foot diagrams refer to top photograph and indicate preferred feet positions. However, these positions are always modified based on individual preference and end-use requirements.

Small black circle indicates approximate center of gravity based on weight distribution given in text. When a range is given (e.g., 50–70% back foot), a black and a white circle indicate the range of gravity values.

Large black circle indicates knee placement on the ground. A black ellipse indicates the placement of curled toes in kneeling or seated stances. The dotted outline in #10 Seated Guard, indicates torso placement.

1. Forward Step

6. Back Shuffle

11. Side Slide (front left)

16. Side Slide–Step (right)

2. Forward Slide

7. Side Step–Front Pivot (left)

12. Side Slide (front right)

17. Turn Step (face forward)

3. Forward Shuffle

8. Side Step–Front Pivot (right)

13. Side Slide (back left)

18. Turn Step (face behind)

4. Back Step

9. Side Step–Back Pivot (left)

14. Side Slide (back right)

19. Pivot (face side)

5. Back Slide

10. Side Step–Back Pivot (right)

15. Side Slide–Step (left)

20. Pivot (face behind)

Most standing footwork derives from about 40 basic steps, which are combined or altered to create innumerable possibilities. During grappling, short steps with wider stances are usually preferred for stability and to prevent an opponent from sweeping your feet or throwing you. Steps 31–40 are variations modified for close-range grappling.

Outlined feet indicate start position; *solid* feet indicate ending. Numbers indicate which foot moves first.

P Pivot
B Back Foot
F Front Foot
1, 2 Sequence

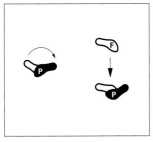

21. Step-Pivot (front step)

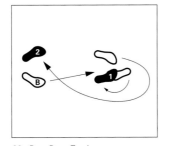

26. Rear Draw Turning

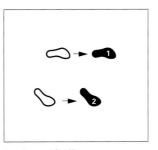

31. Forward Shuffle

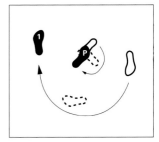

36. Forward Turn (right pivot)

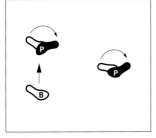

22. Step-Pivot (back step)

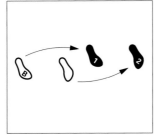

27. Cross Step Behind

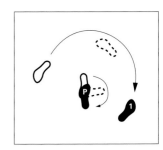

32. Back Shuffle

37. Back Turn (left pivot)

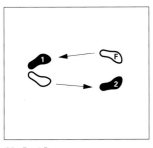

23. Front Draw

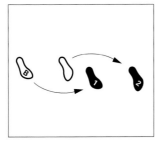

28. Cross Step Front

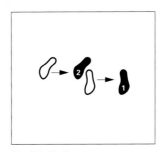

33. Side Shuffle

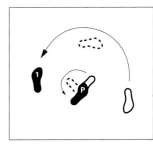

38. Back Turn (right pivot)

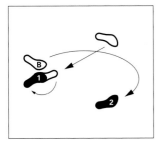

24. Front Draw Turning

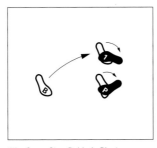

29. Cross Step Behind–Pivot

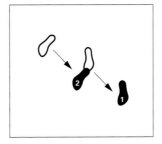

34. Diagonal Shuffle

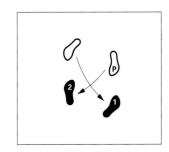

39. Two Step Turn (left)

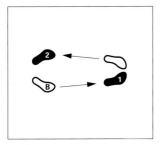

25. Rear Draw

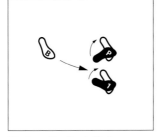

30. Cross Step Front–Pivot

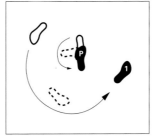

35. Forward Turn (left pivot)

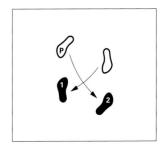

40. Two Step Turn (right)

GROUND MOVEMENT

In martial arts, various forms of ground movement can be executed from a kneeling, sitting, or reclining position against one or more opponents operating from any position, including airborne, standing, sitting, or reclining. As with standing technique, specific movements are used to facilitate execution of offensive or defensive techniques, or to remove oneself from the area of confrontation. Ground movement could become necessary for any of the following reasons:

- You have been thrown
- You have tripped or fallen
- You are executing a sacrifice technique
- You are surprised while seated or resting
- You cannot stand due to foot/leg damage
- You cannot stand due to restricted space
- You need to remain low to avoid hazards (e.g., gunfire, explosions, machinery)
- You have been restrained or tied up
- You prefer to fight on the ground

In this book, ground movements are classified according to method of locomotion. There are eleven basic types of movement:

1 Knee Walk
2 Knee-Foot Walk
3 Knee-Hand Drag
4 Crab Walk
5 Monkey Walk
6 Buttock Pivot
7 Forward Shoulder Roll
8 Back Shoulder Roll
9 Forward Roll
10 Side Roll
11 Side Crawl

The eleven basic types of ground movement are outlined on the following pages. Some of these movements are quite common, for instance, Shoulder Rolls; others are rarely used except when linked to specific techniques and objectives, for instance, the Crab Walk or Side Crawl. Many other subtle ways to shift your body, to escape or counter when on the ground, are shown in practical applications in the *Reclining Defenses* chapter.

1. Knee Walk

Many of the 40 basic steps described in the Standing Footwork section can also be applied to ground movement from a kneeling stance, by using the knees to step and pivot. Keep the feet together and under the hips, with the balls and toes of your feet against the ground. While stationary, your weight should be evenly distributed over the feet and the knees. When moving, the weight shifts from side to side. The hands should remain free to attack or defend. Use upper body rotation to assist forward or back step movements when changing your stance.

2. Knee-Foot Walk

Knee-Foot Walking is a variation of Knee Walking in which a one-knee posture alternates with a two-knee posture. This permits a greater distance to be covered in a shorter amount of time. Each movement results in a stance change (lead knee changes from left to right, or vice versa). This movement is also the beginning of a basic standing recovery.

3. Knee-Hand Drag

In this movement both hands are used to drag the body in the desired direction, usually forward or backward, while maintaining a two-knee posture. It is the same method used by leg amputees and is useful when the ankles or feet are broken or inoperable. This method allows for very rapid movement but ties up the hands, which can be detrimental.

4. Crab Walk

In this movement both hands and both feet are used to move in any direction. The back faces the ground, the buttocks may be elevated or lightly touching the ground. Various combinations and sequences of hand-foot movement are possible. Crab Walking is often used when defending from a seated position against standing opponents, and is very useful for launching kicks or leg blocks.

5. Monkey Walk

In this movement both hands and feet are used simultaneously to move forward, backward, laterally, or diagonally. Unlike the Crab Walk, the chest faces the ground. This form of motion is usually used when ceiling height is restricted or higher hazards are present. Various combinations of hand-foot movement are possible. Usually weight is transferred to the left hand and foot, while the right hand and foot move—then this is repeated, alternating sides. The legs may be kept close together or spread apart. Monkey Walking resembles a monkey moving on all fours, hence its name. Shifting to a standing posture is easily accomplished, since you are already positioned on the balls of the feet.

6. Buttock Pivot

In this movement, the body spins on the buttocks, rotating anywhere from 0° to 360°. A buttock pivot is usually executed from a Relaxed Seated Stance or a Seated Guard, and is often used to adjust your position against standing opponents who are circling you. There are four basic variations. They vary only in how the hands and feet are combined to generate the pivot.

In the first version (6.1), both hands are used to generate the pivoting motion, while the feet are free to strike, block, or throw.

In the second version (6.2), both feet are used to generate movement, while the hands are free to execute techniques.

In the third version (6.3), one hand and one foot generate movement, while the other hand and foot remain free to execute techniques. Version three has four possible permutations, based on left-right combinations.

In the fourth version (6.4), one foot is used to rotate the body, while the other limbs remain free to execute techniques. This version is effective when minor rotation is needed. It frees up more limbs for attack or defense than the other versions; however, the range of motion is shorter and slower to develop. It is also possible to generate motion with one hand, if one has sufficient arm musculature. A Buttock Pivot easily shifts into a Crab Walk when directional movement is required.

1. Knee Walk

2. Knee-Foot Walk

3. Knee-Hand Drag

4. Crab Walk

5. Monkey Walk (feet together)

5. Monkey Walk (feet apart)

6.1 Buttock Pivot (with two hands)

6.2 Buttock Pivot (with two feet)

6.3 Buttock Pivot (with one hand and one foot)

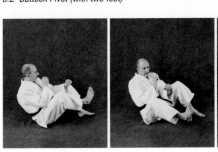
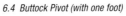

6.4 Buttock Pivot (with one foot)

7. Forward Shoulder Roll

A forward shoulder roll can be used for a variety of offensive and defensive purposes. It is used for protection when being thrown, for movement on the ground, to execute dropping kicks, and for making transitions from reclining to standing postures, or standing to reclining postures. If you are thrown forcefully forward or from a height, you must roll to prevent injury. This is a function of physics: the spinning motion significantly reduces friction and initial impact by redirecting your force upon contact with the ground. When shoulder rolling, the human body resembles a spinning ball glancing across a surface (see diagram later).

Executing a Shoulder Roll

A. Step forward with one foot leading, feet shoulder-width apart. Your leading arm will be used to enter the roll and is always on the same side as the leading foot. The outside of your arm and the knife-edge of your hand are turned outward toward the ground, with the elbow and wrist slightly bent, forming a curved arc with the arm.

B–C. Bend forward, thrust your lead hand forward, down and back between your legs in a vertical circular motion (as if reaching around a barrel). Your entire body follows this motion. Coordinating arm movement with the vertical rotation of the hips and shoulders is essential for generating motion. The trailing hand may be used for support if desired. The fingers are placed on the ground pointing forward (palm elevated), with your hand forming a triangle with both feet. As shoulder rolls increase in height and distance, use of both hands for catching, absorbing, and guiding the roll becomes essential.

D–E. Roll along the outside of your arm and shoulder, on a diagonal across your upper back to the opposite hip and leg (e.g., leading with the left arm means exiting on the right hip and leg). Tuck your chin against the chest. The head and lower spine never touch the ground. Both arms appear to form a circle.

F–G. Upon exiting the roll, keep both legs bent in one of the leg formations described in the next paragraph. Use your forward momentum to resume a kneeling or standing position, or to continue rolling. You may also exit a roll into a Seated Guard or side fall. This may become necessary if you wish to remain on the ground, or have been thrown and your opponent continues to hold your arm.

Leg Formations When Exiting

You may exit a forward roll using either a bent-leg or an extended-leg formation. In the *bent-leg* formation the leading leg is vertical, with the knee bent at least 90°. The trailing leg is fully bent and folded under, horizontal

7. Forward Shoulder Roll

Forward shoulder roll using bent-leg exit

Forward shoulder roll using extended-leg exit (note use of hand)

and flush against ground. This leg arrangement is also used in certain breakfalls (shown later in this chapter); it is often called a *figure 4*, since it resembles the shape of that number. The bent-leg formation is generally preferred for rolling, as it naturally leads to kneeling or standing postures, keeps the hands free to attack or defend, positions the legs for a Seated Guard or immediate kick, facilitates transitions into additional rolls, and reduces side stress on the trailing knee. On hard surfaces, the protruding bent-leg ankle bone is prone to damage from contact with the ground. Try to minimize ankle contact by first absorbing impact with the lower leg, or use the extended-leg version.

In the *extended-leg* formation the trailing leg is partially bent and placed alongside the bent vertical lead leg. This variation is usually used when exiting into a side fall, or if you wish to remain on the ground. Rising to a standing posture is more difficult, without use of the hands or greater rotational force. When rolling on hard surfaces, the ankle is better protected than in the bent-leg formation.

8. Back Shoulder Roll

Back shoulder rolls are used for the same purposes as forward shoulder rolls. They are also used during sacrifice throws or as part of a sit-out entry into a seated guard. A back roll is basically a forward shoulder roll in reverse.

Executing a Back Roll

A–B. Sit back from a standing posture, lowering yourself to the ground by using a two-foot, bent-leg, or extended-leg entry.

C–D. Form your body into a tight ball, keeping the back rounded and head tucked. Sit back, rolling across either shoulder. As you exit the roll, place the opposite hand (left shoulder, right hand) on the ground for support.

E. Exit the roll, landing directly on the balls of the feet and palms of the hand. Resume a kneeling or standing position.

Back Roll Entry Options

You may enter a back roll using either a two-foot entry, extended-leg entry or a bent-leg entry (see photos below). The version selected depends upon individual preference or the techniques to which the move is linked. For example, a *two-foot entry* is often selected when both feet will be used simultaneously from a ground position (e.g., twin kicks). An *extended-leg entry* might be used to execute a kick while falling, or when one knee is damaged and can't be bent. A *bent-leg entry* is often used while stepping backward. All three entries can be linked to specific sacrifice throws and ground fighting skills, which are covered in later chapters. You should practice all three methods so that you have suitable options for any situation.

8. Back shoulder roll using two-foot entry

Back shoulder roll using extended-leg entry   *Back shoulder roll using bent-leg entry*

9. Forward Roll

A *forward roll* and a *forward shoulder roll* are entirely different techniques, although the terms are often used interchangeably. In a forward roll, the body is facing straight ahead (no lead leg) and the roll is executed symmetrically by rolling from both shoulders down the length of the back. Both hands, rather than one arm, initially guide the roll. A forward roll can be used for the same purposes as a forward shoulder roll, although it is more difficult to execute safely from heights or when being thrown. In most martial arts schools it is not used as frequently as the shoulder roll, although in specific situations it is quite useful.

A forward roll is normally used when it is not possible to position or guide the upper body properly for a shoulder roll. It is also commonly used when first teaching students the fundamentals of rolling, since it is more psychologically comfortable for people who have no prior experience tumbling.

Executing a Forward Roll
A–B. Place both hands flat on the ground, with the arms slightly bent. Tuck the head by placing the chin against the chest. Form the body into a tight ball by rounding the spine.

C–D. Bend forward, projecting the hips directly overhead. Use both hands to lower and guide your body into the roll, making contact on the upper back and shoulders,

down the spine and buttocks, and exiting onto the soles of both feet. The head must never touch the ground.

E. Upon exiting, keep both legs bent and the body tightly tucked, with the hands and arms extended forward. Use your momentum to stand or to continue rolling. Avoid using your hands to assist exiting from the roll, since they may be required for attacking, defending, or generating the next movement. Reaching back to push yourself forward also stops the forward motion of the shoulders and upper body, which is essential for completing the roll and returning to your feet.

10. Side Roll

A side roll is used to move laterally from kneeling and reclining postures, often against standing opponents. This roll is frequently used during grappling to enter a hold, move away from opponents, or to switch between bottom and top positions. A side roll is also typically used to move from a Seated Guard to a kneeling Back Kick directed at standing opponents. If you are ground fighting against multiple standing opponents, side roll transitions between kneeling stances and Seated Guards will allow you to face 180° opposite (see 10.1 on next page, steps A–C).

Three basic side roll variations are shown opposite. Other variations are possible using various combinations of two-knee, one-knee and Seated Guard postures, for both entries

and exits. These variations include: two-knee to two-knee; two knee to one-knee; one-knee to two-knee; one-knee to one-knee; two-knee to Seated Guard; one-knee to Seated Guard; Seated Guard to two-knee; Seated Guard to one-knee; and Seated Guard to Seated Guard.

Executing a Side Roll
Pull the leading arm in tight to the body, roll across the back, and keep your knees tucked. In the first two sequences shown, the roll is executed with both legs bent. During the roll you will make contact with both knees and the balls of the feet. At the midpoint of the second sequence (10.2, steps C–D) a Back Kick is often launched. In the third sequence (10.3), both legs are extended during the middle portion of the roll and are partially contracted at the beginning and end. If you were rolling from a lying position, they would be extended throughout the movement.

11. Side Crawl

This movement is used to escape from a reclining position when grappling or being held with a body pin. It can also be used for ground movement if the hands and feet are tied together separately, the leg(s) are severely damaged, or when it is important to remain very close to the ground for safety reasons (e.g., gunfire, environmental hazards, you don't want to be detected). Movement is on the side of the body and is generated by using the abdominal muscles, hand, arm, and shoulder to pull your hips forward.

9. Forward Roll

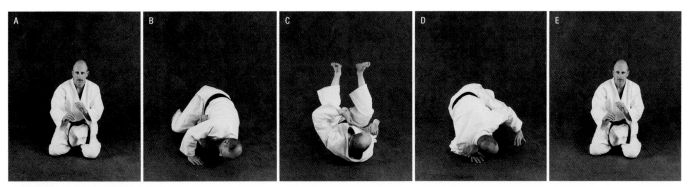

10.1 Side Roll (from Two Knee Stance)

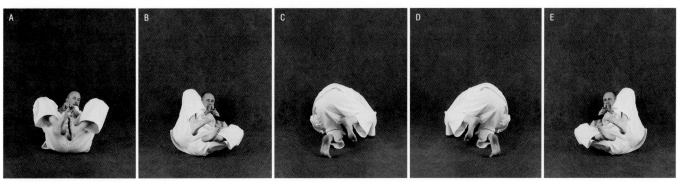

10.2 Side Roll (from Seated Guard)

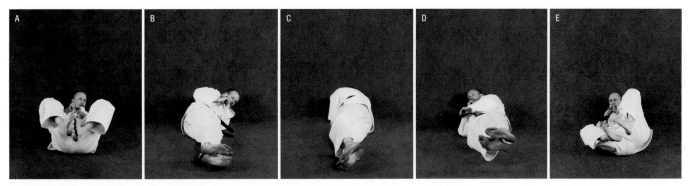

10.3 Side Roll (from Seated Guard, with extended legs)

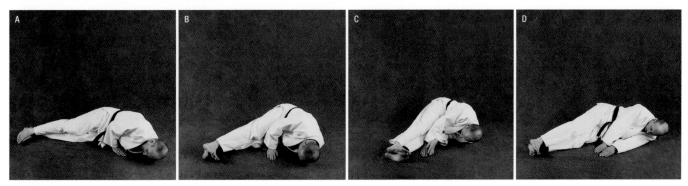

11. Side Crawl

Practicing Shoulder Rolls

Roll entries should be practiced and mastered from aerial, standing, walking, running, kneeling, seated, and reclining positions, on both sides. Practice exiting into reclining, seated, kneeling, and standing postures.

When first learning, start from a kneeling position. When this is mastered, try standing and running, gradually increasing height and distance. Always practice on a well padded surface until mastery is obtained. Practice on grass next, and later, wood or concrete to simulate actual conditions. Remember, too much practice on very hard surfaces can cause cumulative damage to joints, tendons, and bone regardless of the quality of your technique. Practice with common sense. Injuries to the shoulder, collarbone, rotator-cuff, and scapula are very slow to heal (six months plus is typical) and often result in recurrent or permanent conditions.

Common Problems

When initially learning shoulder rolls, a common problem is landing forcefully on the leading elbow or shoulder during the roll. This is usually a result of: collapsing the elbow, not generating enough circular force, placing body weight against the arm during the roll, or failing to extend the leading arm back between your legs. These mistakes are painful and will result in injury if not immediately corrected. A qualified teacher is essential to eliminate faulty technique before it leads to bad habits or bodily injury.

Another common problem is the inability to complete the roll or rise to one's feet. If you fall backwards or use your hands to assist returning to a kneeling or standing position (by pushing against the mat), you have not generated sufficient inertia during the roll. You may also be failing to maintain a tight tuck, causing the upper body to stop your momentum. A one-hand assist is only used during an extended-leg exit. When exiting a roll, the hands should be free to attack or defend, particularly during sacrifice techniques or when rising to face an attacker.

The importance of *relaxing* and *feeling* the movement cannot be overstated. If you are rolling properly you should make very little noise and sustain minimal impact with the ground. Check to make sure you have rolled straight ahead, and not off to the side. If the feet or body make a loud slapping noise against the mat, this indicates hard contact, which on hard surfaces will result in foot or ankle injuries. Historically, one was expected to be able to roll on rice paper without making a sound or tearing the paper. Today, this "quietness" or "harmony between body and ground" is still an important goal when rolling.

The diagrams below illustrate the basic impact reducing factors present in all forms of rolls. You will note that "spinning motion" is crucial in reducing impact and redirecting energy. Common applications and practice methods for shoulder rolls are shown at right.

Force Redirected by Rolling

Left: Normal force and friction at impact is absorbed by body, sustaining damage. Right: Force and friction is reduced and redirected by spinning motion.

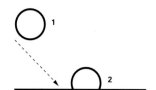
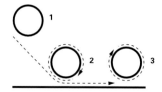

Practicing shoulder rolls for distance (top two photos show the entry sequence).

Practicing shoulder rolls for height (note: jumper is same height as standing people).

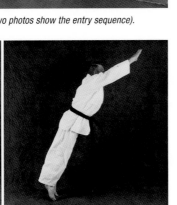

To initiate a high roll: Take a running start, jump and plant both feet, spring off.

This sequence illustrates how a shoulder roll protects a faller during a sacrifice throw.

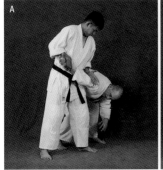

This series illustrates two types of ground movement: Defender uses a shoulder roll to escape arm bar hold (A–B), then a buttock pivot to reposition the legs (C) for a throw (D).

TRANSITIONAL MOVEMENT

The following transitional movements are used to switch between standing and ground positions. This may become necessary, or even desirable, for the reasons listed at the beginning of the *Ground Movement* section. The movements shown may be executed separately or combined into a continuous sequence. Practical applications linking movement with specific strikes, holds, and throws are shown in chapters covering the various aspects of ground fighting.

Entering a Ground Position

The following movement techniques are used to enter a Seated Guard or a kneeling stance from a standing posture. They are typically called *sit-out* or *ground-entry* techniques, and are usually used in conjunction with falls and sacrifice techniques involving kicks and throws. Common methods follow.

1–3 Sit-Out Entry

There are three methods of executing a sit-out to a Seated Guard: two-foot entry, extended-leg entry, and bent-leg entry. They are the same entries used to execute a Back Shoulder Roll and were previously discussed.

4. Back Shoulder Roll Entry

This entry is used to move backward while entering a ground position, often while being pushed or tripped. Back shoulder rolls may be executed using any of the three entry methods listed in the previous paragraph.

5–6 Forward Shoulder Roll Entry

When you wish to move forward while making a transition to the ground, execute a shoulder roll into a kneeling stance or Seated Guard.

7–8 One-Hand and Two-Hand Drop Entry

These methods are used when you wish to drop straight down, often in preparation for ground kicking. The one-hand method is used when you wish to keep a hand free for blocking or grabbing. The two-hand method provides better support and is often linked to twin kicks, leg traps, scissor throws, or other double-leg techniques.

1. Sit-Out Entry (using two-foot entry)

2. Sit-Out Entry (using extended-leg entry)

3. Sit-Out Entry (using bent-leg entry)

4. Back Shoulder Roll Entry

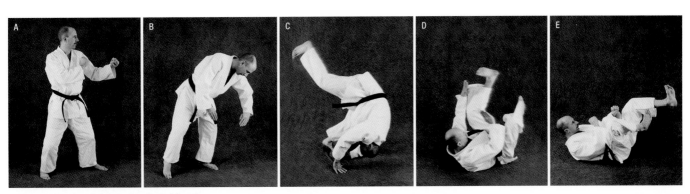

5. Forward Shoulder Roll Entry (into Seated Guard)

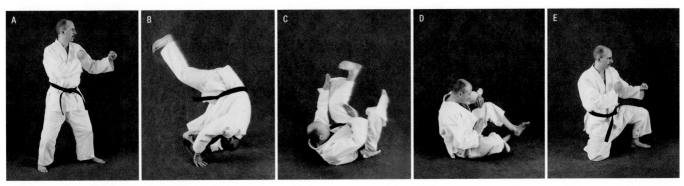

6. Forward Shoulder Roll Entry (into One Knee Stance)

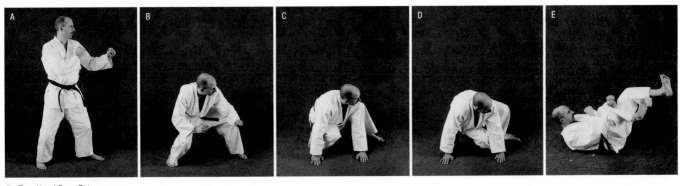

7. Two-Hand Drop Entry

8. One-Hand Drop Entry

Recovering a Standing Position

The following movements are used to enter a standing posture from a seated, kneeling, or fall position. They are called *recovery* techniques and are usually used to regain a standing position after falling or being thrown. Speed, timing, and economy of movement are crucial, since you may be under constant attack. Common methods are as follows:

9. Forward Shoulder Roll Recovery

This movement is used to move forward while changing from kneeling to standing postures, or to move off an opponent you are straddling on the ground. The body can be shifted as you rise, to face any direction.

10. Back Shoulder Roll Recovery

This movement is used to move backward while changing from a seated or kneeling position to standing. It is used to create distance, avoid an attack, or initiate a retreat.

11. Side Roll Recovery

This movement is used to move laterally while changing from a kneeling or seated guard to a standing posture. The technique often incorporates a Back Kick to create space by driving the opponent backwards. Use the kick delivery to assist rising to a standing position as you push off with both hands.

12. Figure-4 Recovery

This movement is used to change from a Seated Guard to a standing posture. It is basically the last part of a forward shoulder roll. However, since you begin from a stationary position, it is necessary to first generate forward momentum before attempting to rise, or you will fall backward. To execute, generate momentum by drawing the upper body forward (into a tuck) as you pull the legs down, folding one leg under the other. Drive forward (leading with one hand) as you press off with your bent leg, allowing your

forward momentum to carry you to a standing position. Do not rise too soon, as your balance can be easily upset by an unexpected push. You may also generate momentum by rocking backward then forward, although this takes more time, which creates greater risk.

13. Two-Knee Recovery

This movement is used to change from a Two Knee Stance to a standing posture. Shift your weight back to the balls of both feet, which are placed under the buttocks. Rise straight upward by extending the legs.

14. One-Knee Recovery

This movement is used to change from a One Knee Stance to a standing posture. Shift your weight forward to the raised knee. Rise straight upward. The majority of your weight should be placed over the front leg, so that the unweighted rear leg is free to block or kick if required.

9. Forward Shoulder Roll Recovery

10. Back Shoulder Roll Recovery

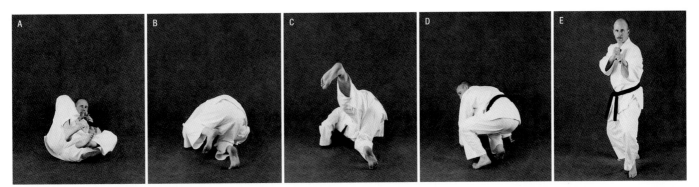

11. Side Roll Recovery (with optional Back Kick)

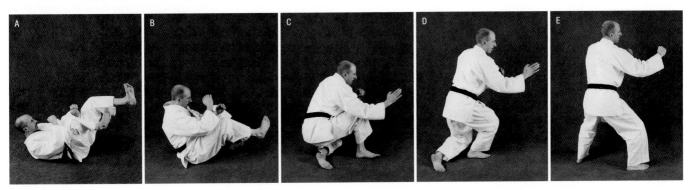

12. Figure-4 Recovery

13. Two-Knee Recovery

14. One-Knee Recovery

15. Roll-Up Recovery

This movement is used to change from a Seated Guard to a standing posture. It is basically the end of a forward roll. Generate momentum by rocking backward then forward. With legs fully bent, pull both feet to your buttocks, keeping them slightly wider than shoulder-width apart. Whip the upper body and arms forward, drawing the chest to the knees, as you roll up onto both feet. If you find yourself falling backwards, you have probably placed your feet too close together, failed to generate sufficient momentum, or are not tightly tucked. Learning a *roll-up recovery* is a precursor to learning a *kip-up*, since both use a similar whipping motion.

16. Kip-Up Recovery

This movement is used to change from any reclining position to a standing posture (e.g., recovering from a Back Fall). A kip-up requires good flexibility, speed, and some aptitude for gymnastics. Although not difficult to learn, it requires good flexibility, supple joints, and a healthy back and knees. To execute, rock back onto the upper back, with your head tucked and both hands planted near the shoulders. Rapidly whip your legs forward, pulling them under the buttocks as you arch your back. Push off with both hands, whipping the arms and shoulders forward, drawing the chest to your knees, as you land on both feet. Kip-ups can also be executed without planting the hands if you develop adequate body motion.

17. Two-Hand Recovery (extended-leg)

This technique is used to regain a standing position after taking an *extended-leg* side fall. To execute, support yourself with both hands as you bring the extended leg back to the rear. Do not move the other leg, as it is already properly positioned. Transfer your weight to both feet, bringing the hands up to a guard position for protection, as you stand up.

18. One-Hand Recovery (extended-leg)

This is the same as the previous technique, except one hand supports the body, while the other hand remains in a guard position. This method provides better protection, since one hand is available for blocking or grabbing (particularly important if an opponent is at close range). Individuals with poor balance or weak arms may feel more comfortable using the two-hand method.

19. Two-Hand Recovery (bent-leg)

This technique is used to regain a standing position after taking a *bent-leg* side fall. It is similar to #17, except the bent-leg is brought to the rear before standing.

20. One-Hand Recovery (bent-leg)

This is the same as the previous technique, except one hand supports body, while the other remains in a guard position. It has the same advantages and limitations as #18.

15. Roll-Up Recovery

16. Kip-Up Recovery

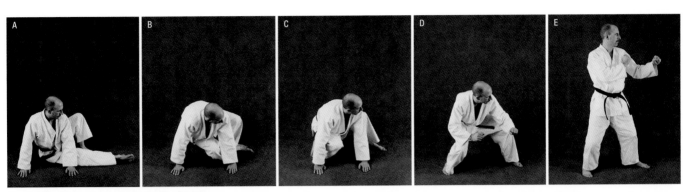

17. *Two-Hand Recovery (from extended-leg side fall)*

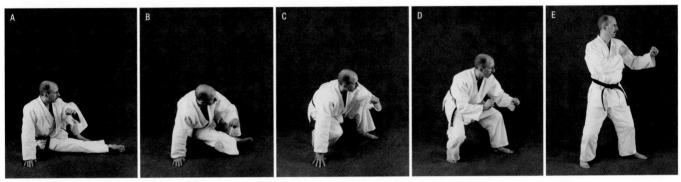

18. *One-Hand Recovery (from extended-leg side fall)*

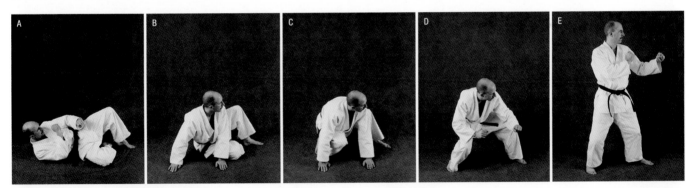

19. *Two-Hand Recovery (from bent-leg side fall)*

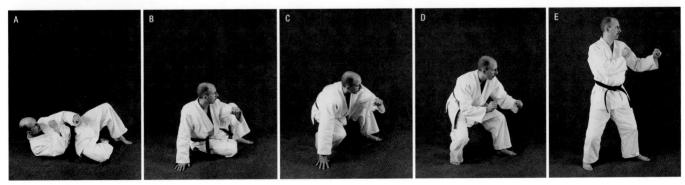

20. *One-Hand Recovery (from bent-leg side fall)*

Breakfalls

If you do not know how to fall, many holds and throws will produce serious injuries. A *breakfall* is a specific method of falling, designed to protect your body from damage as you hit the ground. This involves specific formations of your body which minimize impact by dispersing force over a large surface area. Eight basic types of breakfalls, common to many martial arts, are shown on subsequent pages. The photo(s) above each sequence shows each breakfall being used during a typical throwing technique. All breakfalls should be learned from a qualified instructor to avoid injuries. The breakfall you will use is based on how you are thrown. In all breakfalls, you will attempt to control your body position while airborne. As your body lands in the proper position, you will usually *slap* and emit an *energy-shout* at the same time. In some martial arts an energy-shout is not used; practitioners will instead either exhale or hold their breath during impact.

The Slap

In most breakfalls you will slap with your hand and forearm, or entire arm, to distribute the force of impact. This also helps to position your body and assists in timing. The force of your slap must be adjusted based on the hardness of the surface you are falling onto. While it is common to see students endlessly practicing forceful slaps on the mat, these same slaps will cause you to injure or break your hand when falling on hard surfaces like concrete. In some soft-style martial arts, the slap is barely articulated or nonexistent, since the focus is on blending with the ground.

The Energy-Shout

An energy-shout is an abrupt shout designed to focus your energy and power, and was covered previously in this chapter, under *Energetic Concepts*. During breakfalls, an energy-shout helps protect the body from injury, keeps the wind from being knocked out of your lungs, and causes your body to naturally relax on impact. Some martial arts do not use a shout, but instead focus on relaxing and blending with the ground. In some Chinese arts, practitioners are taught to tense their body and hold their breath during a breakfall, the idea being that this prevents organ damage from the force of impact.

Self-Initiated Breakfalls

In some martial arts, such as Hapkido, you will often initiate your own fall, in order to counter joint locks or throws. This saves your joints from serious injury, and propels you ahead of a thrower's force. Self-initiated falls are the basis of many counters and escapes.

Improvised Breakfalls

In the beginning, good form is important to prevent injury. As you obtain experience, you will notice that there are many ways to fall, some quite unorthodox. In the end, how you fall is irrelevant, since the ultimate objective is to survive and consistently remain injury free.

In this double-throw defense against two simultaneous kicks, the left attacker is executing a Back Fall, as the right attacker executes a Front Fall.

In some throws, the thrower must also use a breakfall to prevent injury. These photos show a Scissor Throw. The thrower uses a Side Fall, the receiver a Back Fall.

Self-initiated breakfalls are often required to save your joints from serious injury. This photo shows two attackers executing Flip Side Falls.

1. Front Fall

As you fall forward, position your hands in front of your face, with your bent-arms at a 45° angle, hands aligned with forearms. While airborne, spread your feet shoulder-width apart or wider. As you approach the ground, slap downward with both hands and forearms, as you shout or exhale. Your hands should make contact slightly before your forearms. The underside of your toes should make contact at the same time.

Important Points

As you fall, turn your head sideways to avoid accidentally breaking your nose. Do not allow your knees or torso to hit the ground. Try to absorb some of the shock by flexing your elbows and shoulders as you land. *Do not* land directly on the elbows (fracture), or reach out with your palms (broken wrist). When first learning to fall, practice from a kneeling position, progressing to squatting, then standing, and eventually airborne.

2. Soft Front Fall

As you fall forward, reach out for the ground with both hands and withdraw them as your hands make contact. Slow your descent by using your arm and shoulder muscles to lower your chest to the ground. This is similar to doing a *push-up*. Simultaneously, arch your back to slow the descent of your legs, landing on the underside of your toes, with your feet shoulder-width apart or wider. Turn your head to protect your nose.

Important Points

This form of breakfall has become more popular in recent years, since it transmits less shock to the arms and shoulders during impact. This makes it more suitable for older individuals, or people who have initial fears about learning to fall. However, there are many situations when it is not possible to control your landing in this manner. Learning the previous *Front Fall* is still considered very important.

3. Back Fall

As you fall backward, cross your arms and tuck your chin against your chest, to keep your head from hitting the ground. As you land on the back of your shoulders, slap the ground with both hands and arms at a 45° angle from your body, and shout or exhale. Quickly retract your hands to prepare for your next technique. When falling from a standing posture (see photos), keep your hips close to your heels.

Important Points

Do not slap higher than 45°. It is ineffective, and will often stress the shoulders, or cause the wind to be knocked out of you. Keep your back curved as you fall. When first learning, progress from lying to sitting, to squatting, to standing, then airborne. Try to avoid landing on the middle or lower back, since this stresses the spine. High falls can be difficult, since minor errors often result in neck or back injuries.

4. Bridge Fall

This breakfall is used when you are flipped straight over onto your back. You will land on the back of your shoulders and balls of your feet, thus avoiding serious injury to your spine. As you land, tuck your chin, elevate the buttocks, slap the ground with both hands and arms at a 45° angle from your body, and shout or exhale. Quickly retract your hands to prepare for your next technique.

Important Points

Do not land on your heels, since this transmits substantial shock to your ankles and knees, and the nerves at the bottom of your heel. When first learning this fall, practice by executing a forward roll very low to the ground. Then progress to flipping straight over with your arms straight and the body extended (see photos). Eventually you can practice airborne falls without using your hands for support.

5. Sit-Out Side Fall

This breakfall is used when you are falling to your side or rear-corner. As one leg is swept or reaped, you will lower yourself using your supporting leg. Sit back toward your rear-corner, rolling onto your side, as you slap the ground with one arm at a 45° angle from your body, and shout or exhale. Allow the rolling motion to carry your legs upward. The slap is often not needed, but helps time your actions.

Important Points

This is a very low-impact fall, since you are controlling your own descent throughout. It sometimes helps to think of it as a *back roll* executed on the side of your body. Keep your buttock close to your heel as you sit back. This breakfall is often confused with the next technique, however, they are quite different. In this breakfall, one leg supports your fall. In the *Sweep Side Fall,* both feet leave the ground.

6. Sweep Side Fall

This breakfall is used when one or both legs are swept out from under you. You will land on the side of your body, as you slap the ground with one arm (at a 45° angle from the body) and shout or exhale. The entire right side of your body and your left foot contact the ground at the same time. The left leg is bent and vertical, landing on the ball of the foot. The right leg is slightly bent, with the sole turned upward to protect the ankle.

Important Points

Make sure you tuck your chin, turn your right foot upward to protect your protruding ankle from hitting the ground, and land on the back of your right shoulder—not the side, or serious injury will result. When compared to the previous *Sit-Out Side Fall,* this fall involves greater impact, with both legs contacting the ground. The force of the throw will not allow you to *sit-out* as described in the previous breakfall.

7. Flip Side Fall

This breakfall is used when your are flipped straight over onto your side. As you land, slap the ground with one arm at a 45° angle from your body, and shout or exhale. The entire right side of your body and your left foot contact the ground at the same time. Your left leg is bent and vertical, landing on the ball of the foot. Your right leg is either slightly bent with the sole turned up, or fully bent with the heel near the buttock.

Important Points

This breakfall is used during most hip and shoulder throws, or when initiating your own fall to counter a joint lock. There are two common leg formations used when landing. The only difference is the position of your left leg. The *Extended-Leg Landing* is more common, and is also used in the Sweep Side Fall. In the *Bent-Leg Landing,* you will fully retract your left leg, being careful not to strike your left ankle with your right heel.

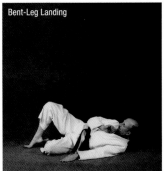

Bent-Leg Landing

Extended-Leg Landing

8. Twisting Side Fall

This breakfall is used when one arm is held behind your back, and you are forced to fall on that same side. Twist your upper body as you fall, bending your legs to control your descent. Land on the side of your right leg, as you slap with your left hand and forearm, and shout or exhale. Twisting your upper body is crucial to prevent your right shoulder from slamming into the ground. Turn your head to protect your nose.

Important Points

This breakfall is rarely needed, which may be the reason it is not taught in most schools. However, during certain types of falls resulting from *Hammer Locks* or *Twisting Arm Locks,* it may provide your only sensible means of protection. In these situations, your opponent may be trying to get you to fall directly onto your shoulder, or backward onto your own arm—resulting in serious injuries (usually to the shoulder).

Blocks from Ground Positions

Blocking techniques are used to avoid being grabbed or hit. Most of the blocks used while standing can also be executed from ground positions, such as kneeling, seated, reclining, straddling, or being straddled. Ground blocks are very similar to standing blocks, they have merely been adapted to ground positions. More than 100 avoiding and blocking techniques are covered in the author's books *The Art of Striking* and *Hapkido: Traditions, Philosophy, Technique.* To avoid redundancy, this material will not be repeated in this text. Instead, a few practical examples will be shown to illustrate the general manner in which blocks are used during ground fighting.

The photographs below show typical ground scenarios with different types of blocks linked to simultaneous counterstrikes. Many other possibilities exist. When blocking from ground positions, the risk of being hit is much greater than standing situations, since your body movement is restricted, your opponent is very close, and your reactions must be quicker. Therefore, short, quick, simple blocks are usually recommended. The following types are generally most useful:

• Short Parries (to deflect)
• Grabbing Parries (to trap the arms)
• Forearm Blocks (inside, outside, rising)
• Shielding Blocks (when other blocks fail)

Shielding Blocks

Shielding blocks absorb the force of a blow by placing your arms or legs in the path of the strike, thereby protecting a more vulnerable target, such as the head, neck, solar plexus, ribs, or groin. Commonly called *covering up,* this type of block is usually used when you cannot avoid being hit, wish to appear helpless, or you are fighting a much smaller opponent whose blows are light and ineffective. Against a very fast striker delivering blows too fast to block or avoid, shielding may be your only defensive option. When skillfully applied, shielding blocks can also provide an excellent base for launching counterattacks. They can also be deceptive.

Inside Parry to straight punch, and Palm Heel Strike to solar plexus at CO-15.

Outside Block to Hook Punch, and Tiger Mouth Strike to throat

Grab Parry to Straight Punch, and Palm Heel Strike to elbow

Elbow Wrap Block to Hook Punch, and Elbow Strike to head

1. Head Block

This shielding block uses the arm to protect the side of the head and neck. Raise your arm with the elbow fully closed and the fist tightly clenched (to reduce damage to the hand). Against very powerful blows, press your arm against your head to prevent the force of the strike from slamming your fist into your own head. Against an opponent in front, this block would be used to defend against circular strikes such as the Hook Punch, Roundhouse Kick, Hook Kick, and Spin Kick. In these instances, try to move toward the opponent's body whenever feasible, placing your head inside the path of the blow. This reduces the blow's impact on your arm and head.

2. Face Block

In this block, you will use both of your arms to protect the front of your face, neck, chest, and solar plexus. Raise your arms with the forearms together, the fists clenched, and the elbows covering the chest. Your arms absorb the force of the strike. During training, try to develop the ability to rapidly switch back and forth between Head Blocks and Face Blocks, as your opponent alternates between circular and straight strikes.

3. Body Block

This shielding block uses the arm to protect the body and head. It is similar to a *Head Block,* except the elbow is placed lower to protect more of your body. Position your arms with the forearms covering your ribs, and the hands protecting your face. Lower your head and tuck your chin in against your shoulder or chest. Allow your body to turn, roll, or sway with the strike, to reduce its impact. This is what is meant by "rolling with the punches."

4. Groin Block

This shielding block is used to protect your groin and genitalia from punches or kicks, by pivoting your hip or thigh into the path of the blow. If you are being overwhelmed, or attacked by several standing attackers while you are reclining, a Groin Block can be combined with a Body Block.

1. Head Block against circular punches to side of head

2. Face Block against straight punches to the face

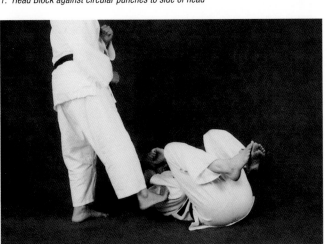

3. Body Block against repeated kicks to the ribs and head

4. Groin Block against attacker crashing in with their knee

PRESSURE POINT TARGETS

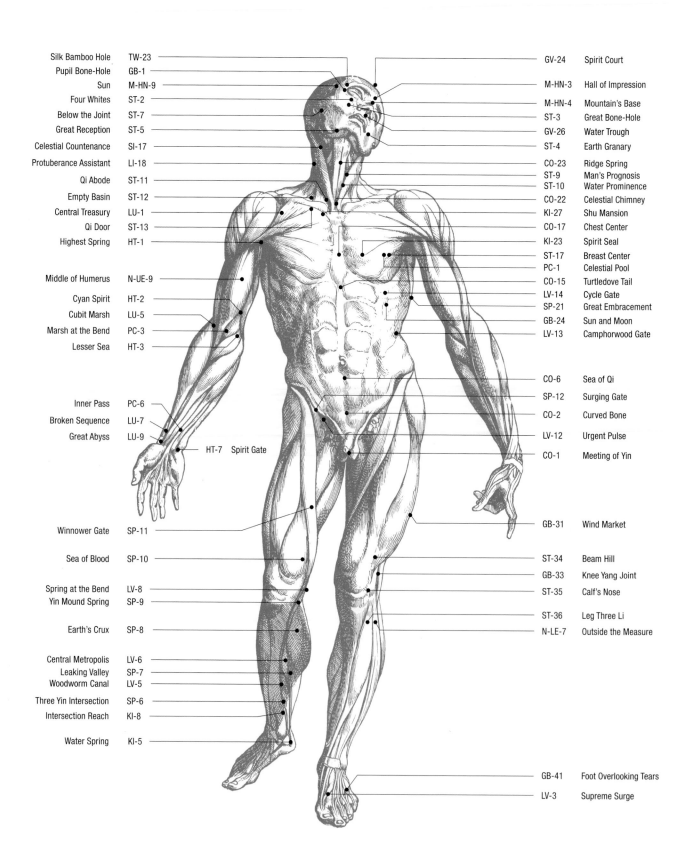

Silk Bamboo Hole	TW-23
Pupil Bone-Hole	GB-1
Sun	M-HN-9
Four Whites	ST-2
Below the Joint	ST-7
Great Reception	ST-5
Celestial Countenance	SI-17
Protuberance Assistant	LI-18
Qi Abode	ST-11
Empty Basin	ST-12
Central Treasury	LU-1
Qi Door	ST-13
Highest Spring	HT-1
Middle of Humerus	N-UE-9
Cyan Spirit	HT-2
Cubit Marsh	LU-5
Marsh at the Bend	PC-3
Lesser Sea	HT-3
Inner Pass	PC-6
Broken Sequence	LU-7
Great Abyss	LU-9
HT-7	Spirit Gate
Winnower Gate	SP-11
Sea of Blood	SP-10
Spring at the Bend	LV-8
Yin Mound Spring	SP-9
Earth's Crux	SP-8
Central Metropolis	LV-6
Leaking Valley	SP-7
Woodworm Canal	LV-5
Three Yin Intersection	SP-6
Intersection Reach	KI-8
Water Spring	KI-5

GV-24	Spirit Court
M-HN-3	Hall of Impression
M-HN-4	Mountain's Base
ST-3	Great Bone-Hole
GV-26	Water Trough
ST-4	Earth Granary
CO-23	Ridge Spring
ST-9	Man's Prognosis
ST-10	Water Prominence
CO-22	Celestial Chimney
KI-27	Shu Mansion
CO-17	Chest Center
KI-23	Spirit Seal
ST-17	Breast Center
PC-1	Celestial Pool
CO-15	Turtledove Tail
LV-14	Cycle Gate
SP-21	Great Embracement
GB-24	Sun and Moon
LV-13	Camphorwood Gate
CO-6	Sea of Qi
SP-12	Surging Gate
CO-2	Curved Bone
LV-12	Urgent Pulse
CO-1	Meeting of Yin
GB-31	Wind Market
ST-34	Beam Hill
GB-33	Knee Yang Joint
ST-35	Calf's Nose
ST-36	Leg Three Li
N-LE-7	Outside the Measure
GB-41	Foot Overlooking Tears
LV-3	Supreme Surge

The illustrations on these pages show 106 common pressure point targets used in the martial arts. Each point is labeled using both its alphanumeric symbol, and the English translation of the point's Chinese name. Korean and Japanese translations are usually similar, if not identical. *Essential Anatomy for Healing and Martial Arts*, by the same author, contains additional pressure point targets and charts, a detailed discussion of pressure point fighting principles, a comprehensive presentation of human anatomy in both Eastern and Western medical systems, and an index listing the precise anatomical location of more than 380 pressure points, cross-referenced to nerves, blood vessels, and other anatomical landmarks.

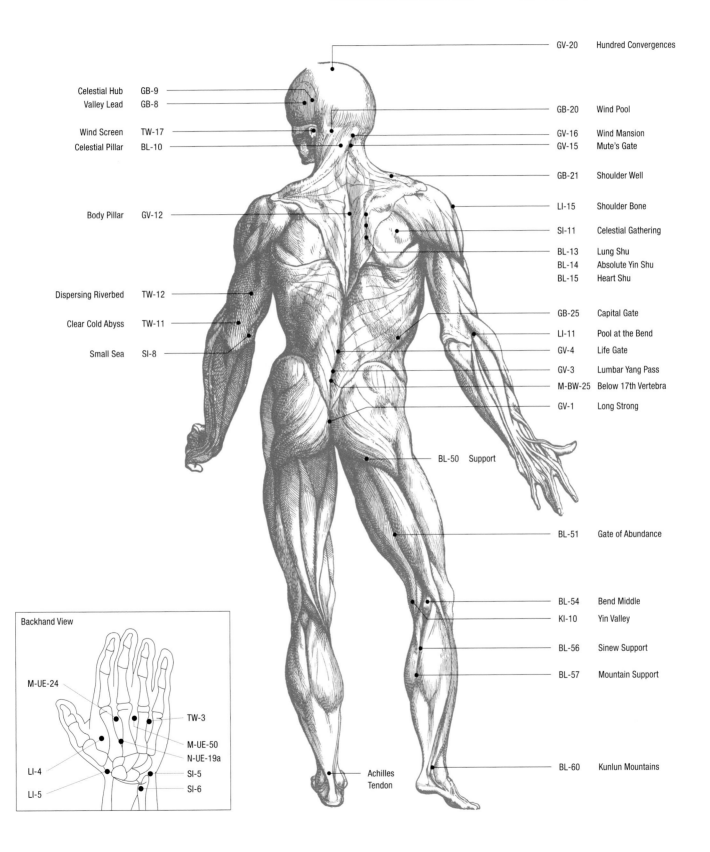

		GV-20	Hundred Convergences
Celestial Hub	GB-9		
Valley Lead	GB-8	GB-20	Wind Pool
Wind Screen	TW-17	GV-16	Wind Mansion
Celestial Pillar	BL-10	GV-15	Mute's Gate
		GB-21	Shoulder Well
		LI-15	Shoulder Bone
Body Pillar	GV-12	SI-11	Celestial Gathering
		BL-13	Lung Shu
		BL-14	Absolute Yin Shu
		BL-15	Heart Shu
Dispersing Riverbed	TW-12	GB-25	Capital Gate
		LI-11	Pool at the Bend
Clear Cold Abyss	TW-11	GV-4	Life Gate
		GV-3	Lumbar Yang Pass
Small Sea	SI-8	M-BW-25	Below 17th Vertebra
		GV-1	Long Strong

BL-50   Support

BL-51   Gate of Abundance

BL-54   Bend Middle
KI-10   Yin Valley

BL-56   Sinew Support

BL-57   Mountain Support

Backhand View

M-UE-24

TW-3

M-UE-50
N-UE-19a

LI-4

SI-5

LI-5

SI-6

Achilles
Tendon

BL-60   Kunlun Mountains

BL-10	Back of neck, 1.3 units lateral to GV-15, within hairline, on lateral side of trapezius muscle.	GB-25	Side of trunk, at lower edge of floating end of 12th rib (lowest rib).	LI-5	Radial side of wrist, in recess between extensor muscle tendons at base of thumb.
BL-13	Upper back, 1.5 units lateral to lower edge of spinous process of 3rd thoracic vertebra.	GB-31	Outer thigh, 7 units above kneecap, at end of middle finger when arm hangs at side.	LI-11	In recess at lateral end of elbow crease, midway between LU-5 and protruding humerus bone.
BL-14	Upper back, 1.5 units lateral to lower edge of spinous process of 4th thoracic vertebra.	GB-33	Outer thigh, in recess above bony knob of femur, between bone and biceps femoris tendon.*	LI-15	With arm raised, in a recess at edge of shoulder joint, slightly forward to middle of deltoid muscle.
BL-15	Upper back, 1.5 units lateral to lower edge of spinous process of 5th thoracic vertebra.	GB-41	Top of foot, in recess distal and between junction of 4th and 5th metatarsal bones.	LI-18	Side of neck, level with Adam's apple tip, directly below ear, on rear part of sternoceidomastoid m.
BL-50	Buttock, at midpoint of crease below buttock (transverse gluteal crease).	GV-1	Halfway between tip of tailbone (coccyx) and anus.	LU-1	Chest, 1 unit below lateral end of clavicle, in first intercostal space, 6 units lateral midline (pulse).
BL-51	Back of thigh, 6 units below BL-50 on line joining BL-50 to BL-54.	GV-3	Midline of back, below spinous process of 4th lumbar vertebra.	LU-5	Crease of elbow, at radial side of biceps tendon, at origin of brachioradialis muscle.
BL-54	Back of knee, midpoint of transverse crease, between biceps + semitendinosus m. tendons.	GV-4	Midline of back, below spinous process of 2nd lumbar vertebra.	LU-7	Thumb-side of forearm, in crevice at lateral edge of radius bone, 1.5 units above wrist crease.
BL-56	Lower leg, 3 units above BL-57, in center of belly of gastrocnemius m. (calf).	GV-12	Midline of back, below spinous process of 3rd thoracic vertebra.	LU-9	Wrist at transverse crease, in recess on radial side of radial artery, where pulse is felt.
BL-57	Lower leg, directly below belly of gastrocnemius muscle, on line joining BL-54 to Achilles tendon.	GV-15	Back midline of neck, in recess 0.5 unit below GV-16, 0.5 unit within hairline.	LV-3	Top of foot, in recess distal and between junction of 1st and 2nd metatarsal bones (above web).
BL-60	Outer ankle, recess halfway between protruding bone at ankle and Achilles tendon, level with tip.	GV-16	Midline of neck, in recess below ext. occipital protuberance, at trapezius muscle attachments.	LV-5	5 units above tip of protruding bone at inner ankle, between posterior edge of tibia and calf m.
CO-1	In center of perineum, between anus and genitals.	GV-20	Midline of head, 7 units above rear hairline, on midpoint of line joining earlobes and ear apexes.	LV-6	Inner ankle, 7 units above tip of protruding bone at inner ankle, on posterior edge of tibia.
CO-2	Front midline, directly above pubic bone (pubic symphysis), 5 units below navel, (pulse is felt).	GV-24	Midline, on top of head, 0.5 unit within front hairline.	LV-8	Inner knee joint. When bent, point is at medial end of crease, above tendons attaching at joint.
CO-6	Front midline of abdomen, 1.5 units below navel.	GV-26	Front midline, in center of groove below nose (philtrum), slightly above midpoint.	LV-12	Inguinal groove, 2.5 units lateral to midline, lateral to pubic symphysis, 5 units below navel.
CO-15	Front midline, 7 units above navel, usually below xiphoid process (depends on length of cartilage).	HT-1	With arm raised, in center of axilla (armpit), on medial side of axillary artery.	LV-13	Trunk, below free end of 11th floating rib, 2 units above level of navel, 6 units lateral to midline.
CO-17	Front midline of chest, level with 4th intercostal space, level and between nipples, on sternum.	HT-2	3 units above medial end of elbow crease and HT-3, in groove medial to biceps muscle.	LV-14	Chest, near medial end of 6th intercostal space (between ribs), 2 ribs below nipple.
CO-22	Front midline, at center of sternal notch (top edge of sternum, at base of throat).	HT-3	With elbow bent, at medial end of elbow crease, in recess anterior to protruding bone at elbow.	M-BW-25	Back midline, 1 vertebra below GV-3, at lumbro-sacral joint (5th lumbar and 1st sacral vertebras).
CO-23	Front midline of throat, above Adam's apple, in recess at upper edge of hyoid bone.	HT-7	On transverse wrist crease, in recess between ulna and pisiform bones, radial side of tendon.	M-HN-3	Front midline, in recess halfway between medial ends of eyebrows (glabella), also called GV-24.5.
GB-1	About 0.5 unit lateral to outer corner of eye, in recess on lateral side of orbit (bony eye socket).	KI-5	Inner heel, in recess above and in front of bulge in heel bone, 1 unit below level of ankle.	M-HN-4	Front midline, lowest point on bridge of nose, halfway between inner canthi of left + right eyes.
GB-8	Side of head, above apex of ear, in recess 1.5 units within hairline (point is felt when biting).	KI-8	Inner lower leg, 2 units above level of protruding bone at ankle, posterior to medial edge of tibia.	M-HN-9	Temple, in recess 1 unit posterior to the midpoint between outer canthus of eye and tip of eyebrow.
GB-9	Side of head, above and behind ear, 2 units within hairline, about 0.5 unit behind GB-8.	KI-10	Medial side of back of knee, between semitendi-nosus + semimembranosus tendons, level BL-54.	M-UE-24	Back of hand, between 2nd and 3rd metacarpal bones, 0.5 unit proximal to base joints of fingers.
GB-20	Back of neck, below occipital bone, in recess between sternoceidomastoid m. and trapezius m.	KI-23	Chest, in 4th intercostal space (between ribs), 2 units lateral to body midline, level with nipple.	M-UE-50	Back of hand, between 3rd and 4th metacarpal bones, 0.5 unit proximal to base joints of fingers.
GB-21	Shoulder, halfway between C7 vertebra and protruding bone at top of shoulder (acromion).	KI-27	Chest, in recess at lower edge of medial head of clavicle, 2 units lateral to body midline.	N-LE-7	Outer lower leg below knee, 1 unit lateral to ST-36.
GB-24	Below nipple, between cartilage of 7th+8th ribs, one rib space below and slightly lateral to LV-14.	LI-4	Center of muscle between 1st + 2nd metacarpals on back of hand (web of thumb), slightly to 2nd.	N-UE-9	Front upper arm, in center of biceps brachii muscle, 4.5 units below axillary (armpit) fold.

N-UE-19a	Back of hand, at forked recess where 2nd and 3rd metacarpal bones merge.	SP-9	In recess below protruding tibia at inner knee, between rear edge of tibia and gastrocnemius m.	ST-11	Front base of neck, in recess between two heads of sternocleidomastoid m., at end of clavicle.
PC-1	Chest, 1 unit lateral to nipple, in 4th intercostal space.	SP-10	Thigh, 2 units above top medial edge of kneecap, on medial edge of vastus medialis m. (on bulge).	ST-12	In a recess at top edge of middle of clavicle, aligned with nipple, 4 units lateral to midline.
PC-3	Inner elbow, on transverse crease, slightly medial to tendon of biceps brachii muscle.	SP-11	Thigh, 6 units above SP-10, at medial side of sartorius m., between SP-10 + 12 (pulse is felt).	ST-13	In a recess at lower edge of middle of clavicle, above and aligned with nipple.
PC-6	Forearm, 2 units above wrist crease, between tendons of long palmar m. and radial flexor m.	SP-12	In inguinal crease, lateral side of femoral artery, 3.5 units lateral to CO-2, where pulse is felt.	ST-17	Chest, in center of nipple. This acupoint is often used as a landmark to locate other acupoints.
SI-5	Ulnar side of wrist, in recess between ulna bone and triquetral bone (wrist joint).	SP-21	Trunk, on midaxillary line, 6 units below armpit, halfway between armpit and free end of 11th rib.	ST-34	Thigh, 2 units above top lateral edge of kneecap, between rectus femoris and vastus lateralis m.
SI-6	With palm facing chest, 0.5 unit proximal wrist, in bony recess on radial side of head of ulna bone.	ST-2	In a recess on top edge of cheekbone, aligned with eye pupil.	ST-35	In a recess below kneecap, lateral to patellar ligament when knee is bent.
SI-8	In recess on flat spot between elbow point (ulna) and medial bony knob of humerus (arm flexed).	ST-3	Directly below eye pupil and ST-2, level with lower edge of nostril.	ST-36	Lower leg, 3 units below ST-35, about 1 unit lateral to crest of tibia bone (shinbone).
SI-11	Flat part of scapula, halfway between left + right edges, 1/3 the distance between ridge and base.	ST-4	Slightly lateral to corner of mouth, directly below ST-3, a faint pulse is felt close below.	TW-3	Back of hand, between 4th and 5th metacarpal bones, in recess proximal base joints of fingers.
SI-17	Directly behind corner of jaw (angle of mandible), recess at anterior edge of sternocleidomastoid m.	ST-5	In a groove-like recess along bottom of jaw bone, on front edge of masseter muscle (pulse is felt).	TW-11	Back of upper arm, 2 units above point of elbow, on triceps brachii tendon.
SP-6	3 units above protruding bone at inner ankle, on rear (posterior) edge of tibia.	ST-7	In front of ear, in recess at lower edge of zygomatic arch, forward of jaw joint.	TW-12	Back of upper arm, at end of lateral head of triceps brachii muscle.
SP-7	6 units above protruding bone at inner ankle, 3 units above SP-6.	ST-9	Side of neck, level with Adam's apple tip, at front edge of sternocleidomastoid m., along carotid a.	TW-17	In recess behind ear lobe, between mastoid process (on skull) and jawbone (mandible).
SP-8	3 units below protruding tibia bone at inner knee, on line joining SP-9 and protruding anklebone.	ST-10	On front edge of sternocleidomastoid muscle, halfway between ST-9 and ST-11.	TW-23	Side of head, in recess at lateral end of eyebrow.

Locating Pressure Points

Pressure points (also called *acupoints*) are usually located in depressions at bones, joints, and muscles. The area affecting each point is usually the size of a dime, but can be as small as a pin head. Some points are easy to locate by simply probing around, since they are very sensitive to pressure. Others are well hidden and require very precise targeting. The angle of attack is often critical. Feel for a slight depression or hollow at each point. This might be a perceived as a slight depression in the bone, or a small space between muscle fibers, tendons, and muscles.

Location Methods

In ancient China, a system using body landmarks and a relative unit of measurement called a *cun*, assisted practitioners in locating points. This system is still in use today. A cun (also called a body inch, unit, or finger unit) varies in length based on the proportion and size of the individual being measured. The length or width of different parts of the fingers are used to make rough estimates of point locations, as shown at right.

Terms Used in This Reference

When describing the locations of pressure points on the human body, it is necessary to use precise anatomical terms to avoid confusion. For example, "above the wrist joint" can refer to either side of the wrist, depending on how the arm is oriented (raised, lowered); whereas, "proximal" is precise, regardless of orientation.

Superior:	Toward the head or upper part of a structure.
Inferior:	Away from head, or toward lower part of a structure.
Anterior:	Nearer to, or at the front of body.
Posterior:	Nearer to, or at the back of body.
Medial:	Nearer to the midline of body, or a structure.
Lateral:	Farther from the midline of body, or a structure.
Proximal:	Nearer to the attachment of an extremity, to trunk or a structure.
Distal:	Farther from the attachment of an extremity, to trunk or a structure.
Superficial:	Toward or on the surface of body.
Deep:	Away from the surface of body
Unit:	Relative unit of measurement based on use of the fingers.

Abbreviations: (m.) muscle, (n.) nerve, (a.) artery, (v.) vein

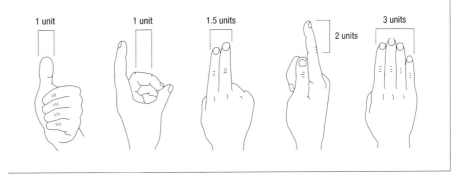

GROUND SUMMARY

This book outlines 195 ground-fighting techniques used in martial arts. They are summarized at right and shown in subsequent chapters. Techniques are organized as follows:

32 Chokes and Head Locks
38 Pinning Holds
38 Ground Kicks
20 Seated Defenses
32 Reclining Defenses
6   Kneeling Defenses
29 Sacrifice Techniques

Technique names are based on commonly used terms. However, within the martial arts there still remains a great deal of variability in term use. Many different terms are often used to represent the same technique. Whenever possible, the clearest or most widely accepted nomenclature is used.

Chokes + Head Locks

1   Front Naked Choke
2   Rear Naked Choke
3   Front Lapel Choke
4   Rear Lapel Choke
5   Front Double Lapel Choke
6   Rear Double Lapel Choke
7   Rear Cross Choke
8   Half-Nelson Choke
9   Double Sleeve Choke
10 Single Sleeve Choke
11 Arm Trap Choke
12 Rear Interlock Choke
13 Front Interlock Choke
14 Arm Scissor Choke
15 Arm Brace Choke
16 Thrust Choke
17 Knuckle Choke
18 Index Knuckle Choke
19 Thumb-Hand Choke
20 Spear-Hand Choke
21 Tiger-Mouth Choke
22 Pincer-Hand Choke
23 Knife-Foot Choke
24 Knee Choke
25 Leg Interlock Choke
26 Leg Scissor Choke
27 Full Nelson 1 (palms)
28 Full Nelson 2 (Knife Hands)
29 Full Nelson 3 (compress)
30 Twisting Neck Lock
31 Scooping Neck Lock
32 Smothering Neck Lock

Pinning Holds

1   Knee Arm Bar Pin
2   Foot Arm Bar
3   Buttock Arm Bar Pin
4   Inside Inverted Arm Bar
5   Shoulder-Kneel Arm Bar
6   Knee Choke Arm Bar
7   Elevated Arm Bar Pin
8   Armpit Arm Bar Pin
9   Armpit Arm Bar + Shoulder Lock
10 Reclining Arm Bar (one leg over head)
11 Reclining Arm Bar (one leg over body)
12 Reclining Arm Bar (both legs over)
13 Reclining Arm Bar (no legs over)
14 Reclining Leg Arm Bar
15 Reclining Knee Arm Bar
16 Entangled Arm Bar 1
17 Entangled Arm Bar 2
18 Entangled Front Shoulder Lock
19 Entangled Rear Shoulder Lock 1
20 Entangled Rear Shoulder Lock 2
21 Entangled Rear Shoulder Lock 3
22 Seated Bent-Arm Lock
23 Seated Bent-Arm + Wrist Lock
24 Seated Bent-Arm Lock (leg assist)
25 Leg Bent-Arm Lock
26 Elevated Shoulder Lock Pin
27 Planted Shoulder Lock Pin
28 Straight Shoulder Lock Pin
29 Driving Shoulder Lock Pin
30 Elbow Hammer Lock Pin
31 Bent-Wrist Hammer Lock Pin
32 Gooseneck Hammer Lock Pin
33 Scarf Hold
34 Reclining Ankle Lock 1
35 Reclining Ankle Lock 2
36 Knife-Foot to Calf Pin
37 Knife-Foot to Knee Pin
38 Bent-Leg Lock

Ground Kicks

1 Drop Front Kick
2 Drop Roundhouse Kick
3 Drop Side Kick
4 Drop Back Kick
5 Drop Turning Back Kick
6 Drop Axe Kick
7 Drop Hook Kick
8 Drop Spin Kick
9 Drop Twin Front Kick
10 Drop Twin Roundhouse Kick
11 Drop Twin Side Kick
12 Drop Twin Back Kick
13 Drop Twin Overhead Kick
14 Drop Front Split Kick
15 Drop Side Split Kick
16 Drop Overhead Split Kick
17 Seated Front Kick
18 Seated Front Blade Kick
19 Seated Front Toe Kick
20 Seated Roundhouse Kick
21 Seated Reverse Roundhouse Kick
22 Seated Side Kick
23 Seated Back Kick
24 Seated Stamp Kick
25 Seated Circular Inner-Heel Kick
26 Seated Inside Crescent Kick
27 Seated Outside Crescent Kick
28 Seated Cutting Crescent Kick
29 Seated Axe Kick
30 Seated Inside Hook Kick
31 Seated Hook Kick
32 Seated Twin Front Kick
33 Seated Twin Roundhouse Kick
34 Seated Twin Side Kick
35 Seated Twin Overhead Kick
36 Seated Side Split Kick
37 Seated Front Split Kick
38 Seated Overhead Split Kick

Seated Defenses

Twenty typical ground techniques executed from a seated position against standing opponents are covered in a later chapter.

Reclining Defenses

Thirty-two typical ground techniques executed from a variety of reclining positions are covered in a later chapter.

Kneeling Defenses

Six typical ground techniques executed from a kneeling position against reclining opponents are covered in a later chapter.

Sacrifice Techniques

Twenty-nine typical sacrifice techniques used in a variety of circumstances are covered in a later chapter.

Chokes and head locks are specific types of holds that are applied to the neck and head. "Chokes holds" typically involve strangulation techniques designed to impede or stop the flow of blood or air to the brain, whereas "head locks" are joint lock techniques used to apply stress to the cervical spine. Both types of holds are potentially very dangerous and can easily produce life-threatening injuries. For this reason, these techniques should only be learned and practiced under qualified instructors, who are also skilled in revival techniques. When

CHOKES + HEAD LOCKS

these techniques are properly and skillfully applied in appropriate situations, they provide one of the most powerful and effective methods for controlling an opponent, without causing serious or permanent injuries. As opponents become larger and more powerful, any martial technique tends to lose its effectiveness, although chokes remain useful longer than most other skills. The following pages will provide an overview of basic principles, followed by a description of 32 chokes and head locks commonly used in the martial arts.

BASIC CONCEPTS

Chokes and head locks are specific types of holds applied to the neck and head. They are typically used to control or restrain a person, and work in one or more of three ways: by reducing the flow of blood or air to the brain via strangulation, by applying painful pressure to nerves and pressure points, or by twisting the head to stress the cervical spine.

Chokes

Choke holds are commonly applied to the neck, using your hands, arms, legs, or feet. The surfaces of your body used to apply chokes will vary by technique, and are mostly the same as surfaces used for striking (see *Attack Points* at right). Chokes can be used to render an opponent unconscious, assist throws, or weaken an attacker during grappling. There are three types of chokes:

• Vascular Chokes (restrict blood flow)
• Windpipe Chokes (restrict air flow)
• Nerve Chokes (control movement and pain)

Vascular Chokes

Vascular chokes reduce or eliminate the flow of blood to the brain, resulting in progressive disorientation, loss of consciousness, or death. This usually involves clamping holds to the carotid artery, jugular vein, and vagus nerve, all in close proximity on the side of the neck. By compressing blood vessels, blood flow is decreased and pressure increases. The vagus nerve, which normally acts to slow the heart rate in response to supply demands, further reduces blood flow, compounding the effect. When a vascular choke is properly applied, an opponent can pass out in 10 to 15 seconds. While this person may regain consciousness naturally, many chokes lead to a loss of breathing and heart functions, in which case it is vital to revive the person, or brain damage and death will quickly occur. When using vascular chokes, accuracy is essential if the choke is to be effective. Primary targets are ST-9 and ST-10 (where a pulse is felt). Chokes at SI-17 are also possible, but require greater accuracy. Vascular chokes are not usually painful unless nerves are also being pressed.

Windpipe Chokes

Windpipe chokes reduce or eliminate the flow of air to the brain, resulting in progressive disorientation, loss of consciousness, or death. Chokes to the windpipe are very dangerous and should only be used in life-threatening situations. A collapsed trachea is likely, which requires immediate expert medical attention to prevent death. Windpipe chokes do not require the precise accuracy of vascular chokes to be effective. They are easier to learn and often applied accidentally by novices attempting to learn vascular chokes. Generally, vascular chokes are preferred for most situations, since they are safer.

Nerve Chokes

Nerve chokes attack nerves or pressure points in order to control an opponent's movements by producing pain or damaging motor functions. Many of these sensitive points will work even on powerful opponents. Targets include LI-18, SI-16, TW-17, CO-22, ST-9, ST-10, and the spinal nerves at the back of the neck. Properly directed, nerve chokes can produce intense pain, forcing a submission or causing a loss of consciousness. Nerve chokes are often combined with vascular chokes.

Head Locks

Head locks are typically characterized by twisting the head to stress the cervical spine and its nerves. Head-twisting holds limit mobility by damaging the spine, or pinching spinal nerves where they pass through the vertebrae. Violent head-twisting is *extremely dangerous*, and should only be used in life-threatening situations. A broken neck is likely and can cause permanent paralysis or death. In contrast, gentle head-twisting is safer, and a very efficient way to control body movement, particularly on the ground. Some head locks also incorporate choking techniques.

Practical Concerns

In terms of application, there are two forms of chokes: those that rely on clothing or the environment for support (lapel, wall, ground), and those that do not. It is important to evaluate a situation before applying a choke.

For example, a Lapel Choke is not used on an opponent clothed in a T-shirt (or shirtless), since this choke requires strong clothing to be effective. In this situation, you might use a Naked Choke or an Interlock Choke. Another example: if your opponent is backed against a wall, a Forearm Thrust Choke (using your arm to pin the neck against the wall) is far more efficient than attempting to wrap your entire arm around the head (Front Naked Choke).

Limitations of Chokes

It is important to understand the limitations of various chokes. Some individuals possess tremendous ability to resist all forms of chokes; others are easily restrained, even when your technique is bad. Only by sparring or engaging in competition can you become fluent with choke techniques. Work lightly and sensibly, under qualified supervision.

It is also important to realize that some chokes used in competition (e.g., Judo) were specifically modified for sport use. Rules often limit technique or encourage methods of application that would be inherently risky in self-defense. For example, when applying a Rear Naked Choke in Judo, your head is often placed to the side of an opponent's head, to secure a stronger hold and restrict head motion. In a real fight, this places your face within striking distance, allowing an opponent to poke your eyes or punch back to the face. This response is not legal in Judo competition, hence not a concern. If you were originally trained to choke in competitive martial arts, you may need to modify certain aspects of your technique—although basic principles remain the same.

Choke Transitions

Skillful opponents may negate your attempts to choke them. Switching between vascular, windpipe, and nerve chokes is often useful if an opponent protects one area. For example, if an opponent drops the chin to protect the windpipe, circle your hand around to the side of the neck and attack the carotid artery or great auricular nerve (LI-18). Strikes can also create the space needed to apply a choke.

Types of Chokes

Windpipe Choke (restricts air flow)

Vascular Choke (restricts blood flow)

Nerve Choke (controls movement, causes pain)

Major Targets

A. Windpipe (CO-23)
B. Base of Windpipe (CO-22)
C. Jugular Vein ····
D. Carotid Artery ---
E. LI-18 (4 nerves)
F. SI-16 (2 nerves, cervical a.)
G. SI-17 (carotid a., jugular v., 3 nerves)
H. ST-9 (branching of carotid a., thyroid a., jugular v., 3 nerves)
I. ST-10 (common carotid a., cut. cervical n., superior cardiac n.)
J. TW-17 (auricular n., jugular v.)
K. Spinal Nerves

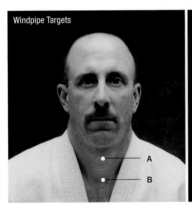

Windpipe Targets

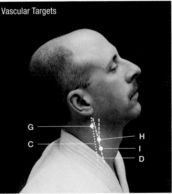

Vascular Targets

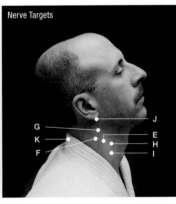

Nerve Targets

Attack Points

The following attack points are generally used to apply chokes. Many other possibilities exist.

A. Fingertips
B. Tip of Thumb
C. Finger Knuckles
D. Index Finger Knuckle
E. Pincer Hand
F. Tiger Mouth Hand
G. Knife Hand (edge of hand)
H. Wrist (protruding bones)
H. Forearm (edge of bone)
I. Lower Leg (edge of bone)
J. Foot (blade, heel, or toes)

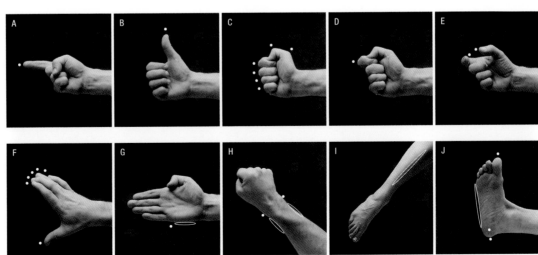

Basic Entries

When applying chokes in which you wrap the neck, there are two basic methods of entry: A) Circle the neck, raking with your thumb knuckles; or B) Execute a strike which places your attack point at the target to be choked.

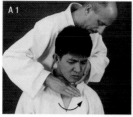

Forced Entries

If an opponent drops the chin to protect the neck, press sensitive points to move their head.

C. TW-17 (behind ear)
D. ST-4 (jaw)
E. GB-1 or TW-23 (temple)
F. Eyes and ST-2 (cheek)

Wrist Action

Regardless of how a choke is applied, wrist movement is very important when pressing your attack points into the neck. Three methods of executing a Naked Choke are shown as a typical example. Although the method of clasping the hands varies, wrist action is the same. The first method (1A–1B) is widely used and may be the most difficult grip to break. The second and third methods (2A–2B; 3A–3B) sometimes permit deeper penetration and greater force. Generally, body position, individual anatomy, and personal preference will all influence grip choice. The subtle differences are best grasped by experimentation.

Ki-Flow and Grip

When gripping your fist in methods 2 and 3, place HT-8 (palm between 4th and 5th metacarpal bones) against SI-3 (back of the smallest base-knuckle) Biomechanically, this provides a strong, secure grip.

Aligning these acupoints is also thought to increase physical strength, since the natural flow of Ki is enhanced (HT meridian connects with the SI meridian) In method 2, your smallest fingers will overlap each other, also aligning HT-9 and SI-1.

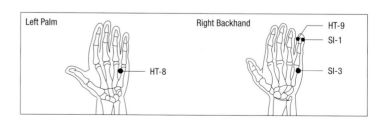

Eliminating Free-Play

The effectiveness of a choke is reduced when there is any free-play or movement in the hold. To restrict movement:

A. Use Lapel
B. Use Wall
C. Use Ground
D. Use Your Arm
E. Use Your Head
F. Use Opponent's Weight
G. Use Your Weight

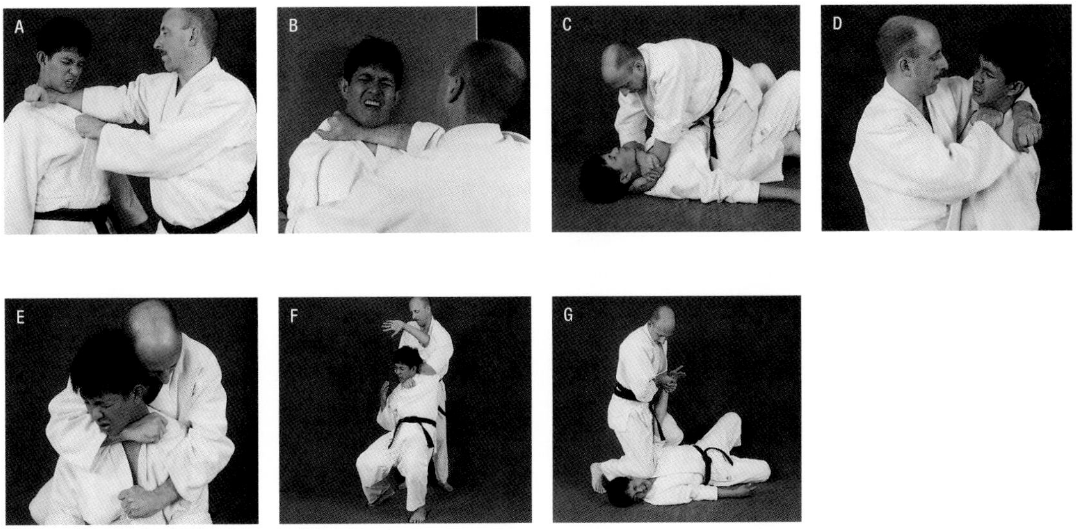

Body Positions

Most chokes can be executed from a variety of positions. Typical examples are shown opposite. Many other body relationships are possible.

A. Front Standing (upright)
B. Front Standing (bent over)
C. Side Standing
D. Rear Standing
E. Overhead Hanging
F. Rear Kneeling
G. Front Kneeling
H. Side Mount
I. Front Top-Mount (supine attacker)
J. Rear Top-Mount (prone attacker)
K. Front Reclining
L. Rear Reclining

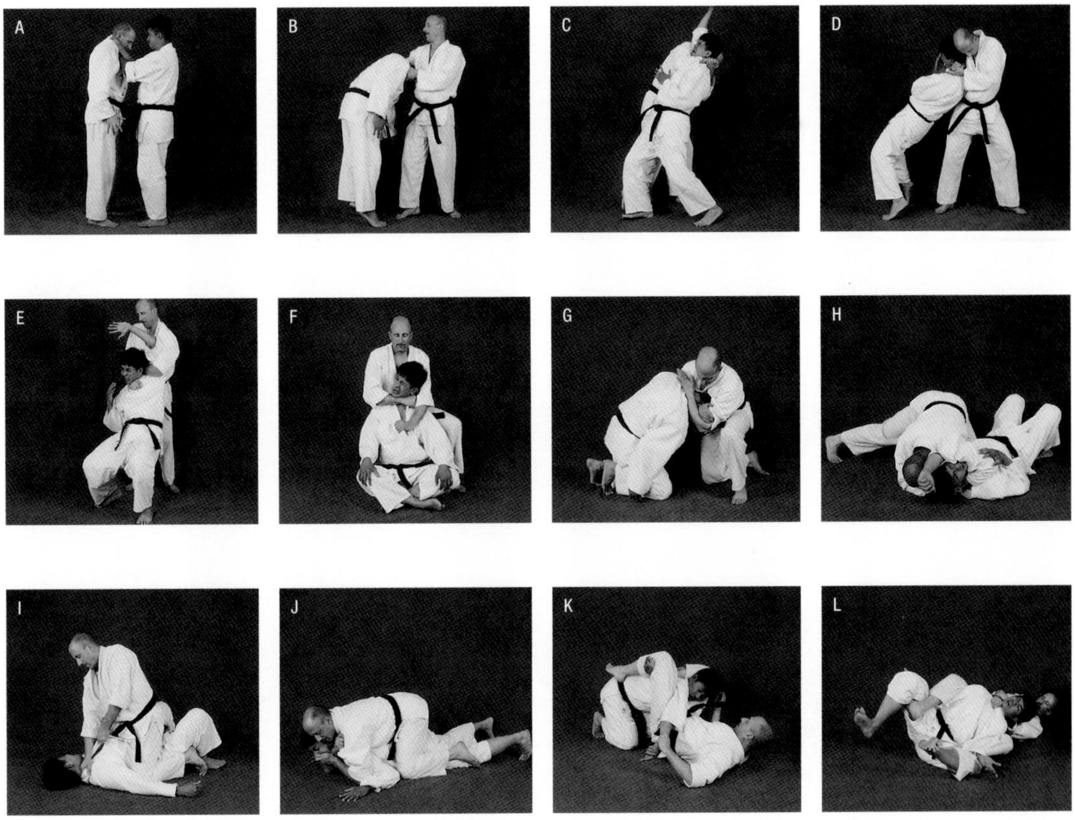

1. Front Naked Choke

Press your opponent's head downward (A), as you tightly wrap your arm around the neck, placing the bony part of your wrist or forearm against the throat. Join your hands as shown previously, using *wrist action* to apply (B, C). Lifting up and leaning back will place extreme stress on the cervical spine. This choke is a useful counter against a low charge or throws in which an opponent tries to scoop your legs from the front.

2. Rear Naked Choke

This is a very strong, practical choke. Tightly wrap your arm around the neck, placing the bony part of your wrist, forearm, or thumb-knuckles against the desired target. When standing, quickly unbalance an opponent to their rear by using a hip butt or palm strike (A) to the lower spine. This prevents counter-throws or escapes. Join your hands and use *wrist action* to apply (B, C). Opponent's *hanging body* will increase pressure.

1. Front Naked Choke

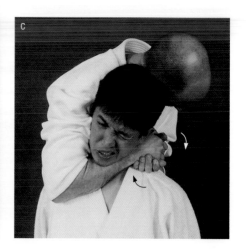

2. Rear Naked Choke

3. Front Lapel Choke

This choke requires strong clothing, since it uses an opponent's collar for support. Pull the lapel out and down with one hand; grip the collar at the side of the neck with the other hand (A). Rotate your fist, extending your wrist bone into the target. Pull the opposite lapel across the neck to create a *noose-like* effect (B). The choke is made stronger by using a wall (C) or the ground for support, to keep the neck from moving away.

4. Rear Lapel Choke

This is similar to the previous choke, except it is applied from the rear. Reach around as far as possible and grip the collar at the far side (A). Extend the wrist into the throat as you pull the opposite lapel down and across the neck (B, C). The choke is stronger when using an opponent's hanging weight to increase pressure. When kneeling, stand up as you apply pressure. When standing, unbalance an opponent backward.

  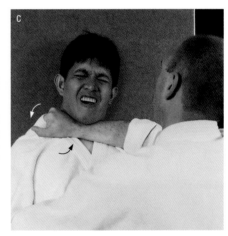

3. Front Lapel Choke

  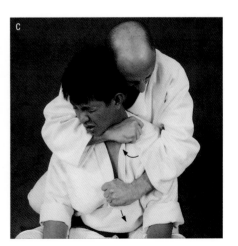

4. Rear Lapel Choke

5. Front Double Lapel Choke

This is similar to a *Front Lapel Choke*, except you will use both hands. With your arms crossed, grip high on both sides of the collar. Apply pressure with both wrists. When choking from a straddle position, lean forward and press your elbows toward the ground (A–B). When standing, pull an opponent close and spread your elbows (C). Be cautious when using this choke, since it leaves you open to strikes (your hands are occupied; opponent's are free).

Double Lapel Grip Variations

There are three methods of gripping. In method 1 (D), both hands grip with the thumbs *outside*. Rotate your wrists and spread the elbows to apply. In method 2 (E)3, both hands grip with the thumbs *inside*. Use *wrist action* and spread your elbows to apply. In method 3 (not shown), the top hand grips with the thumb inside, the lower hand with the thumb outside. In the photos, the choker's head is dropped low to provide a better view of the choke (don't do this).

5. Front Double Lapel Choke

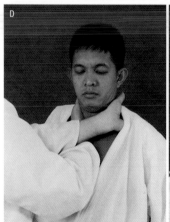
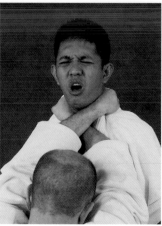
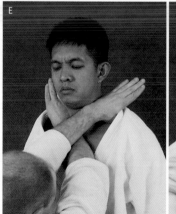
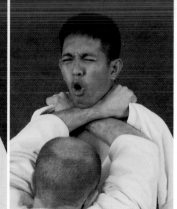

Method 1 (thumbs outside)

Method 2 (thumbs inside)

6. Rear Double Lapel Choke

This is like a *Rear Lapel Choke*, except you will use both hands. With your arms crossed, grip high on both sides of the collar (A). Apply pressure by using *wrist action* and spreading your elbows (B, C). Since both arms cross under the chin, this hold also locks the neck backward (immobilizing the head), as you press to both sides of the throat at the carotid artery (ST-9, ST-10). This choke is very strong if your grips are properly placed.

7. Rear Cross Choke

This is basically a *Rear Lapel Choke*, except you will use your other forearm to apply additional pressure to the opposite side of the neck, often to nerves or pressure points (A–C). This eliminates free-play and neck motion, which often reduces the efficiency of lapel chokes. The other wrist presses the carotid artery or windpipe. This choke can also be used to counter a throw when the opponent's body is placed in front of you (e.g., a hip throw).

  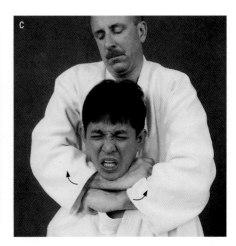

6. Rear Double Lapel Choke

  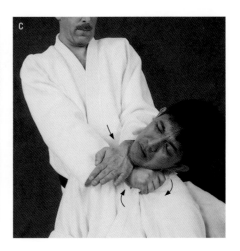

7. Rear Cross Choke

8. Half-Nelson Choke

This is similar to the previous *Rear Cross Choke,* except you will trap one arm by reaching under it and lifting, as you wrap your hand behind the head, turning your palm outward (A–B). Drive your hand around to the side of the neck, pressing with your Knife Hand as you choke with the other hand (C). This choke is useful if an opponent reaches back to attack your face during other chokes. When standing or kneeling, unbalance an opponent rearward and hang them from the choke (C).

Half-Nelson Variations

Provided the opponent is hanging, you can choke with your wrist placed at either side of the neck (D, E). Grip placement is not critical, since a loose choke will become tight as you apply it. When executed on the ground (F), drive or kick your heels into the groin. Keep your eyes away from the fingers of the held arm. Generally, these are very secure chokes, and are very difficult to counter or escape once they have been applied. The Half-Nelson Choke is also commonly referred to as a *Single-Wing Choke.*

8. Half-Nelson Choke

Half-Nelson Choke variations (wrist placed at either side of neck)

Half-Nelson Choke applied from reclining position

9. Double Sleeve Choke

In this choke you will use both of your sleeves for support. Place your arms on both sides of the neck. Grip your inner sleeves with both hands, and extend both wrists (or forearms) into the targets. This choke can be applied from any position (front, rear, side, ground). When ground fighting, this choke is difficult to detect, since your arms do not provide the usual clues to an opponent (e.g., wrapping the neck, gripping the collar, clasping your hands).

10. Single Sleeve Choke

This is similar to the previous choke, except you will grip one sleeve only. This is not by choice, but usually because your opponent does not allow you to secure the second grip—or you may feel that your hold is strong enough and does not warrant further maneuvering. If possible, use the ground, wall, or your body weight to assist the hold. Many different body positions are possible, including top (A), bottom (B), and side (C).

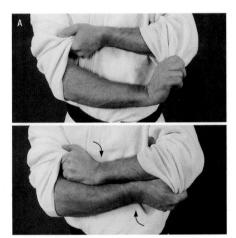

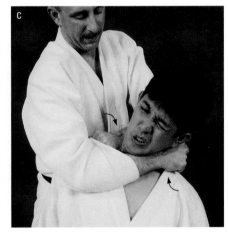

9. Double Sleeve Choke

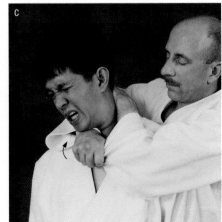

10. Single Sleeve Choke

11. Arm Trap Choke

This is basically a *naked choke* applied from the side, with the opponent's arm trapped between your shoulder and their head. The choke can be entered by either wrapping or striking into the far side of the neck. Join your hands as shown previously, pressing your wrist or thumb-knuckles into the carotid artery or nerves (LI-18 is typical). Because the entry is very fast, it is often used to counter straight punches or pushes, by using a parry to deflect as you enter.

Ground Variations (D)

This choke is used to force a takedown, or is applied during ground fighting. On the ground, the hold varies slightly: Wrap your arm further around the neck. Press your wrist and the edge of your tensed arm muscles into nerves or the carotid artery. To secure the hold, press down with your neck and head, place one leg against the side of the attacker's body (with your knee and ball of the foot planted), and brace outward with your other leg (ball of the foot planted).

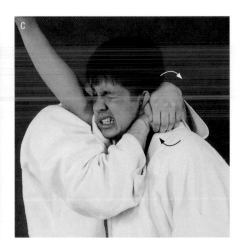

11. Arm Trap Choke

12. Rear Interlock Choke

This is another variation on a basic *naked choke*. It is mostly applied from the rear. Wrap the choking arm around the neck, locking your hand in the crook of your other elbow (A). Place your other hand behind the head and push forward with the edge of your Knife Hand or wrist, as you pull backward with your choking forearm (B, C). Be sure to use pronounced *wrist action* with both arms. This is mostly a windpipe choke, so exercise caution to avoid life-threatening injuries.

13. Front Interlock Choke

This is the same as the previous choke, except it is executed from the front. Two possibilities exist: Front-over (A) and front-facing (B or C). Front-over can be used from standing or ground postures. Front-facing is also used from standing or ground positions; however, you will be reversing the roles of your arms. The wrapping arm presses nerves at the back of the neck. Your other wrist or hand will press the throat. The choke can be applied from top (B) or bottom (C) positions.

12. Rear Interlock Choke

13. Front Interlock Choke

14. Arm Scissor Choke

This choke is applied from an opponent's side. Enter by placing your wrist at the base of the windpipe (A–B). Place your other forearm on the back of the neck, clasp the hands or interlock your fingers, and choke by extending both wrists (C). If needed, extend your arms to increase pressure. Secure the hold by dropping to one knee. This choke is often used as a transition from a *Front Naked Choke*, if an opponent turns outward to escape before you can clasp your hands.

15. Arm Brace Choke

Wrap one hand behind the opponent's neck, with your fingertips at the far side, gouging nerves or pressure points. Grab your wrist with your other hand, planting your forearm on the windpipe and carotid artery. Drive your elbow toward the back of the neck, as you pull with both hands (A, B). This choke is made more secure by using the ground (C) or wall for support. This choke's weakness is the open end of the hold, which permits an opportunity for escapes.

14. Arm Scissor Choke

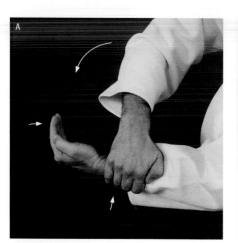

15. Arm Brace Choke

16. Thrust Choke

Pull back on the lapels as you thrust your wrist into the front of the throat (A), or drive your smallest base-knuckle into ST-9 (B). This can be a gentle plant or a forceful strike. Use the wall or ground to eliminate movement whenever possible. You can also execute the choke with one hand, using the other hand to block or grab a strike (C). This choke is also used to initiate a throw, by trapping or reaping a leg as you drive an attacker backward.

17. Knuckle Choke

This choke is executed from the opponent's front, using a *Knuckle Fist* (A). Grip the lapels with both hands, placing your fingers inside the cloth. Take up any slack and apply pressure by turning your fists outward, and driving the second set of knuckles into the front or sides of the neck. Whenever possible, use the wall, ground (B), or a neck wrap (C) to eliminate neck movement. This choke is very effective for targeting nerves or pressure points.

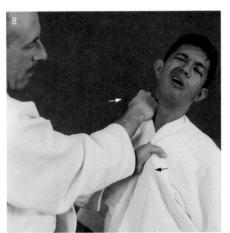

16. Thrust Choke

17. Knuckle Choke

18. Index Knuckle Choke

This is basically the same as the previous *Knuckle Choke*, except you will use an *Index Finger Fist* (A) to apply pressure. The extended knuckle will penetrate more deeply, and is used for pinpoint targeting to sensitive nerves and pressure points. The choke can be applied with two hands holding at the collar (B), or with one hand holding and pressing, as your other hand pulls the opposite lapel to tighten the choke (C).

19. Thumb-Hand Choke

This choke is executed from the front or side, using a *Thumb Hand* (A) to apply pressure. The tip of the thumb is driven into any neck target, particularly nerves and pressure points. This choke can be applied with one or both hands by: gripping the collar for leverage (B), wrapping your fingers around the neck for support (C), or applying a straight thrust (no grips) and using the wall or ground to eliminate neck motion. Exercise caution.

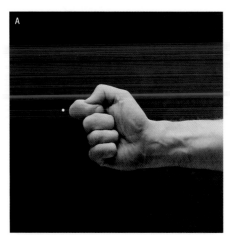

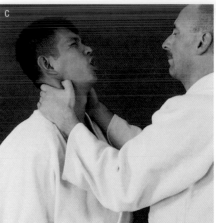

18. Index Knuckle Choke

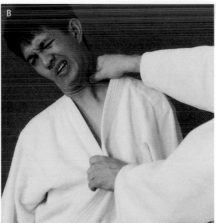

19. Thumb-Hand Choke

20. Spear-Hand Choke

This choke is executed from the front or rear, using a one, two, or three finger *Spear Hand* (A) to apply pressure. The finger may be straight or bent. The most common target is CO-22 at the base of the windpipe. You may trap the head by by pulling the lapel (B) or wrapping the neck (C). This choke is also used to apply throws, by pushing the throat as you pull the lower spine or trap a leg.

21. Tiger-Mouth Choke

Use a *Tiger Mouth Hand* (A) to clamp the windpipe or press into both carotid arteries (A). Squeeze with all five fingertips, using clothing, holds, or the environment to eliminate movement. In the photo (B), the thumb and index fingers are pressing both SI-17 points; the other fingers are pressing ST-9 and ST-10, and along the carotid artery. Do not crush the windpipe or you will produce life-threatening injuries.

22. Pincer-Hand Choke

Use a *Pincer Hand* (A) to clamp nerves or pressure points on the throat with the thumb and index fingers. You can also assist by pressing with your lower knuckles into additional pressure points on the neck. The photo (B) shows an attack to CO-22 and ST-11. You can also grip mid-throat at both ST-9 pressure points (a pulse is felt); or higher on the neck at both SI-17 pressure points (a pulse is felt).

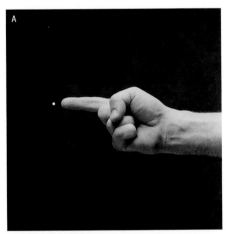
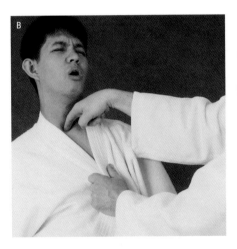

20. Spear-Hand Choke

21. Tiger-Mouth Choke

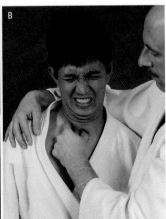

22. Pincer-Hand Choke

23. Knife-Foot Choke

This is often used to choke and pin an opponent immediately after you have thrown them. Press the blade of your foot into the throat or side of the neck, as you pull up on the arm (A–C). Shift your weight to the choke-leg as needed. You may enter the choke by planting the foot gently or striking forcefully. You may also apply an arm bar to the held-arm, to strengthen the hold (B). Do not step on the windpipe (life threatening).

24. Knee Choke

Like the previous choke, this choke is also used to choke and pin, immediately after throwing an opponent. Sink your knee into the throat or side of the neck, as you pull up on the arm (A–C). Your planted knee remains on the ball of the foot, ready to rise or shift balance if an opponent counters. You can apply joint locks to strengthen the hold. If the situation justifies it, you may drop forcefully, thrusting your knee into the neck.

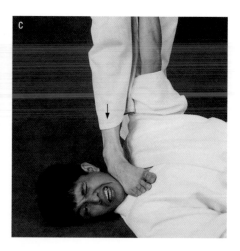

23. Knife-Foot Choke

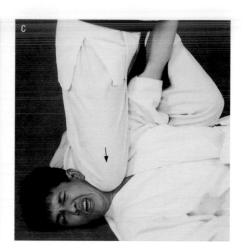

24. Knee Choke

25. Leg Interlock Choke

Wrap one leg over an opponent's shoulder and around their neck, locking your foot in the back of your other knee (the other leg passes under their armpit). Fully bend both feet and drive your heel toward your buttock to tighten the choke (A). The opponent's arm must be trapped against their neck to eliminate space. You may also apply an arm bar (see A). If an opponent rolls, maintain your hold (B). There are many other variations.

26. Leg Scissor Choke

This hold is often used to counter chokes from the side, when you are reclining. Roll back and plant the back of one leg against the side of the neck (A). Reach around the head with your other leg and hook the ankles together (B). Drive both legs toward the ground. Press the knees together and extend the legs to choke (C). As you enter, grab the opponent's wrist with both hands to keep them from turning away. Arm bars are often possible.

25. Leg Interlock Choke

26. Leg Scissor Choke

27–29 Full Nelson Locks

This head lock is very dangerous and will break the neck if forcefully applied. Reach under both arms, slipping both hands behind the head. There are three methods of applying force to the spine:
1) Push forward with overlapped *palms* against the back of the opponent's head.
2) Push forward with *Knife Hands* projecting around the side of the neck, with wrists crossed. 3) *Compress* the cervical spine by pushing the head down.

30. Twisting Neck Lock

If forcefully applied, this head lock will break the neck or dislocate the jaw (if the jaw is unclenched). However, if detected, the hold is easily countered by using strength. Push with the heel of your palm against the chin; pull with the other palm at the back of the head (C), or pull hair. When applied gently, it can be used to control the body, throw, or pin. Generally, the body will follow the head. Execute from ground (A) or standing (B) positions.

27. Full Nelson Lock (method 1)

28. Full Nelson Lock (method 2)

29. Full Nelson Lock (method 3)

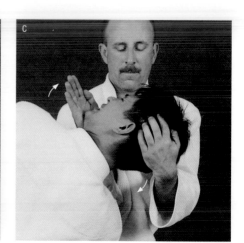

30. Twisting Neck Lock

31. Scooping Neck Lock

Drive your thumb-knuckles into nerves at the side of the jaw (ST-4), and scoop upward using one or both hands to twist the head and neck (A–B). Attacking nerves is very important, otherwise an opponent can resist the hold (C). You can also press into the gums or teeth. Be *extremely careful* when twisting, or you may break the neck. This hold is often used to force your way into a *Front Naked Choke*, or to throw an opponent.

32. Smothering Neck Lock

Apply a *Rear Naked Choke* with one arm, to control head motion (A); try to clamp the windpipe or carotid artery. Place your other palm tightly over the opponent's mouth, pinching the nose closed with your thumb and index finger (B). Cup your hand to prevent being bitten. Tight holds totally block air intake. Even if air slips in, volume is greatly reduced, particularly if winded. "C" shows a ground choke using a hair-pull to assist (C).

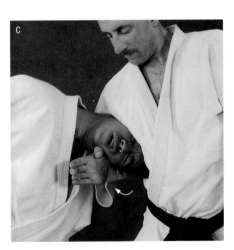

31. Scooping Neck Lock

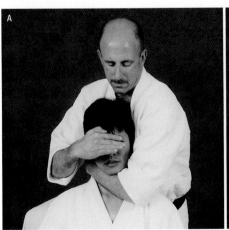
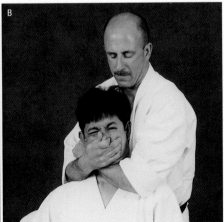

32. Smothering Neck Lock

Pins are specific types of holds that are used to restrain movement by pinning an opponent to the ground, or against a wall or other obstacle. Pinning holds can consist of joint locks or chokes, or may simply involve the use of your body weight. Pins used in sport martial arts are often quite different than those used in self-defense and combat. For example, pinning an opponent's back to the mat using certain sport holds that do not incorporate joint locks or chokes may win a match, but rarely accomplishes a self-defense objective.

PINNING HOLDS

If you release your opponent, they can merely return to the attack. Also realize that many of these sport holds leave an opponent's hands free to strike vital points, such as the eyes. Because virtually all pins possess limitations that eventually cause them to fail under certain circumstances, it is important to constantly test these techniques, so you have a sense of their limits and vulnerabilities and know how best to use them. This chapter shows 38 typical pins used in self-defense oriented martial arts. Many other possibilities exist.

1. Knee Arm Bar Pin

Use your body weight to press your knee into the triceps tendon at TW-11, just above the back of the elbow joint. Press with the bony edge of your tibia bone (just below the knee). This pins the arm and is very painful. You can also lock the wrist by bending the opponent's palm toward their forearm as you twist their hand forward. This increases the amount of pain generated by the hold, and helps to keep the opponent from twisting their arm to protect their triceps tendon. Even without the wrist lock, this hold is very strong.

2. Foot Arm Bar

Use your body weight to press your heel or the blade of your foot into the triceps tendon at TW-11, just above the back of the elbow joint. This pins the arm and is very painful. When using your heel, be aware that the heel can easily slip off the opponent's arm if you are not accurate when planting it, or if the arm shifts as attacker struggles. In contrast, the blade of the foot offers a longer, harder surface. This results in a greater margin for error (your foot is less likely to slip off) and more effective targeting of the nerve.

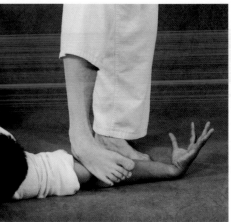

3. Buttock Arm Bar Pin

Plant your buttock or the base of your sacrum on the opponent's elbow and sink downward, as you pull their wrist upward with both hands. This locks the elbow and will break it if you pull forcefully. You can also apply this hold by sitting on the opponent's shoulder joint. If you pull the wrist upward and toward your *right*, you can also lock the shoulder. If your opponent counters by rolling sideways to force you to fall backward, maintain your grip on their wrist and make a transition to a Reclining Arm Bar (see pin 12).

4. Inside Inverted Arm Bar

After trapping the opponent's wrist in your armpit, lift upward with your forearm against TW-11, as the opponent falls backward. Brace your right hand on your left arm. Lock the elbow: extend the bony edge of your forearm upward by bending your wrist, as you press downward on their upper-arm or shoulder with your left hand. Plant your L shin against opponent's side or back to prevent them from turning toward you to grip or hit you with their free hand. You can also kneel on the opponent's neck with your R knee (choke).

5. Shoulder-Kneel Arm Bar

Kneel on the shoulder using your body weight to restrain the opponent. Lock their elbow against your inner thigh by pulling their wrist back toward your R hip with both hands. From this pin, you can easily make a transition to the next technique (see pin 6) by dropping your L knee to the neck. You can also shift to a Reclining Arm Bar (see pins 10 and 13). When shifting to pin 10, thrust your L heel into the chin (forcing the head to turn sideways) as you slide your L leg over the head. This can be a forceful kick if justified.

6. Knee Choke Arm Bar

Kneel on the opponent's throat at the carotid artery, using your body weight to prevent movement. Lock their elbow against your inner thigh by pulling their wrist backward with both hands. Press your L knee into the ribs. Squeeze your legs together to restrict their arm movement. Exercise caution when applying weight to your R knee, since this choke can cause serious injuries to the neck, windpipe, jaw, or temple. From this pin, you can easily make a transition to a Reclining Arm Bar (see pin 13).

7. Elevated Arm Bar Pin

Kneel on the opponent's shoulder. Lock their elbow by pressing the bony edge of your forearm (ulna bone) into the triceps tendon at TW-11 (just above the elbow joint), as you lift their wrist with your other hand. You can also assist the hold by planting your knee under the opponent's wrist for additional lift or support. If possible, try to also lock the opponent's wrist by forcing their palm toward their forearm as you twist their hand forward (see photos). This increases pain and helps keep the elbow properly positioned.

8. Armpit Arm Bar Pin

Clamp the opponent's elbow in your armpit and pull their wrist upward with both hands, locking their elbow. Press the side of your body downward against their shoulder and torso to restrict movement, and spread your legs for stability. Keep your opponent flat on their belly. Adjust your hip and torso placement as needed to maintain control and keep attacker from rising to their knees or rolling to their side. You can also lock the opponent's shoulder (in addition to the elbow) by levering the arm forward as shown in the next pin.

9. Armpit Arm Bar + Shoulder Lock

This is basically the same as the previous hold, except you will lever the opponent's hand forward toward their head. This locks the shoulder in addition to the elbow. As you push their hand forward, pull your R elbow and upper arm tightly to your side to increase stress on their shoulder and elbow. Transitions back and forth between pins 8 and 9 can be used to maintain control when either hold is in danger of failing. You can also lock the opponent's wrist by forcing their palm toward their forearm as you twist their hand forward.

10–13 Reclining Arm Bars

Lock the opponent's elbow against your inner thigh as you lift your hips and pull downward on their wrist with both hands. The opponent is usually weaker if their thumb faces up. Keep your hips close to the shoulder. There are four common methods of using your legs, which are listed and shown below. You can also lock the elbow with your inner leg (pin 14) or inner knee (pin 15).

10. Reclining Arm Bar (one leg over head)
11. Reclining Arm Bar (one leg over body)
12. Reclining Arm Bar (both legs over)
13. Reclining Arm Bar (no legs over)

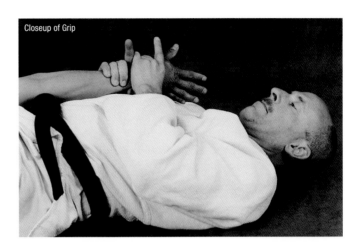

Closeup of Grip

10

11

12

13

14. Reclining Leg Arm Bar

Grab the opponent's R wrist with both hands, turn to your R side, and slide your hips to the left. Wrap your L leg over their arm, planting your thigh on the back of their elbow, and the front of your ankle on their throat. Pull the opponent's wrist toward you to straighten their arm if it is not already so. Lock their elbow by pressing your leg just above the joint, as you pull their wrist in the opposite direction. The direction of your leverage depends on the orientation of their elbow. If desired, you can shift to a side position by rolling laterally as you maintain the arm lock.

15. Reclining Knee Arm Bar

Wrap the opponent's wrist, trapping it in your L armpit. Plant your L foot on their ribs and lock their elbow by pressing your inner knee downward, as you lift their wrist. Press your R sole into their L thigh to help control their body and keep them face down.

16–17 Entangled Arm Bars

Hold an opponent's wrist with one hand, as you reach under their elbow and grab your forearm for support. Push down on their wrist as you lever the bony edge of your forearm into TW-11 (elbow). The hold can be applied in one of two ways, based upon which hand grabs the wrist and which one locks the elbow. Variation 16 is often preferred by some practitioners, since it permits transitions to stronger holds if an opponent counters by bending their arm. When executing any *Entangled Arm Bar* or *Entangled Shoulder Lock* (shown next), it is important to pin the opponent's opposite wrist between your crossed ankles. Push downward with your legs, as you sink your weight into the chest. Press firmly against the wrist, or the opponent's hand can slip free and attack your groin or other vital targets.

18–21 Entangled Shoulder Locks

These holds apply stress to both the elbow and shoulder. These holds are closely related to the *Entangled Arm Bars* shown previously (pins 16 and 17). Pull the opponent's hand tight to your body and grasp your own wrist for support (called a *figure-4* hold). Elevate the opponent's elbow, locking the shoulder and elbow. Their are four common variations:

18. Entangled Front Shoulder Lock
19. Entangled Rear Shoulder Lock 1
20. Entangled Rear Shoulder Lock 2
21. Entangled Rear Shoulder Lock 3

18. Entangled Front Shoulder Lock
The opponent's elbow is fully bent and pressed against the side of their body. Coordinate three actions: pull opponent's wrist downward and inward with your L hand, pull your L wrist with your R hand, and lift your R elbow. Bending your wrists is crucial for increasing your range of motion.

19–21 Entangled Rear Shoulder Lock
When compared to hold 18, this hold rotates the arm and locks the shoulder in the opposite direction, similar to a hammer lock. Three grip variations are shown in the photos.

Transitions
Transitions between Entangled Arm Bars and Entangled Shoulder Locks are often required. If an opponent counters the previous Entangled Arm Bars (pins 16 and 17) by bending their elbow, you will naturally transition into one of the following holds:

Entangled Arm Bar 1 (pin 16), shifts to Entangled Front Shoulder Lock (pin 18)

Entangled Arm Bar 2 (pin 17), shifts to Entangled Rear Shoulder Locks 1, 2, or 3 (pins 19, 20, and 21)

22–25 Seated Bent-Arm Locks

Force the opponent's elbow to close tightly around the protruding bones of your wrist (pins 22–24) or ankle (pin 25). Press the opponent's wrist toward their shoulder, as you twist your bone against the inner elbow. This causes intense pain at the biceps tendon and median nerve as you force the arm to close. Their are four common variations:

22. Seated Bent-Arm Lock
23. Seated Bent-Arm + Wrist Lock
24. Seated Bent-Arm Lock (leg assist)
25. Leg Bent-Arm Lock

Pin 23 is like pin 22, except the opponent's wrist is locked forward to create additional pain. Press the opponent's palm toward their forearm, as you twist your trapped wrist to apply pain. In pin 24, wrap your inner knee over the opponent's wrist and plant your instep under their neck. Extend your leg and twist your trapped wrist to apply pain. In pin 25, use your inner thigh to press the opponent's wrist, closing their elbow around your ankle as you twist your trapped ankle to apply pain. These holds are often used when an opponent counters a Reclining Arm Bar (pins 10–13) by bending their elbow.

26. Elevated Shoulder Lock Pin

The following are alternate methods of applying an Elevated Shoulder Lock Pin. Variation A is most typical and is applied by pressing your knee downward against the opponent's shoulder and laterally against their upper arm, as you pull their wrist laterally away from their body. Their elbow is bent and pointing up, with their hand against the ground. This lock stresses both the elbow and shoulder. You can also add a wrist lock if needed (A1). If the opponent tries to counter by pivoting on their back (their head circles toward the lock as their hips circle away from you), you must block their head to prevent movement. Do this by pushing against the side of their head with your free hand (B), or by sliding your knee down between their head and shoulder (C). As a general rule, restricting head movement prevents body movement. This hold can also be applied by pressing your L shoulder (at the chest) down against the elbow, pinning the wrist. This usually works well when you are having trouble keeping a stronger opponent's arm down on the ground.

A. Knee pressing shoulder and arm
B. Same as A, except hand blocks head
C. Knee planted between head and arm

27. Planted Shoulder Lock Pin

Press the opponent's elbow downward to the ground with your palm, as you pull their hand toward their shoulder, trapping it underneath. Their elbow is fully bent. You can now release your hold on the wrist and use your hand to strike, or to block a punch from the opponent's free hand. Use your body weight to maintain the arm pin. You can also apply this hold by reversing the roles of your hands. Transitions between pins 26, 27, and 28 are commonly used to maintain control as an opponent struggles or counters.

28. Straight Shoulder Lock Pin

Plant an opponent's wrist against the ground, with their arm fully extended and their palm facing down. Use one or both of your hands. Pin the opponent's elbow by kneeling on their triceps tendon at TW-11, which is located just above the elbow joint. This is very painful, so do not apply your full body weight unless necessary. Keep the opponent's arm pressed against their head. Transitions between pins 26, 27, and 28 are commonly used to maintain control as an opponent struggles or counters.

29. Driving Shoulder Lock Pin

Plant your knee on the opponent's upper arm using your body weight to restrict movement. Lock their bent-wrist by forcing their palm toward their forearm, as you crank their hand forward to lock their shoulder. The opponent's bent-arm resembles the crank on a winch. If an opponent straightens their arm to counter, shift to a Knee Arm Bar (pin 1). If they attempt to escape by raising their hips to execute a roll (flipping over to their back), block their hips with your L elbow or by briefly leaning into them with your body.

30. Elbow Hammer Lock Pin

Pin the opponent face down, using your body weight to assist the hold. The opponent's arm is placed behind their back. Place your forearm behind and above their forearm, trapping their wrist in your inner elbow. Lock their shoulder by lifting their wrist toward their head with your elbow, as you drive downward with the blade of your hand against their inner elbow. Keep your hips planted over their lower back to prevent them from rising to their knees. A Hammer Lock can also be applied using two hands, as shown next.

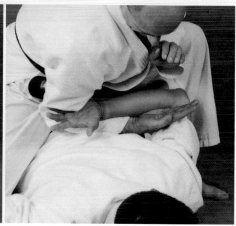

31. Bent-Wrist Hammer Lock Pin

Pin the opponent face down on ground, using your body weight to assist the hold. The opponent's arm is placed behind their back. Grip their wrist with one hand and their elbow with the other. Lock their shoulder by lifting their wrist toward their head, as you drive their elbow inward. At the same time, lock the wrist by bending their palm toward their forearm. Keep your hips planted over their lower back to keep them from rising to their knees. You can also strengthen the hold by using your legs to press against the wrist and elbow.

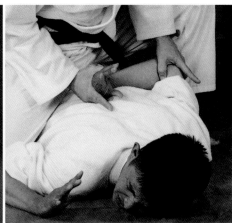

32. Gooseneck Hammer Lock Pin

This hold can be applied from ground positions or by lowering an opponent backward onto their buttocks (you are kneeling). The opponent's arm is placed behind their back. Trap their elbow between your inner elbow and body. Slip one hand behind their arm and wrap the back of their hand. Bend their wrist to lock it, by forcing their palm toward their forearm. Reach around with your free hand and apply a Rear Lapel Choke or Rear Naked Choke as described in the *Chokes + Head Locks* chapter.

33. Scarf Hold

This Judo pin is used to restrain an opponent for a set amount of time. It does not incorporate chokes, joint locks, or finishing techniques. Hence, its use in self-defense is limited (if you release your opponent, they can continue to fight). You can also be struck with the free R hand. To apply: Wrap the neck with your L arm (like a scarf), gripping your pant leg, or clothing at opponent's L shoulder. Grip their arm or sleeve with your R hand and trap their arm in your armpit. Spread your legs, lower your head, and press down with the side of your body.

34–35 Reclining Ankle Locks

Tightly wrap your arm around the opponent's ankle, trapping their extended foot in your armpit. Join your hands. Lever your wrist (radius bone) upward into the Achilles tendon as you recline backward. This hold is very painful at the Achilles tendon, as along as the opponent's foot remains fully extended. If an opponent's foot is bent, their tolerance to pain will increase substantially, and they will possess greater leg strength to resist or kick-out of the hold. Two variations of this hold are shown below, distinguished by the manner in which your legs are used.

34. Reclining Ankle Lock 1

Trap the opponent's ankle in your armpit as previously described. Wrap their leg with your leg, kicking their groin with your heel as you enter. Recline backward as you lever your wrist up into the Achilles tendon and press your knee downward. Lift your hips to increase stress. Use the sole of your other foot to keep the opponent's arm away from your leg. Otherwise, they will try to apply the same hold to you. If this happens, thrust your R heel into their groin (Stamp Kick), or lift your R leg and drop your heel forcefully downward into the solar plexus (Axe Kick).

35. Reclining Ankle Lock 2

This is similar to the previous hold, except you will use your feet to restrain the opponent's left leg and right arm. As you press their leg and arm, pull back on the ankle lock, forcing their legs and arm to form a "T". If they have limited flexibility, this will stretch or tear muscles. If an opponent is substantially taller than you, your legs may not be long enough to apply this hold. If you lose control, turn the opponent onto their belly and shift to a *Single-Leg Crab Lock* (shown in the author's other works, *The Art of Holding* and *Hapkido: Traditions, Philosophy, Technique*).

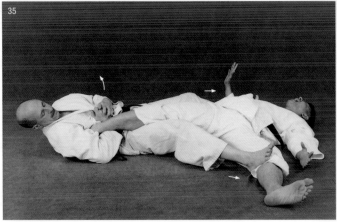

Opposite view of 35

36. Knife-Foot to Calf Pin

In this hold, you will pin an opponent's leg against the ground by using your body weight to apply pressure to sensitive nerves and pressure points. Press the blade of your foot (Knife Foot) into the back of the calf at BL-56 or BL-57 (medial sural cutaneous nerve), or into the Achilles tendon. Both sites are very painful. Standing on the opponent's calf anchors their leg and keeps their foot extended. If they manage to bend their foot, pain will be greatly reduced. This pin can be used against a kneeling or prone opponent.

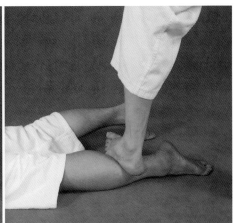

37. Knife-Foot to Knee Pin

In this hold, you will pin an opponent's leg against the ground by using your body weight to apply pressure to sensitive nerves and pressure points. Press the blade of your foot (Knife Foot) into the back of an opponent's knee at BL-53, BL-54, and KI-10 (posterior and medial femoral cutaneous nerves, tibial nerve). This pin can be used against a kneeling or prone opponent. Against a kneeling opponent, the hold can be made more secure by adding a Rear Naked Choke, as shown at right.

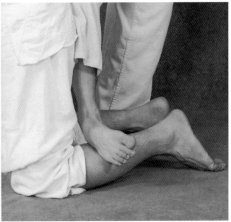

38. Bent-Leg Lock

Your opponent is reclining on their belly. Plant your foot between the legs, near the groin. Grab their foot and force their leg to bend forward, with your ankle trapped in their inner knee, pressing the calf at BL-57. Keep their foot extended by pressing on the instep or toes. Bend the toes downward toward the sole of the foot, by pressing with the palm of your hand. There are many other types of Bent-Leg Locks, which are covered in the author's other works, *The Art of Holding*, and *Hapkido: Traditions, Philosophy, Technique*.

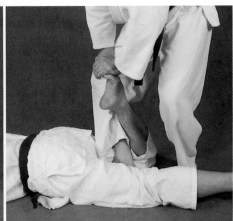

Kicks are striking techniques that use specific surfaces of the foot for delivering blows anywhere on the body. Ground kicks are very similar to standing kicks, except they are delivered from a kneeling, seated, or reclining position. These kicks are usually directed to standing opponents; however, kneeling or reclining targets are also possible. There are two basic categories of ground kicks: drop kicks and seated kicks. Drop kicks are executed while making a transition from standing to ground positions, often returning to

GROUND KICKS

standing postures at the completion of the kick, possibly to face other attackers. They are also called sacrifice kicks or falling kicks. Seated kicks are executed from a kneeling, seated, or reclining position, when you are already on the ground. This chapter outlines 38 kicks commonly used in Hapkido, which are also found in other arts. The following pages provide an overview of basic principles, followed by a description of each kick, outlining their biomechanical qualities, appropriate uses, and relationships to each other.

DROP KICKS

Drop kicks are very similar to standing kicks, except they are delivered from a crouching, kneeling, or reclining position, after transition from a standing posture. Upon completing the kick, you may either return to a standing posture or remain on the ground. Drop kicks can be directed to standing, kneeling, or reclining opponents. When attacking standing opponents, there is always an element of risk. If your strike is ineffective or your opponent avoids the kick, you are left in a vulnerable position (you are on the ground, they are standing). For this reason, drop kicks are usually used: when standing skills fail; as an unexpected surprise; while falling; or to take your opponent to the ground where you believe you possess an advantage. Whenever possible, execute a preliminary feint to disguise your kick. This might involve looking high, standing tall, throwing a high strike, etc. Generally, drop kicks should be very fast, continuous, and end in a standing posture.

In many martial arts systems, students will first learn standing kicks, so that they can refine basic biomechanical motions associated with specific kicks, before attempting their ground versions. Standing kicks are covered in the author's books *The Art of Striking* and *Hapkido: Traditions, Philosophy, Technique*.

Planted Knee vs Elevated Knee

When executing most drop kicks from crouching or kneeling positions (see kick 2), there are two methods of supporting your body. In the first method, the knee and ball of the foot are planted. In the second method, the ball of the foot is planted, with the knee elevated above the ground. Generally, a particular martial art will prefer one method over the other. Both have advantages and disadvantages best grasped by experimentation. Drop kicks in which the knee is planted are usually easier for beginners to learn.

Movement Preceding the Kick

Drop kicks begin from a standing posture and transition to the ground by one of three methods: 1) attacking footwork, 2) defending footwork, or 3) a ground-entry technique such as a sit-out or roll.

1. Attacking footwork involves moving toward the opponent, usually to seize the initiative. The type of step used depends upon the kick to be executed (e.g., a forward step for a front kick, a cross step for a side kick). The step can also be used as a feint or to avoid an attack.

2. Retreating footwork involves moving away from the opponent, usually to counter a charge or diminish the power of an incoming attack, particularly against an overpowering opponent. Retreating footwork is usually executed by performing the opposite steps you would use for moving forward.

3. A ground-entry technique is used when you wish to remain on the ground or are in the process of falling or running backwards. Ground-entry techniques are specific methods by which you transition to a kneeling or seated guard, prior to kicking. A sit-out entry (sitting down backwards onto your back) or a shoulder roll are the most common methods. Other options are outlined in the *Fundamentals* chapter, under *Ground Movement*.

Since there are many footwork and ground-entry variations, only the most common methods are shown in the examples. The particular type of footwork depicted (attacking, retreating) is labeled below the last photo in each series, at the bottom of the pages.

Returning to a Standing Posture

Many drop kicks are designed to permit rapid return to standing postures, in order to reduce the element of risk when confronting standing opponents. This is accomplished by using the fingertips of both hands and the ball of the foot for support. To return to a standing posture, simply push off with both hands and your supporting foot.

Ball Foot

Bottom Heel

Knife Foot

Spear Foot

Instep Foot

1. Drop Front Kick

Drop Front Kicks are directed straight forward, or forward and upward, using one of the following five attack points: *Ball Foot* (greater reach), *Bottom Heel* (greater power), *Knife Foot* (greater penetration), *Spear Foot* (pinpoint targeting), or *Instep Foot* (rising strikes, usually to the groin). The specific attack point used depends upon target size and shape, and the method of execution (snap or thrust). In terms of the kick's delivery, there are two basic methods of executing a front kick from the ground: snapping and thrusting. In *snap kicks,* the foot follows an upward circular path, with the knee acting as fulcrum as the hips thrust forward. The foot is quickly withdrawn. In *thrusting kicks,* the knee is extended as the foot follows a straight path.

Whether you attack or retreat, the kick is the same; only the footwork preceding it differs. To attack, the rear foot steps forward. To retreat, the front foot steps backward. After the step, shift balance to the rear leg, planting the rear hand on the ground (front hand guarding). As you reach back to plant the other hand, snap or thrust your foot forward into the target, using either leg. Raise the hips forward to assist the kick. To remain on the ground, sit-out into a seated guard, then kick. Targets include the knee, groin, ribs, solar plexus, chin, and head.

Footwork used for attacking or retreating

Sit-out to a seated guard

95

2. Drop Roundhouse Kick

This kick follows a horizontal circular path. Delivery is primarily characterized by the snapping of your lower leg, with your knee acting as a fulcrum. The kick may be executed using either the Ball Foot or Instep Foot (see below) to strike targets at any height, with either leg. The attack point (hitting surface) used depends upon the target selected. Instep kicks are mostly directed to the head, ribs, abdomen, hip, thigh, or knee. Ball Foot kicks are usually used to strike the groin, solar plexus, neck, or jaw. Make sure the toes are curled back to prevent damage. When wearing shoes, the tip may be used instead.

Front or rear leg strikes are possible, based on the preceding steps. To attack, step forward (straight or 45°), or drop directly to the ground. Plant both hands, lower the front knee, and execute a rear-leg kick (see photos). To retreat, the front foot steps to the rear. Lower the rear knee, plant both hands, and execute a front-leg kick (not shown). To remain on the ground, execute a sit-out into a seated guard, then kick. Targets include the knee, groin, solar plexus, and head.

Instep Foot

Ball Foot

Footwork used for attacking

Sit-out to a seated guard

3. Drop Side Kick

This kick is often executed from a Side Stance. It is powerful, versatile, and assists rapid return to a standing posture. The Drop Side Kick is safe to execute in a variety of situations, since your groin and frontal targets are well protected.

Whether you attack or retreat, the technique is the same; only the footwork preceding it differs. To attack, cross-step forward (rear foot passes behind front foot). During the cross step, plant both hands on the ground, lower the knee, and cock the opposite leg. Thrust the foot straight outward (parallel to the ground), striking with the Bottom Heel or Knife Foot. Before retracting the foot along the same path, the leg is momentarily locked-out to add force to the strike. To retreat, cross-step backward (front foot passes in front of rear foot), plant both hands, lower the rear knee, cock the opposite leg, and kick. To remain on the ground, execute a sit-out into a seated guard, then kick. Targets include the ankle, knee, groin, midsection, neck, and head. The kick may also be directed to the underside of an attacker's leg to counter a Side Kick.

Bottom Heel

Knife Foot

Footwork used for attacking or retreating

Sit-out to a seated guard

4. Drop Back Kick

This kick is directed to an opponent behind. To attack, the front foot steps backward past the rear foot (toward opponent). To retreat, the rear foot steps forward past the front foot (away from opponent). While looking over your shoulder at the target, plant both hands and lower the knee of the stepping-foot. Cock the opposite leg. When the lower leg aligns with the target, thrust the foot straight backward, striking with your Bottom Heel or Knife Foot. Quickly retract your kick to prevent your leg from being grabbed, and to prepare for the next technique. Place your chest close to the ground for higher kicks. Targets include the shin, knee, groin, midsection, throat, or the head if an opponent is bent over.

Bottom Heel

Knife Foot

Footwork used for attacking opponent behind you

Footwork used for retreating from opponent behind you

5. Drop Turning Back Kick

This is the same as the previous kick, except you will pivot 180° to deliver a kick to an opponent in front. Whether you attack or retreat, the kick is the same; only the footwork preceding it differs. To attack, step forward or drop to the ground without stepping. To retreat, the front foot steps to the rear foot (but not past). In one continuous motion: lower your body, pivot and turn toward your posterior side, plant both hands, and cock the rear leg as you pivot on the ball of the foot. Lower or plant the support knee and thrust your foot straight backward, striking with your Bottom Heel or Knife Foot.

6. Drop Axe Kick

This kick is directed to an opponent in front. Slam the back of your heel forcefully forward and downward into the target, as you exit a forward shoulder roll (see *Fundamentals* chapter). The rolling motion powers the kick, as your forward momentum propels you to a kneeling or standing position afterwards. Depending upon how the shoulder roll is executed, the kick can be used to strike targets at a variety of distances. Since the shoulder roll complicates timing and distance, this kick requires extensive practice to develop accuracy. If you do miss, continue to execute hand strikes as you move upward into the opponent, assuming a standing posture. This kick is rarely used but can be very effective in specific circumstances. Targets include the abdomen, groin, thigh, knee, toes, top of the foot, or anywhere on an opponent who is reclining on their back.

Back Heel

Dropping and turning, without stepping

Footwork used for attacking

7. Drop Hook Kick

This circular kick normally uses the same attacking or retreating footwork, or sit-out entries, as the Drop Side Kick. Drop Hook Kicks are usually directed to the side or back of the knees, to cause a fall. You may also strike to the side of the head if an opponent is leaning over, or to the groin if an opponent is in a side stance. To execute, extend your leg out to the side and pull your heel outward and across your body in a circular motion, toward the target. Rapidly bend the knee at impact to add force to the blow. Because the Hook Kick is not inherently powerful, it is most effective when striking sensitive nerves or pressure points, particularly on the leg. Common targets include: SP-6 (inner shin); SP-9, SP-10 and ST-34 (knee area); SP-11 (inner thigh); GB-31 (outer thigh); LV-12 and SP-12 (cluster at hip-leg junction); and the testicles. Strikes to these pressure points will usually weaken or buckle the legs. Takedowns that use your non-kicking leg to trap an opponent's foot as you kick, are covered in the *Seated Defense* chapter.

8. Drop Spin Kick

This is a devastating circular kick to the knee, shin, or ankle, in which your entire body rotates about 360° to power the blow. The Drop Spin Kick is used to knock an opponent to the ground by upsetting the balance or damaging the lower leg. Targets are outlined in the previous kick. Very fast Drop Spin Kicks are a hallmark of Hapkido. There are two basic ways to execute a Drop Spin Kick: *foot pivot* and *knee pivot*. In the first method, the supporting leg is fully bent as you pivot on the ball of the foot. In the second method, the knee is planted and serves as pivot-point. The first

Back Heel

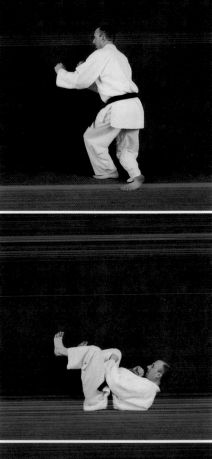

Footwork used for attacking or retreating

Sit-out to a seated guard

method (foot pivot) is arguably faster, more powerful and permits rapid return to a standing position. The second method (knee pivot) is easier to execute, permits greater height (hit to the groin or upper leg), and can be used by individuals who cannot fully bend the knee due to previous injuries. In order to execute these kicks safely, you will need healthy knees with strong supporting musculature and tight ligaments. In both versions, you will turn as you drop, allowing hip rotation to propel your extended leg inward. Your foot traces a 360° arc, parallel to the ground, hitting with the back of your heel.

Drop Spin Kick (foot pivot)

This kick is used to strike targets at knee height or lower. The technique is very similar to a standing Spin Kick, except the supporting leg is fully bent at the knee. As you step across to initiate the spin, lower yourself *straight down* to the ground. If you lean forward or backward as you drop, you will upset your balance during the spin. When first learning, plant both hands for support (fingertips, not palms). Later, the hands only touch lightly to stabilize your balance, or not at all. The key to speed and fluidity is staying relaxed and focusing on hip rotation. Do not allow the hips to rise. If you miss the target, continue spinning to a standing posture by rising on the support-ing leg, as you set the kicking leg down to the rear. The entire kick (stand-drop-stand) is applied in a very fast, continuous motion.

Drop Spin Kick (knee pivot)

When using the knee as pivot-point, the hand plant is used for balance and power. This version begins like a Drop Turning Back Kick. Rotate on the lower knee (not the kneecap), with the supporting foot lightly brushing against the ground. The hands push forward near the end of delivery to assist the spinning motion. When using the knee as a pivot, it is possible to raise the kick higher than is possible with a *foot pivot*. This is useful when striking higher targets such as the upper leg, groin (when countering a kick), or head (when an opponent is leaning over). To return to a standing posture, push off with your hands and supporting leg, similar to other drop kicks.

Drop Spin Kick with foot pivot

Drop Spin Kick with knee pivot

DROP TWIN KICKS

Drop twin kicks are ground strikes in which you simultaneously kick with both legs. The kicks are directed to either the same or to two different targets. These kicks can be practical in certain circumstances, such as: defending against multiple attackers, driving back an overpowering attacker (extra power needed), or fighting when your feet are tied together. Twin drop kicks are executed with the hips planted or airborne, based on your entry method. You will often use the same footwork and ground-entry methods as single-leg drop kicks.

When both feet and hips are airborne, the most difficult part of the kick is landing. You may land on either the balls of the feet or side of body. When landing on the balls of the feet, it is possible to quickly return to standing postures. In comparison, body landings can be fairly jarring, and should not be used until you are proficient in breakfalls. Remember, landing on a padded mat is very different than landing on concrete or asphalt. Twin kicks are also executed from a seated posture or jump (shown later in this chapter).

9. Drop Twin Front Kick

Execute two front kicks at the same time, with both feet very close together, buttocks planted on the ground. Either snapping or thrusting deliveries are possible. Strike with the Bottom Heel or Ball Foot. Use the attacking, retreating, or sit-out entries previously discussed (see Drop Front Kick). Thrusting deliveries can be used to drive a converging opponent or grappler backward.

Sit-out to a buttock pivot

Sit-out to a seated guard

10. Drop Twin Roundhouse Kick

Execute a two-foot Roundhouse Kick
with both feet close together, using either
the Instep Foot or Ball Foot. When using
attacking or retreating footwork, the entire
body is airborne, with both hands planted
and supporting. Land on the balls of the
feet or side of the body. When using a
sit-out entry, the hips and side of the torso
are planted during the kick, with the hands
maintaining a guard. Power comes from
lower-leg speed and use of the abdominal
muscles as you bend at the waist.

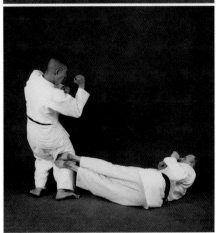

Kicking with body airborne

Kicking with hips planted

11. Drop Twin Side Kick

Execute a two-foot Side Kick with both feet very close together. When using attacking or retreating footwork, the body is airborne, with both hands planted and supporting. The entire body travels in the direction of the kick, to add force to the strike. If you fail to use body momentum, you may be knocked off-balance by the force of impact. Land on the balls of the feet or side of the body. The force of impact can be used to assist returning to a standing position. When using a sit-out entry, the hips and side of the torso are planted during the kick, with the hands maintaining a guard.

Kicking with body airborne

Kicking with hips planted

12. Drop Twin Back Kick

When compared to other twin kicks, this technique is quite powerful and fairly easy to perform. Execute a two-foot Back Kick with both feet very close together. Regardless of footwork, the body is always airborne, with both hands planted and supporting. The entire body travels in the direction of the kick, to add force to the strike. Land on both feet, returning to a standing posture. Use the attacking or retreating footwork shown for the Drop Back Kick. Sit-out entries are impractical.

13. Drop Twin Overhead Kick

This kick is directed to an opponent behind, as you sit-out or fall backward. Its primary use is against two attackers standing in front and behind. As the front attacker pushes or throws you backward, execute a sit-out, using the rolling motion to deliver a Twin Front Kick to the rear attacker. Strike using the Ball Foot or the hard tips of your shoes. Grasp the attacker's ankles to increase power and keep them from stepping backward, which forces a fall to their rear.

14. Drop Side Split Kick

This twin kick is directed to two opponents standing in front, at your left and right sides. To execute, rotate your body so that one side is facing the ground. The top leg executes a side kick (Bottom Heel), while the bottom leg executes a front kick (Ball Foot or Bottom Heel). This is a difficult kick requiring good flexibility and much practice. When using attacking or retreating footwork, the entire body is airborne, with both hands planted and supporting. Land on your feet or the side of the body. When using a sit-out entry, the side of one hip is planted during the kick, with your hands maintaining a guard. In this situation, it is possible to execute multiple Side Split Kicks, in repetition. Targets include the thigh, knee, shin, or ankle. This is also called a *Scissor Kick*.

Kicking with body airborne   *Kicking with hips planted*

15. Drop Front Split Kick

This kick is directed to two opponents standing in front, at your left and right sides. As you sit-out or fall backward, pull both feet together toward your buttocks with the knees fully bent. Angle your knees outward, pointing at both targets. Simultaneously snap both lower legs outward to either side, hitting with the Ball Foot or Bottom Heel. Immediately retract your feet, assuming a seated guard or continuing to other techniques. Common targets are the groin, knee, or shin.

16. Drop Overhead Split Kick

This is basically a *Side Split Kick* (see kick 14) executed with your body resting on the upper back or shoulders. The kick is directed to two opponents standing in front and behind. As you sit-out or fall backward, execute the twin kicks. It is usually executed in continuous repetition, or linked with other ground kicks and takedowns. Depending on target and distance, hit with the Ball Foot, sole, or Back Heel. Targets include the groin, ribs, abdomen, and solar plexus.

SEATED KICKS

Seated kicks are very similar to standing kicks and drop kicks, except they are executed from a seated guard, relaxed seated posture, or during ground movement. Various forms of ground movement are outlined in the author's books *Hapkido: Traditions, Philosophy, Technique* and *The Art of Ground Fighting*.

Seated kicks are used for ground fighting against either standing or reclining opponents. They can be used to: take an opponent to the ground, defend against an unexpected attack while relaxing, attack grapplers during ground fighting, or keep attackers at a distance until you can recover a standing posture. Since seated kicks are basically the same as standing kicks, or drop kicks using a sit-out entry, entire sequences will not be shown. The seated kicks shown are among those most commonly used in martial arts with extensive ground-kicking repertoires, such as Hapkido. However, almost any standing kick can be modified for use from ground positions. Experimentation is suggested.

17. *Seated Front Kick (to underside of chin)*

18. *Seated Front Blade Kick (to groin)*

19. *Seated Front Toe Kick (to throat, CO-22)*

20. *Seated Roundhouse Kick (ball foot to SP-10)*

21. *Seated Reverse Roundhouse Kick (to head)*

22. *Seated Side Kick (to knee, with leg trap at ankle)*

23. *Seated Back Kick (from side roll, to throat)*

24. *Seated Stamp Kick (to top of foot, LV-3)*

25. *Seated Circular Inner-Heel Kick to kneecap*

26. *Seated Inside Crescent Kick (to side of head)*

27. *Seated Outside Crescent Kick (blocking knife)*

28. *Seated Cutting Crescent Kick (slashing the eyes)*

29. *Seated Axe Kick (to nose and cheekbone)*

30. *Seated Inside Hook Kick (to kneecap)*

31. *Seated Hook Kick (to knee, with leg trap at ankle)*

32. *Seated Twin Front Kick (to base of rib cage)*

33. *Seated Twin Roundhouse Kick (ball foot to groin)*

34. *Seated Twin Side Kick (to floating ribs)*

35. *Seated Twin Overhead Kick (to throat)*

36. *Seated Front Split Kick (to both inner knees)*

37. *Seated Side Split Kick (to both ankles, takedown)*

38. *Seated Overhead Split Kick (to both groins)*

Seated defenses are ground-fighting techniques employed when you are sitting on the ground and must engage a standing opponent. These techniques can be used if you are surprised or attacked while relaxing—for instance, sitting in a park or at the beach—or if you are being restrained or guarded, such as in a hostage situation where must initiate an attack from a disadvantaged position. All of the defenses in this chapter are shown being initiated from a Relaxed Seated Stance, which was previously described in the

SEATED DEFENSES

Fundamentals *chapter. Like all relaxed stances, it is designed to camouflage your intent while giving you the ability to respond very quickly to a variety of attacks. In most seated defenses, the objective is to force a fall, after which you will either execute finishing blows, shift to a restraining hold, or move quickly to a standing posture. Most seated techniques can also be applied from kneeling or reclining postures. This chapter contains 20 self-defense techniques used in Hapkido, which are also found in other martial arts.*

A

Index Finger Fist

1. Instep Gouge + Leg-Twist Throw

You are seated with your legs crossed. Attacker is standing. Reach outside attacker's ankle and grab their heel with your cross-hand. Gouge their instep at LV-3 with your opposite Index Finger Fist (A). As attacker lifts their leg, twist their foot by pulling their heel as you press their instep (B). Plant one or both wrists on their calf at BL-57 and press down. Force a Front Fall (C). Pin their leg with your shoulder as you press BL-57 (D).

Important Points

This throw can be gentle or destructive, based on force. Violent twisting will damage the knee. Forceful throws will smash the kneecap into the ground. When pinning the leg, press your wrist into BL-56, BL-57, or the Achilles tendon, as you push downward with your shoulder against the instep and toes (the knee is fully bent, the foot is fully extended). If you allow attacker to bend their foot or open their knee, they will possess greater leg strength and can kick-out of the hold.

B

C

D

A1

LV-3

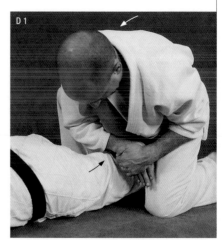

D1

2. Ankle Hold Throw

You are seated with your legs crossed. Attacker is standing (A). Grab the back of their opposite ankle with your L hand. At the same time, reach across with your R hand and grip their inner ankle, planting your index-finger base joint (palm-side) against SP-6 (B). Grip their ankle tightly and extend your knuckle into the nerve, as you pull their heel toward you. This generates immediate pain, forcing a Back Fall (C–D).

Important Points

Your L hand keeps attacker from pulling their leg away, as your R hand presses the nerve on the inner ankle. This hold works well if you are accurate. This pressure point is located on the inner ridge of the tibia, above the protruding bone at the ankle. Grip tightly *before* extending your inner knuckle into the nerve. Occasionally, some individuals will not experience pain. In this situation, shift your attack to pressure points at the inner knee, such as SP-9 or LV-8 (see next technique).

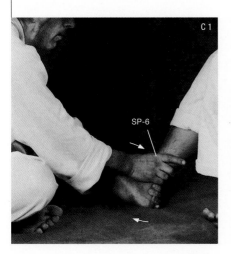

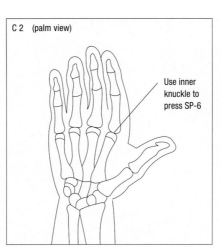

C 2 (palm view)

Use inner knuckle to press SP-6

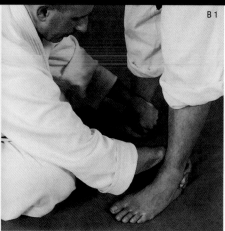

3. Twin Ankle Hold Throw

You are seated with your legs crossed. Attacker is standing in front (A). Reach between attacker's legs and grab the backs of both ankles, using both hands (B). Press the outer edge of your wrists or forearms (ulna bone) into SP-6 on both inner ankles. Lean your upper body forward and pull with your hands to assist leverage (C). This generates immediate pain, forcing a Back Fall (D). Execute a Back Shoulder Roll and rise to a standing posture (E–F).

Important Points

Your hands keep attacker from pulling their legs away, as your bony forearms press nerves at their inner ankles. This hold can be difficult to execute, since accurate targeting is needed. Nerves are located at the inner ridge of the tibia, above the protruding bone at the ankle. Occasionally, some individuals will not experience pain at this point. In this situation, shift your attack to other points (e.g., attack the groin or inner knee).

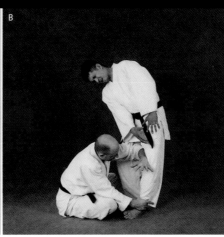

4. Forearm-to-Leg Throw

Standing attacker grabs your wrist (A). Grip the back of the opposite ankle with your R hand. At the same time, leverage your L wrist free, as you reach across and press the bony edge of your L Outer Forearm into nerves on the inner shin or lower knee (B). Press the shin as you pull the ankle toward you. This generates pain, forcing a Back Fall (C). Wrap the ankle, trapping the instep in your armpit. Lift as you drive your radius bone (bony edge of Inner Forearm) up into the Achilles tendon (painful), keeping the foot fully extended and the ankle locked (D). Pivot as you leverage and turn attacker over onto their belly. Step over their back, sit on their lower spine and lean backward, forcing the leg muscles, ankle, and spine to travel beyond their normal limits (E). Exercise extreme caution. Dropping forcefully will fracture spinal vertebrae.

Outer Forearm (left)
Inner Forearm (right)

Important Points

Although this example shows a defense against a wrist grab, it can be used in a variety of situations. Your R hand keeps attacker from pulling their leg away, as your L forearm presses nerves on their lower leg. Potential nerve targets exist at different heights. Common pressure points from low to high are at SP-6, LV-5, LV-6, SP-8, SP-9, and LV-8. You can also reverse the roles of your hands (grip with your L hand, press the L shin with your R wrist). You can also use your hands or knuckles to attack nerves.

Palm Heel Hand

Middle Finger Fist

5. Hand-to-Knee Throw

You are seated with your legs crossed. Standing attacker grabs your sleeve (A). Grip the back of the opposite ankle with your L hand. At the same time, reach across and press your R Palm Heel into base of the kneecap, or into nerves at the inner knee (B). Press attacker's knee forward or toward their rear-corner, as you pull the ankle toward you, forcing a Back Fall (C). You can drive the knee in one of two directions: If you press forward into the kneecap, the joint locks (B1). If you press sideways, the knee buckles (B2).

Important Points

Your L hand keeps attacker from pulling their leg away, as your R hand presses their knee. You can direct pressure in two possible directions: 1) push your Palm Heel forward into the base of the kneecap to lock the joint (B1), or 2) push your Middle Finger Fist or Palm Heel sideways into the inner knee at SP-9 or SP-10 (B2). Pushing sideways is usually more difficult to resist, since the knee is less stable in this direction.

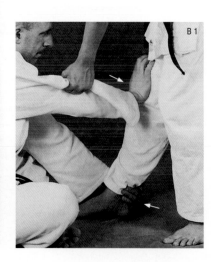

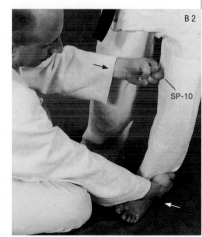

SP-10

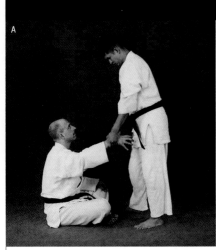

A

B

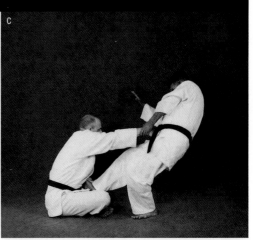

C

D

E

6. Spear-to-Groin Throw

You are seated with your legs crossed. Attacker grabs your arm (A). Grip the back of the opposite ankle with your L hand. Press your R Spear Hand into the groin at SP-12 and LV-12 (B). Press forward and downward toward their right rear-corner, as you pull the ankle toward your R armpit, forcing a Back Fall (C–D). Wrap the ankle in your armpit, with your wrist pressing the Achilles tendon (foot fully extended). Apply a Reclining Ankle Lock (E) as described in the *Pinning Holds* chapter. Stomp the groin if justified.

Important Points

Your L hand keeps attacker from stepping away, as your R hand presses their groin. You can scoop their heel toward either armpit, although pulling across your body will keep you from being kicked in the chin as they fall. It also puts you outside attacker's legs, which is a safer position. Once you wrap their ankle, use both your feet to restrain their L leg and R arm (E). You can also turn attacker over onto their belly and pin them.

Spear Hand

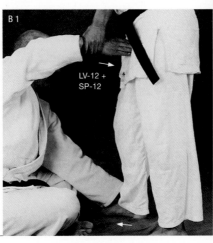

B 1

LV-12 + SP-12

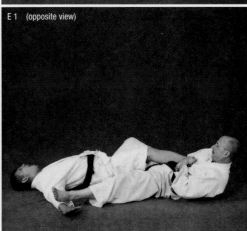

E 1   (opposite view)

7. Twin Shin-to-Shin Throw

You are seated with your legs crossed. Attacker is standing in front (A). Plant your hands for support. Pass both of your feet between attacker's legs and trap the backs of both of their ankles, using your insteps (B). Press the front edges of your tibia bones into attacker's inner shins at LV-5, LV-6, or SP-7. Lift your hips and drive forward, using your hands to assist. This creates immediate pain, forcing a Back Fall (C). As attacker lands, deliver a Front Thrust Kick with your heel to the testicles (D–E).

Important Points

Your insteps keep opponent from pulling their legs away, as your bony shins press into nerves on both inner shins. This hold can be difficult to execute, since accurate targeting is needed. The nerves you will be pressing are located on the inner ridge of the tibia, above the protruding bone at the ankle. Apply pressure quickly, before opponent can step away. If your throw is not working, shift your attack to other nerves or other techniques (see next technique).

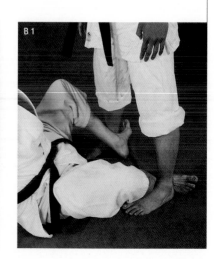

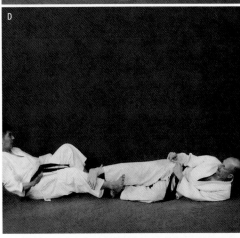

8. Blade-to-Leg Throw

Attacker is standing in front of you, while you are seated (A). Turn onto your left side. Hook your L instep against the back of attacker's ankle (B). Thrust your R Knife Foot into attacker's lower-inner knee at SP-9 (C1); or lower-outer-corner of the kneecap at ST-35 (C2); or inner shin at SP-6, LV-5, SP-7, or LV-6 (C3). Push attacker's knee forward, as you pull their ankle toward you. This generates pain and causes the knee to lock or buckle, forcing a Back Fall (D). When justified, apply this throw by kicking forcefully into the leg.

Important Points

You can hook either ankle, from the inside or outside, making for eight basic variations. The pressure point you will target depends upon your orientation to attacker's leg. The SP-9 point at the inner knee arguably works best, since the knee is also structurally weak in this direction. Even if you miss this pressure point, it will be difficult for an opponent to resist force in this direction, and the knee will invariably buckle outward. LV-8 at the inner knee joint also works well.

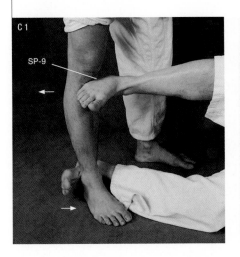

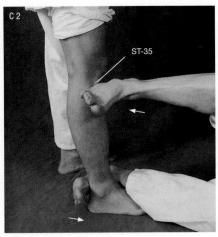

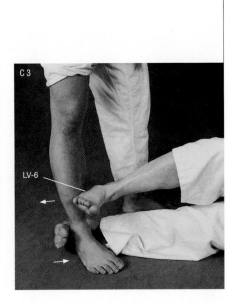

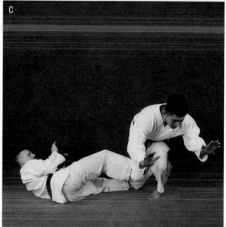

9. Hook Kick Throw

You are seated with your legs crossed. Attacker is standing in front (A). Turn onto your side. Plant your instep on the front or inner-side of their ankle (B). Execute a Hook Kick to the back of their knee at BL-54, as your instep pushes their ankle in the opposite direction (C). Attacker falls forward. Leave your ankle on their knee, as you bend their leg and roll up behind them. Press your wrist into the Achilles tendon (D). Pin by leaning forward, as you lever your knee backward (E).

Important Points

As attacker falls, forcefully scissor your legs so their leg bends up behind them. When entering the Bent-Leg Lock (D–E), grip their foot with your hands, planting their instep on your abdomen. Keep their foot fully extended, as this reduces leg strength. If attacker can bend their foot, they can kick-out of your hold. Force their knee to close tightly around your ankle, as you lean forward. This is very painful and will force a dislocation.

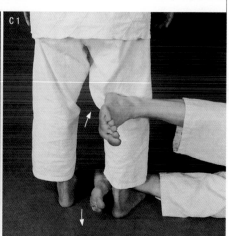

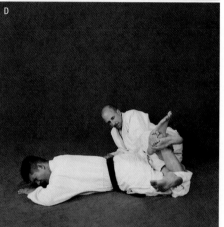

10. Rear Scissor Throw

You are seated with your legs crossed. Attacker is standing in front, facing sideways (A). Turn onto your side. Plant your instep on the front of the far ankle, blocking both legs (B). Kick forcefully into the back of both knees, as you push their ankles in the opposite direction (scissor your legs), forcing a Front Fall (C). Continue to scissor your legs and roll your body, bending their legs behind them (D). Mount and apply a Bent-Leg Lock (E1) or Rear Interlock Choke (E2).

Important Points

This is similar to the previous technique, except you will attack from the side and scissor both legs. If opponent does not know how to fall, they may fracture their kneecaps or wrist, or hit their head. Two pins are shown. E1 is like the previous pin (see technique 9), except you will cross and lock both legs. In E2, attacker attempts to straighten their legs before you enter. Let them, then straddle their hips and apply a Rear Interlock Choke.

E 1 (Bent-Leg Lock)

E 2 (Rear Interlock Choke)

B

A

C

D

11. Circle Throw

Attacker is standing in front, choking you or grabbing your lapel or pushing you backward (A). Grip their lapel with one hand; grip their sleeve under the elbow with your other hand (B). If attacker is sleeveless, grip their bare elbows or upper arms. Pull attacker toward you. Kick your foot into their groin, belly (C1), solar plexus, or hip joint (C2). Roll backward and pull them over your head, as you extend your leg to lift (D). You can also throw by planting your shins against their shins (C3).

Important Points

You must pull forcefully and maneuver your hips *under* attacker's hips. Try to initiate the throw as attacker is leaning or pressing forward, otherwise the throw can be easily countered. Plant your foot vertical (C1), or angled outward (C2). *Angled* provides slightly better control of attacker's hips, but may produce greater stress on your knee. Circle Throws can also be executed by directing attacker to the side, rather than overhead. This is faster and more difficult to counter, but is also less destructive to your opponent.

C 1

C 2

C 2

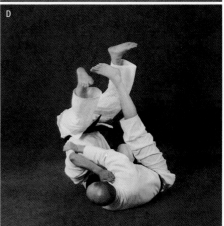

12. Corner Throw

Attacker is standing in front, choking you or grabbing your lapels, with their arms bent (A). Pull one elbow inward and down, as you lift their other elbow toward their head, unbalancing them toward their right side or right front-corner (B). As you drive their elbows in a vertical circle, block their outer ankle with one foot. Use your other foot to lift their leg at the inner knee or ankle. Throw attacker sideways or toward their right front-corner (C–D). Roll on top, choke, and punch (E–F).

Important Points

You can direct this throw in a variety of directions, depending on how attacker reacts to your initial pull. Assess their foot placement and balance, to decide which direction you should pull. Lifting their leg at the knee works well when directing them over your shoulder toward their front-corner. Lifting at the ankle works well when throwing them sideways. You can also lift at the buttock. Forcefully turning attacker's elbows (like a wheel) as you roll your body are the key actions that power the throw.

B

A

C

D

13. Thumb Lock + Outward Wrist

You are seated with your legs crossed. Standing attacker grabs your lapel (A). Reach across with your L hand and lock their L thumb: use the heel of your palm to jam the tip of their bent-thumb toward its base joint, as you squeeze with your fingers to assist (B). As attacker releases the lapel, continue locking their thumb and turn their hand outward (B2). Grasp four fingers with your R hand (overhand grip), squeeze them tightly (clashing joints), and twist outward (C). This locks the wrist and fingers, forcing a fall (D).

Important Points

The thumb lock is a very strong hold and can be used by itself to force a fall. Adding the Outward Wrist Lock strengthens the thumb lock by also locking the wrist and all four fingers. This technique illustrates how joint locks typically used from standing positions are made more efficient by locking the fingers and modifying grips. These type of adjustments are mandatory, since your ability to use your body or footwork is limited.

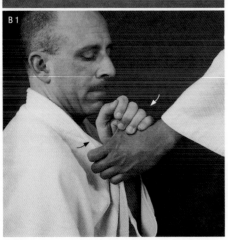

B 1

B 2

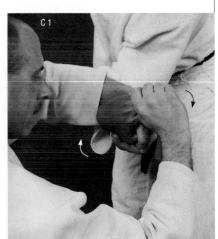

C 1

A

B

C

D (option: wrist bent back)

14. Bent-Arm Wrist Lock (2 fingers)

You are seated with your legs crossed. Standing attacker grabs your wrist (A). Circle your held-hand outward and over their wrist. Grip the two smallest fingers with your L hand, placing your pinky on their base joints. Lock attacker's fingers and wrist by rotating their hand forward, as you pull downward and backward on their wrist (B). Attacker will drop to relieve pain (C). If they straighten their wrist during step B, redirect the finger lock toward the back of their hand, forcing a Back Fall (D, D1).

Important Points

Like the previous technique, this hold also shows how wrist locks used from standing positions are made more efficient by also locking the fingers. These type of adjustments are mandatory, since your ability to use your body or footwork is limited. It is very unlikely that the standing-method of gripping and applying this hold (see *The Art of Holding* by the same author) would ever work from a seated position against a standing attacker.

B 1 (wrist bent forward)

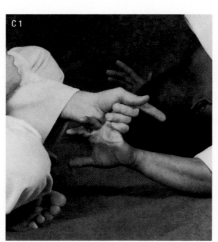

C 1

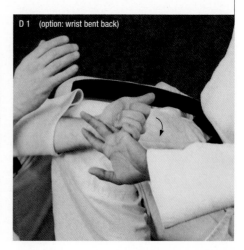

D 1 (option: wrist bent back)

A (against Front Kick)

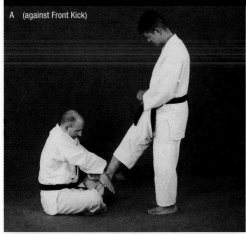

B

C

D

A 1 (against Roundhouse Kick)

15. X Leg-Twist Throw

Attacker executes a Front Kick (A). Execute an X Block and grab their ankle (right hand over left, for right kick). Twist their foot as you pull it toward you, trapping it between your inner elbow and shoulder (B). Plant one or both wrists on their calf at BL-57 and press down, forcing a Front Fall (C). Pin by pressing your wrist into BL-56, BL-57, or the Achilles tendon, as you push their instep down with your shoulder (D). Their foot is fully extended.

Important Points

The orientation of your hands when blocking kicker's foot, determines the type of Leg-Twist Throw that is possible. Don't worry about mixing up the orientation of your hands (e.g., left over right), since they are always setup for either technique 15 or 16. Just focus on trapping and twisting the foot, as you press the nerve on the calf. This throw can also be used against a Roundhouse Kick by blocking as shown in A1, then applying the throw as previously outlined.

B 1

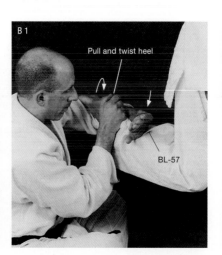

Pull and twist heel

BL-57

D 1

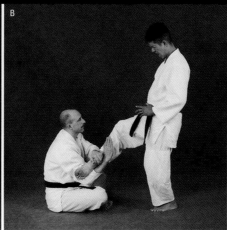

16. Reverse X Leg-Twist Throw

Attacker executes a Front Kick (A). Execute an X Block and grab their ankle (left hand over right, for right kick). Twist their foot as you pull it toward you, trapping it between your inner elbow and shoulder (B). Press down and twist, forcing a Side Fall (C). Continue twisting to turn them onto their belly (D). Pin by sitting on their upper back, as you trap one leg inside the other (E). Pull the instep of one foot backward, with both hands (F).

Important Points

The orientation of your hands when blocking kicker's foot, determines the type of Leg-Twist Throw that is possible. Don't worry about mixing up the orientation of your hands (e.g., left over right), since they are always setup for either technique 15 or 16. Just focus on trapping and twisting the foot, as you press BL-56 or BL-57 on the calf, or the Achilles tendon. When executing steps C–D, be on guard against a Roundhouse Kick to your head from opponent's free leg.

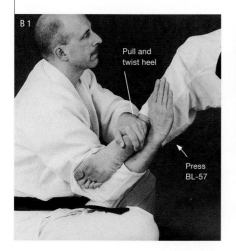

Pull and twist heel

Press BL-57

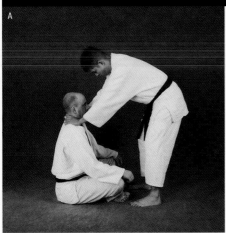

A

B

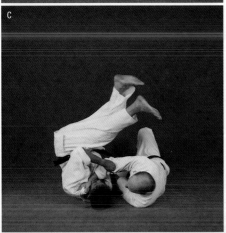

C

17. Front Drop Throw

Attacker grabs your shoulders or throat, and attempts to push you backward to force you to recline (A). As they lean forward and push, grip their body, clothing, or limbs. Pull their upper body toward you, unbalancing them forward as you roll back onto your left side. Your body blocks their legs (B). Continue pulling attacker forward and downward, forcing them to crash on their head or shoulder. A skilled attacker will flip over and land on their side, using a Flip Side Fall to prevent injury (C–D).

Important Points

Control attacker's balance by leading their upper body. The more your opponent leans forward, the easier it will be to unbalance them. If you meet resistance, use your grips to lift your body off the ground, then use your body weight to help unbalance attacker. You can also enter this throw by resisting attacker's initial push, then suddenly pulling them forward as they push harder. As you roll to your side, pull forcefully to your left toward a point well past your body, then downward.

D

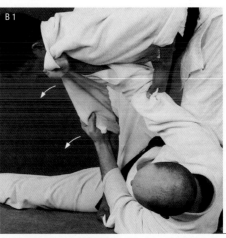

B 1

18. Side Kicks + Wrist Nerve Throws

You are seated with your legs crossed. Two attackers grab your wrists. Form Live-Hands (A). Lead both hands forward to weaken attackers' grips. Circle both your hands backward and under attackers' wrists. Grip their inner wrists in the "V" between your thumb and index finger. Press your index-finger base joints (palm side) into LU-7, by extending your index fingers (B). Throw attacker on right by pulling their wrist forcefully downward toward your left front-corner, as you execute a R Side Kick to their L knee (C–D). Repeat the same throw to attacker on right (E–F). When gripping attacker's wrist, you must be accurate targeting the nerve at LU-7. Otherwise, it will be difficult to unbalance attackers forward.

LU-7

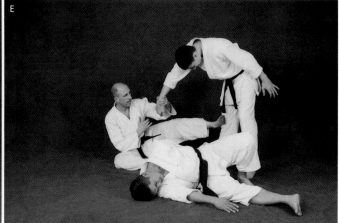

B

A

19. Forearm-to-Leg Throw, Back Fist, Kick

Two attackers grab your wrists. Form Live-Hands (A). Lever both
hands free (B). Throw right-attacker by gripping their L ankle at SP-6
with your L hand, as you press their L knee with your R wrist (C–D).
Keep your head down to avoid a R falling kick. Target back of knee at
BL-53 or BL-54, side of knee at GB-34, or front of knee at ST-35 or
kneecap. Execute a L Back Fist Strike to left-attacker's inner shin at
SP-6 or LV-5 (E). Plant both hands, roll onto your L knee, and deliver a
R Roundhouse Kick to the groin or head (F). Stand up. When gripping
the ankle, press your index-finger base joint (palm side) into SP-6, by
extending your index finger (C1). Opponent will lean or fall backward
to relieve pain. This assists the primary leverage at the knee.

C

C1

SP-6

D

E

Hit SP-6 or LV-5

F

20. Passing Cross Arm Bars (front)

Two attackers grab your wrists. Form Live-Hands. Circle both your hands backward and over attackers' wrists (A). Grip their wrists in the "V" between your thumb and index finger. Press LU-7 with your index-finger base joints. Twist their arms outward, as you raise your R knee (B). Pass under right-attacker's arm and pivot 180° (C). Raise your L knee and plant your R knee, as you cross attackers' straight-arms, forcing them to collide. Twist and lever their arms, locking their elbows against each other (D). Lower your body as you throw attackers in opposite directions (E–F). This technique can also be executed by gripping four fingers on each hand, to twist and lock joints. Locking the fingers allows greater control of your opponents.

Reclining defenses are ground-fighting techniques employed when you are reclining and must engage a standing, kneeling, or reclining opponent. These techniques can be used if you are surprised or attacked while relaxing (for instance, in a park or at the beach), if you have been thrown or forced to the ground, or during the course of ground fighting. The defenses in this chapter are organized based on the relationship between you and your opponent. These situations include: reclining against a standing attacker, reclining

RECLINING DEFENSES

against an attacker kneeling between your legs, reclining against a straddling attacker, and reclining against an attacker entering from the side. In most reclining defenses, the objective is to force a fall (if an opponent is standing), and either execute finishing blows, shift to a restraining hold, or move quickly to a standing posture. Many reclining techniques can also be initiated from kneeling or seated postures. This chapter contains 32 self-defense techniques commonly used in Hapkido, which are also found in other martial arts.

1. Kick Combo + Rise to Standing

Attacker advances from the front. From a Seated Guard, execute an Outside Crescent Kick and Inside Crescent Kick (A–B). The kicks are used to block strikes or grabs. If attacker is close, hit the head with the second kick (B). Turn to your L side, deliver a R Side Kick to the shin, knee, or belly; retract the L leg as the R kicks (C). Plant your hands, turn, and deliver a L Back Kick (D). Push upward with both hands and stand (E).

Important Points

This particular combination of kicks is designed to deter an attack, as you transition to a standing posture. The Crescent Kick combination can also be performed in repetition to provide a shielding effect. The velocity of your Back Kick will help you stand up. Many other kick combinations are possible. The example shown merely illustrates the basic way in which multiple kicks are executed from ground positions.

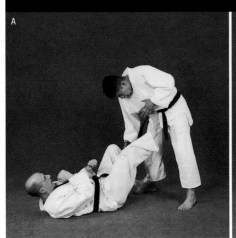

A

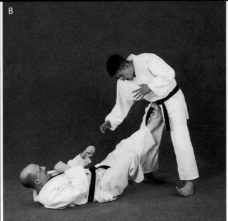

B

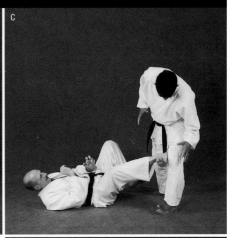

C

2. Kick Combo + Takedown

Attacker advances from the front. From a Seated Guard (L foot lead), execute two Front Blade Kicks to the groin (right first, then left) (A–B). Snap your R heel outward, executing a Circular Inner-Heel Kick to the kneecap or inner knee (C). Hook your R heel inward, executing an Inside Hook Kick to the outer knee (D–E). Hook the ankle with your R leg. Thrust your L Spear Foot into the groin at SP-12 and LV-12, forcing a fall (F–G).

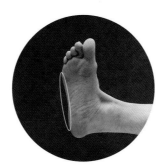

Knife Foot (steps A–B)

D

Important Points

The series of kicks shown are designed to damage attacker's groin and lower legs, as you force them to the ground. The entire combo is executed very quickly. The initial blade kicks can also be executed continuously to provide a shielding effect; the circular motion of your feet resembles *pedaling a bicycle backwards.* Retract one leg as the other kicks, to protect your groin and prepare for the next kick.

Spear Foot

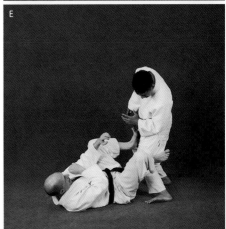

E

G

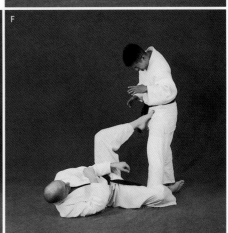

F

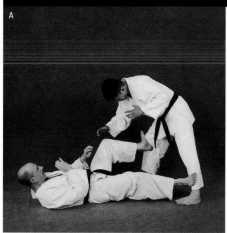

3. Leg-Push Reversal

This counter is used to keep a standing attacker from moving in on top of you. Assume a Seated Guard with your legs facing attacker. As they try to mount you, arrest their movement by blocking their lower legs with the soles of your feet (A). This keeps them at a distance. If attacker attempts to circle to your side, pivot on your buttocks (B), using your hands to generate motion (see *Ground Movement* in *Fundamentals* chapter). At your first opportunity, grab attacker's arms or clothing. Plant the soles of your feet on both ankles (C). Pull attacker's upper body toward you as you recline backward. At the same time, push both of their ankles away by extending your legs (D). You can also push one ankle and one knee, or both knees. As attacker falls forward, roll sideways and redirect them onto their back (E). You can either: 1) roll on top and straddle their chest, as you apply a choke or execute strikes (F); or 2) roll safely away and stand up. In photo F, the L hand applies a Knuckle Choke, as the R hand delivers an elbow strike to the head.

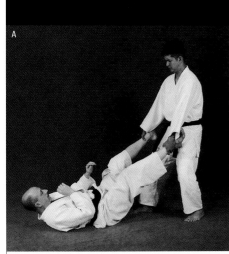

A

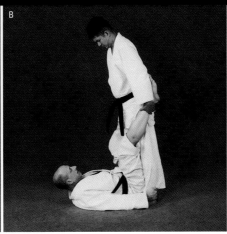

B

C

D (punch groin)

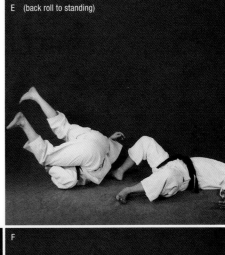

E (back roll to standing)

4. Legs-to-Hip Throw

This counter is used to throw a standing attacker, who has grabbed your ankles and is dragging you or pulling you toward them (A). Bend both your legs, which pulls your hips close to attacker. Grab the back of both ankles, with your fingers and thumbs on the outside (B). Push your lower legs against attacker's hips (your knees push their knees), as you pull their ankles, forcing a Back Fall (C). Sit up and strike the groin (D), then roll backward to a standing posture (E–F).

Important Points

This throw causes a hard fall onto the buttocks, jarring the lower spine. Do not sit up during step B, or you will reduce your throwing leverage. Unbalance attacker straight backward. You can also lock their knees as you throw, by planting the back of your knees on their kneecaps. After throwing, you can either: 1) roll away to safety and stand up (E–F); or 2) continue to move forward, roll up onto your knees, and straddle attacker, applying chokes or strikes.

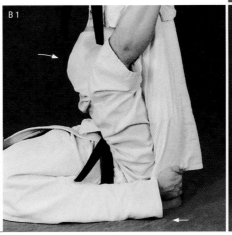

B 1

F

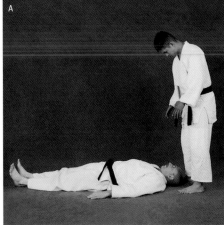

5. Seated Twin Overhead Kick

Attacker is standing to your rear (A). Reach back and grab the back of both ankles, with your fingers on the outside. Swing both of your feet back overhead and kick into attacker's belly, ribs, or throat (B–C). Strike using the balls of the feet (C1), or shoe tips. The force of your kick will cause attacker to fall backward. Swing your legs forward, planting your feet under your buttocks, and rise to a standing posture (D).

Important Points

This technique can be executed from a sitting or reclining posture, or a Seated Guard. Gripping attacker's ankles keeps them from stepping back to regain their balance, as they are knocked back. When kicking, move your feet in unison. Targets include: CO-6 at the belly, both ST-25 pressure points (lateral to navel), both LV-14 and GB-24 pressure points (lower rib cage), both PC-1 and ST-17 pressure points (nipples), or the throat.

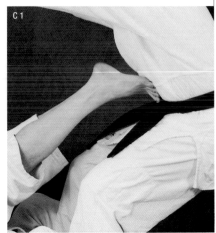

6. Shin-Press Throw

Attacker approaches from your side. Adopt a Seated Guard, as attacker executes a Front Toe Kick to your head or ribs (A). Roll to your side and block their inner shin at SP-6 or LV-5, using your top forearm. At the same time, hook your bottom forearm behind their ankle (B). Clasp your hands together. Press your outer wrist into SP-6 or LV-5, as you twist their leg (C). This causes immediate pain, forcing a Back Fall (D).

Important Points

After clasping your hands, scissor your forearms and use *wrist action* to apply pressure. Attacker will usually fall backward to relieve pain. If attacker does not respond to pain, press their inner knee at SP-9 or SP-10, with your L wrist. The knee is structurally weak in this direction and will usually buckle outward, regardless of whether pain is present. Direct the throw toward the rear-corner of the leg you are holding.

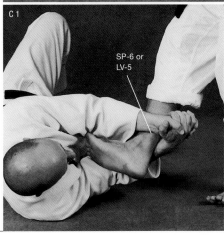

SP-6 or LV-5

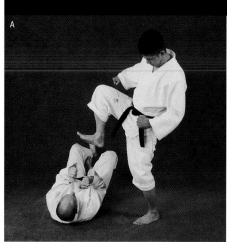

A

B

C

C 1

7. Arm Block + Leg-Twist Throw

You are defending from a Seated Guard, as standing attacker executes a Stamp Kick to your head (A). Block to the sole with both forearms, with fists clenched for strength (B). Grip their foot at the toes and heel (C). Twist the foot as you roll to your right, forcing a fall (D–E). As attacker falls prone, lift your leg and deliver an Axe Kick to their coccyx (tailbone) or lumbar spine (F). If attacker falls to their back, target their groin or kneecap.

Important Points

Blocking a Stamp Kick with your forearms (instead of your hands) provides the greatest strength, and offers the largest area of protection. Keep your forearms parallel and close together. You can also attempt to catch the kick with your hands. This is much more difficult, but provides a quicker throw. However, unless you are quite strong, you may not be able to stop the kick, and your hands will be driven into your face.

D

E

F

8. Leg Block + Leg-Twist Throw

Standing attacker delivers an Axe Kick to your groin or belly (A). Cross your lower legs and block to the ankle (B). Grip their foot with both hands and twist it, as your legs redirect the kick sideways (C). Press your shin into SP-6, LV-5, or LV-6, forcing a Back Fall (D). Wrap the ankle in your armpit, with your wrist on the Achilles tendon, keeping their foot extended. Thrust your heel into the groin (E). Wrap your leg over their knee. Lock the ankle (F).

Important Points

To lock the ankle, recline backward as you lever your wrist up into the Achilles tendon and press your knee downward. Lift your hips to increase stress. Use the sole of your other foot to keep attacker's arm away from your leg. Otherwise, they will try to apply the same hold to you. If this happens, thrust your R heel into their groin (Stamp Kick), or lift your R leg and drop your heel forcefully downward into the solar plexus (Axe Kick).

A

B

C

D (Thumb-Hand Choke)

9. Knee-Belly Reversal

This technique is used to escape from the bottom position. You are reclining in a Leg-Wrap Guard and attacker is kneeling between your legs (A). Grip their arms and/or lapels. Pivot onto your side, plant your knee in their belly, and drop your other leg to the ground (B). Turn attacker over by coordinating four actions: kick your R heel into their lower leg (sweep), extend your L leg, pull their L arm, push their R shoulder (C). Roll sideways, straddle attacker, and choke (D) or strike.

Important Points
The Leg-Wrap Guard (A) is used to restrict attacker's movements. It also prevents them from straddling your chest or circling to your side. This reversal is executed by releasing your leg-wrap, at a moment when attacker is not expecting it. Planting your knee in their belly (B), momentarily prevents them from mounting you, as you execute the reversal. Use your heel to forcefully hit into nerves on the lower leg or knee, sweeping their leg.

10. Twin Sole-Push Reversal

This is used to reverse your position during strikes or chokes, or to prevent a straddle. Attacker is kneeling between your legs (A). Grab their wrists with both hands. Plant your soles on both of their knees (B). Push your body away by extending your legs. Pull their arms at the same time, forcing them to lie flat (C). Their balance is now vulnerable. Roll sideways and flip them over (D). Straddle and pin one wrist over the other. Execute elbow strikes to their face if justified (E–F).

Important Points

Gripping attacker's wrists prevents them from using their hands to maintain their position or counter your reversal. Do not plant your soles on the upper-thigh or hip, or you will be unable to extend attacker's legs. When you extend your legs, you will either push your body away from theirs, or push their legs away (based on the relative weights of your bodies). Regardless, the result is the same: attacker is lying flat, vulnerable to a reversal.

A

B

C

11. Reclining Leg Arm Bar

Attacker applies a front choke with both hands, while kneeling between your legs (A). If their arms are straight, break their elbow by hitting it with your forearm (B). Otherwise, grab their R wrist with both hands, pull their arm straight, and turn onto your side as you slide your hips to your left (C). Wrap your L leg over attacker's arm, planting the front of your ankle against their throat. Lock their elbow by pressing your thigh against the joint, as you pull their wrist in the opposite direction (D). If desired, shift to a side position by rolling laterally as you apply the lock (E).

Important Points

Your initial strike to the elbow uses a twisting delivery, which is the same motion used for an Inside Block. Shifting your hips to your left (C) is necessary, otherwise you may not be able to wrap your leg over attacker's arm. Techniques 11 and 12 are closely related: one technique often leads into the other, depending on an attacker's reactions.

D

E   (option: transition to side position)

12. Reclining Arm Bar

Attacker applies a front choke with both hands, while kneeling between your legs (A). Turn onto your side and slide your hips to your left. Wrap your L leg over their arm (B), planting your lower leg against their head or throat (C). Grab their R wrist with both hands and push their head to your left, forcing them onto their back (D). Lock the elbow: pull the wrist down, press your inner thigh up against the elbow, and lift your buttocks (arch). Pin the head with your L leg (E).

Important Points

This hold begins like previous counter, except you will turn attacker in the opposite direction. Transitions between these two holds are common when trying to overcome resistance. When applying the arm bar, pull attacker's arm to keep your buttocks pressed against their shoulder. Squeeze your knees together to prevent them from rolling up between your legs. If you turn their hand so their thumb faces up, they may be weaker.

13. Seated Bent-Arm Lock

This hold is often used with the previous technique, a Reclining Arm Bar (A–B). If opponent bends their arm to prevent the arm bar, trap your R wrist inside their elbow as you push it closed (C). Press downward on their wrist as you twist your R arm, driving your protruding wrist bone into their biceps tendon (D, D1). This is very painful. Make sure their arm is completely bent before twisting your wrist. You can also use a wrist lock to assist the hold (D2).

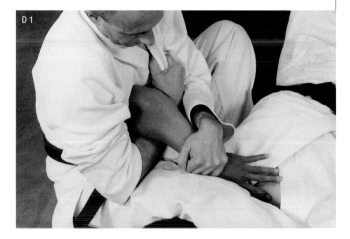

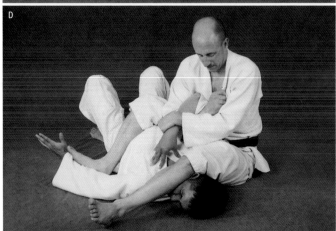

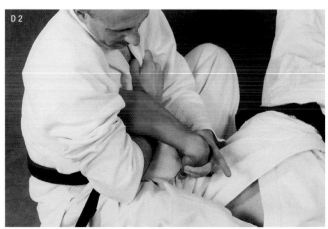

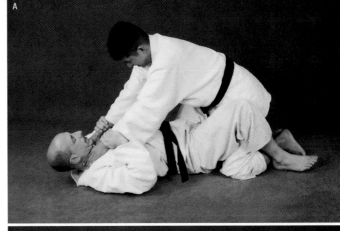

14. Reclining Knee Arm Bar

Attacker applies a front choke with both hands, while kneeling between your legs (A). Bring your L arm up between their arms, and break their choke by wrapping and trapping their wrist in your L armpit. At the same time, plant your R sole on their L thigh or groin and push, as you turn your hips and unbalance attacker forward (B–C). Plant your L foot on their ribs, and your L inner knee against their elbow. Lock the elbow by pressing your inner knee downward, as you lift the wrist (D).

Important Points
The success of this hold (D) depends on coordinating three basic actions: 1) pushing against opponent's R side with your L foot (into nerves along the ribs); 2) breaking their balance forward; and 3) pressing your knee downward to lock the elbow. Use your soles to control attacker's body movement, as you maintain the arm bar. There are many variations in how you use your legs and arms. You can also trap their elbow by squeezing your bent-knees together.

A

B

C

C 1   (option: Double Sleeve Choke)

15. Chop + Front Interlock Choke

Attacker applies a front choke with both hands, while kneeling between your legs. Drop your chin to protect your throat. Raise your L hand (A). Hit downward into their inner elbow with your L forearm (B). This lowers attacker's head, reduces their leverage, and makes it difficult for them to punch. Wrap your R arm around their neck and pull it toward you. Lock your R hand in the crook of your L elbow. Press your L wrist into their throat (C). Sleeve Chokes also work well (C1), and are described in greater detail in the *Chokes + Head Locks* chapter.

Important Points

The Front Interlock Choke is very powerful. However, sometimes your arms are not long enough to permit you to grip your elbow or position your wrist. Make sure you are placing your R elbow near the back of attacker's neck, since this increases your reach. If your arms are too short to apply this choke, the Double Sleeve Choke and Single Sleeve Choke are both excellent alternatives. You can also wrap their neck with your R arm and pull it toward you as you apply a Spear Hand Choke to CO-22, or a Knuckle Choke to ST-9 or ST-10 (see *Chokes + Head Locks* chapter).

16. Legs-to-Hip Throw

This technique is used to throw an attacker as they stand up. They will often do this to: escape from your leg-wrap (A); lift and slam your upper body; or move higher so they can punch downward. As attacker tries to stand, grab the backs of both ankles, with your fingers and thumbs on the outside (B). Release your leg-wrap by uncrossing your ankles. Push your lower legs against attacker's hips and thighs, as you pull their ankles, forcing a fall backward (C). Roll up as attacker falls (D). Straddle their torso and execute strikes or apply a choke (E).

Important Points

When releasing your leg-wrap (B), be ready to reapply it at anytime, should attacker return to their knees or drop to punch you. Do not sit up during step B: this reduces throwing leverage and places your head in punching range. The throw causes a hard fall onto the buttocks, jarring the lower spine. You can also lock attacker's knees as you throw, by planting the back of your knees on their kneecaps. After throwing, you can either roll away to safety and stand up (see technique 4); or continue to move forward, roll up onto your knees, and straddle attacker (D–E).

E   (Knuckle Choke)

149

17. Outside-Lift Shoulder Lock

Attacker straddles your torso and executes a R Straight Punch. Parry with your L hand, and grab their wrist with your R hand. Grip their elbow with your L hand and press nerves at LU-5 and HT-3 (A). Circle their hand from right to left, bending their elbow. Attacker's elbow remains fairly stationary and acts as the center of the circular motion. As their wrist and shoulder lock, grip your own wrist (B). Their wrist is now bent fully forward. Lock their wrist and shoulder by pushing down and twisting their wrist, as you lift their elbow with your L wrist (B1). Roll sideways and drive your elbow into their head to assist your throw (C). Roll up to your knees. Pin by maintaining the wrist and shoulder lock, as you press your elbow into their throat (choke) (D). Try to target ST-9 or ST-10 (carotid artery). D1 shows an alternate pin: press the elbow down, trapping the hand under the shoulder. Strike with your free hand. Techniques 17–19 use joint locks based on standing holds. However, since your body movement is restricted, grips have been modified for greater efficiency. Standing grips usually do not allow for sufficient leverage.

18. Poke + Bent-Arm Wrist Lock

Attacker straddles your torso and applies a choke with both hands. Press CO-22 with your fingertips, as you grab their cross-wrist with your other hand (A). As the choke releases, twist their hand inward. Hit their inner elbow with a L Ridge Hand, bending their wrist and elbow (B). Grip their fingers with your L hand. Lock their wrist by rotating their hand toward their body midline. Force a fall sideways (C–D). Maintain the wrist lock as you execute an Axe Kick to the groin or testicles (E).

B

A

C

19. Poke + Outward Wrist Lock

Attacker straddles your torso and applies a choke with both hands. Press CO-22 with your fingertips, as you grab attacker's opposite wrist with your L hand (A). Twist their hand outward to lock their wrist (your thumb presses TW-3, your fingers pull the edge of their palm). Grip attacker's fingers with your R hand (thumb down) and twist to assist the wrist lock. Roll sideways and arch as attacker falls sideways (C). Apply a Tiger Mouth Choke, clamping their windpipe and gouging your fingers into the carotid arteries on both sides. Pull back on attacker's wrist, locking their elbow on your knee (D).

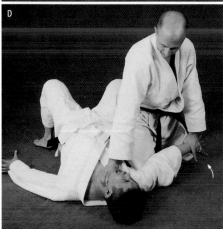

C

Important Points

This technique illustrates how joint locks used from standing positions are made more efficient by locking the fingers and modifying grips. These type of adjustments are mandatory, since your ability to use your body or footwork is limited. Exercise extreme caution when clamping the throat. You can easily produce life-threatening injuries that require immediate medical attention.

D

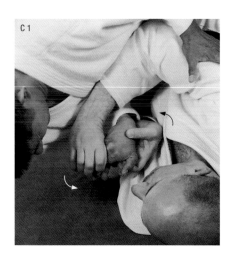

B 1

Twist Fingers

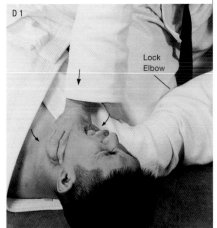

C 1

D 1

Lock Elbow

(hit M-HN-9)

20. Strikes + Twisting Neck Lock

Attacker straddles your torso and chokes you with their wrists crossed. Execute a Twin Hook Punch to the temples at M-HN-9 or TW-23, or the ribs at SP-21 (A). Raise both arms (B). Strike downward to attacker's inner elbows with both of your wrists. This lowers attacker's head and loosens the choke (B). Grab the rear-corner of their skull with your R hand, plant your L palm on their chin. Trap attacker's L ankle with your R foot. Twist their head and lift your hips (D), throwing attacker sideways or toward their left front-corner (E).

Important Points

If an attacker has the proper technique, you can be choked unconscious very quickly, which is why this technique begins with devastating pressure point strikes. Since you will hit the same pressure point on both sides of attacker's body, the effect is magnified. Since attacker's hands are occupied, it is unlikely your strikes will be blocked. Exercise caution and common sense when twisting the neck. Fractured cervical vertebrae can easily result in permanent disabilities or death.

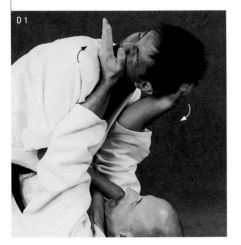

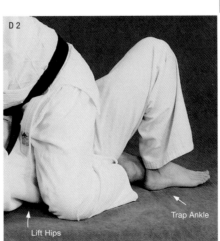

Lift Hips

Trap Ankle

21. Wedge, Wrap, Bridge Throw

Attacker straddles your torso and applies a choke with both hands. Hit both sides of the throat at ST-9 and ST-10, with a Twin Spear Hand Strike (A). Wedge your forearms outward (B). Wrap your arms around attacker's arms, trapping both wrists in your armpits. This breaks the choke. At the same time, trap their ankles with your feet (C). Pull their arms, lift your hips, and roll laterally (D), throwing them toward their front-corner (E).

Important Points

When you try to throw an opponent by lifting your hips (called bridging), they will try to maintain their balance by bracing with their arms or legs. Therefore, to force an attacker to dismount, you must trap their arm and/or leg on the side you will unbalance them toward. In this particular technique, you will trap both arms and legs. Consequently, you can throw to either side. If you meet resistance one way, redirect the throw to the other side. If attacker plants their hands flat on the ground during step C, their fingers will bend backward and lock as you throw.

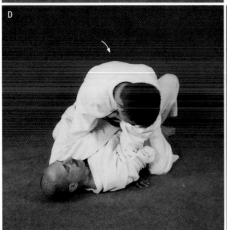

22. Ankle-Lift Bridge Throw

Attacker straddles your torso, kneels on your upper arms, and applies a choke with both hands (A). Grab both of their ankles, placing your thumbs inside and fingers outside (B). You may need to first push your elbows outward, so your hands can reach attacker's ankles. Lift your hips, as you push their ankles over your head (C). Attacker will fall toward their front or either front-corner (D). You can also roll sideways and throw.

Important Points

It is usually fairly easy to unbalance an opponent in this position, since their hips are so far forward on your body. Because there is no weight on your hips, it is usually easy for you to lift them. When throwing, lift and bridge at the same time, before attacker can plant their arms forward or shift their hips backward, to prevent your throw. If your opponent is inexperienced, they will usually slam their head or shoulder into the ground, as you throw them over your head. A more experienced opponent will execute a shoulder roll to prevent injury (D).

A

B 1

TW-17

23. Thumb Choke + Throw

You are prone. Attacker straddles your back and applies a Rear Interlock Choke (A). Drop your chin and hunch your shoulders, to fight the choke. Reach back with both hands. Wrap your fingers around the back of their neck and gouge both thumbs into nerves. Targets include ST-9, ST-10, SI-17, and TW-17 (B). Pull laterally forward, leading attacker off your body (C). Rise to your knees (D). Kneel on their neck and pin them with a choke (E).

Important Points

This is one of the worst positions you can find yourself in. However, there is a small ray of hope. If you can target vital pressure points, you may be able to release the choke or injure attacker, before you pass out. Make your first opportunity count, since they will be on guard against later attempts. If you can rise to your knees, this will assist your throw. However, this is usually difficult. You can also try to bite attacker's arm, or puncture their eardrums by slapping them with your palms.

B

C

D

E

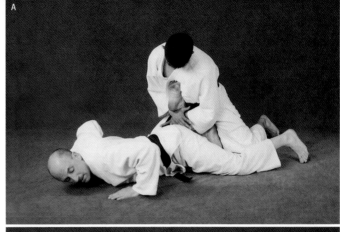

24. Kick-Out + Side Roll

Attacker applies a Bent-Leg Lock (A). Try to forcefully extend your leg, before the hold is tight. If your leg is fully bent, plant your hands under your shoulders and push your body forward, to create slack in the hold. Plant your free L foot on their thigh (B). Twist your R foot so the ankle is bent with the instep on their hip joint. Forcefully extend both legs, throwing attacker backward (C). Roll sideways and hit the groin with an Axe Kick (D), or stand up.

Important Points

The key factor when applying any Bent-Leg Lock is to reduce leg-strength by keeping the foot extended. Many people, including experienced martial artists, are unaware of this. They tend to focus on controlling the ankle or lower leg, instead of the instep. This vulnerability is the basis for your counter. If you can *bend your ankle,* turning the toes outward, you will likely possess enough leg strength to kick-out of the hold. Rolling to your side can also help unbalance your opponent.

A

B

25. Underhand Forearm Arm Bar

Attacker kneels at your side and applies a choke with both arms straight (A). Grab their R wrist with your L hand. Roll to your left and place your R wrist behind their R elbow at TW-11 (B). Reverse direction and roll to your right. Lock their elbow by pulling your wrist into TW-17, as you push their wrist upward. This forces attacker to fall forward. Maintain your hold, pinning them face down (C). If they bend their arm during step B, use a similar motion to lock the shoulder. As you pull their bent-elbow, their fingers will lock backward against your chest (C2).

C

C 1

C 2   (If they bend arm, shift to Scoop Palm Lock)

26. Front Shoulder Lock (trap)

Attacker kneels at your side and applies a
choke with both arms bent. Grab their L wrist
with your R hand. Raise your L arm (A). Strike
down into their inner elbow with your L wrist.
This lowers their head, bends their arms, and
loosens the choke. Pass your L arm under
their L arm, trapping their R wrist in your
armpit (B). Grip their L hand with both hands
and bend it forward, locking the wrist. Twist
and pull their hand to your right, locking the
shoulder (C). Roll right, throwing attacker over
your body (D). Maintain the hold and pin (E).
Their R wrist remains trapped in your armpit.

A

B

C

27. Turnover Arm Bar

Attacker kneels at your side (leaning forward) and attempts to wrap your neck or execute a punch (A). Parry and grab their wrist with your L hand. Lift your R elbow into their elbow (B). Drive your elbow over your head, as you pull back on attacker's wrist, raise your hips (bridge), and flip over (C). These actions lock attacker's elbow and force them to fall forward. Pin attacker by pressing your R wrist downward into the triceps tendon at TW-11 to lock their elbow, as you hold their wrist down with your L hand (D). If attacker bends their arm, transition to a hammer lock (E): lock their shoulder by lifting their locked-wrist toward their head, as you drive their elbow inward. This hold is further described in the *Pinning Holds* chapter.

D (arm bar)

E (If they bend arm, shift to hammer lock)

A (opposite view)

B

28. Leg Scissor Choke

Attacker sits at your side and applies a Scarf Hold (see *Pinning Holds* chapter): their L arm wraps around your neck and their R hand grips your arm (A). Reach up with your free hand and push attacker's chin or head backward. If necessary, gouge your fingers into their eyes or pressure points on their face (ST-2, ST-3, ST-4, GV-26), or press the blade of your hand upward into the underside of their nose (B). Roll backward onto your shoulders, lift your R leg, and wrap their head or neck (C). Cross your ankles, forcefully squeeze your legs together, and apply a choke (D). Pull attacker's head backward toward the ground and apply an arm bar, locking their elbow against your chest. Continue to tighten your leg choke (E).

C

D

E

A

B

C

D

29. Nerve Press, Elbow-to-Groin

Attacker applies a Reclining Arm Bar (see *Pinning Holds* chapter), and pins your head with their leg. Free your head by gripping their ankle and pressing your thumb into SP-6 (A). You can also pinch their thigh. Push their ankle above your head (B). Roll toward attacker. Grab your R hand with your L hand and forcefully bend your elbow to prevent it from being locked. Drive your elbow downward into their groin (C). Pull your elbow toward your hip, freeing your hand. Wrap your R arm under attacker's L knee and flip them over (D). Straddle them and apply a Rear Choke, catching their instep with your inner thigh as you enter. Pin attacker's L leg by pressing your inner thigh downward against their instep (E).

Important Points

You must begin your counter as early as possible, before the Reclining arm Bar is tight and your arm is broken. Pressing nerves, pinching the legs, or biting can all be used to loosen the hold. Turning your elbow can also help to negate the arm bar.

E (Rear Naked Choke + Bent-Leg Lock)

30. Roundhouse Kick + Hook Kick

Attacker applies a Reclining Arm Bar (A).
Roll onto your R side, sliding your hips toward
attacker's right side. Grab your R hand with
your L hand and forcefully bend your elbow
to prevent it from being locked or broken. At
the same time, execute a L Roundhouse Kick
to the temple or jaw, using the ball of your
foot or the tip of your shoe (B). Swing your
foot past attacker's head (C). Execute a Hook
Kick to the other side, by swinging your heel
forcefully into the side of the head, ideally
targeting the temple (D).

Important Points

A hallmark of Hapkido is its use of kicks from
any position, including the ground. In ground
fighting, very few grapplers will be expecting
this type of counter to a Reclining Arm Bar.
If your kicks connect solidly, you can easily
knock them out. At the very least, you will
loosen or release the arm bar, permitting an
escape. The initial position of your hip is very
important, since this affects the distance and
power of your kick. These kicks can also be
repeated as needed.

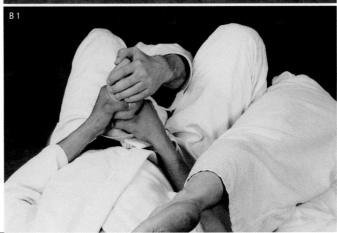

31. Roll + Leg Scissor Choke

Attacker applies an arm bar by pinning your wrist and kneeling on your elbow (see *Knee Arm Bar Pin* in *Pinning Holds* chapter). Bring your knees under your body and raise your hips (A). Execute a Forward Roll to escape (B). As you roll to your back, trap attacker's neck between your lower legs. Cross your ankles, fully bend your R foot, and press your knees together to apply a Leg Scissor Choke (C). Roll sideways and pull attacker to the ground (D). This is a very powerful choke that forces the inner edge of both tibia bones against the carotid arteries at both sides of the neck. Exercise caution: the force of this choke can tear the sternocleidomastoid muscle where it attaches to the skull (near the base of the ear).

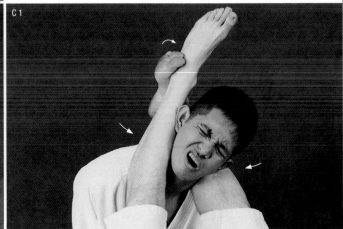

32. Leg Scissor Choke Throw

Attacker kneels above your head and applies a choke with both hands (A). Drop your chin, hunch your shoulders, and grab both of their wrists, to fight the choke (A). Roll backward onto your upper back. Lift both of your legs and swing them backward toward attacker's head. Trap their neck between both of your lower legs. Immediately cross your ankles and press your knees together to apply a Leg Scissor Choke (B). Pull your legs forward, throwing attacker to their front or front-corner (D). You can also throw by rolling sideways, which is often easier. This choke is the same as the choke in the previous technique, except you are applying it from a different position, with your legs reversed.

The kneeling defenses in this chapter consist of ground-fighting techniques employed against a reclining attacker when you are kneeling in one of several positions. These techniques are typically used during the course of ground fighting, or immediately after you have thrown an opponent. It is important to recognize that just because your opponent is in the bottom position on their back, does not mean that you are safe or in a superior, controlling position. You can very easily be choked or punched unconscious by an experienced

KNEELING DEFENSES

grappler, even if you are in a straddle position. In most kneeling defenses, your objective is to force submission by employing joint locks or chokes, or if needed, strikes. This chapter contains 6 typical self-defense techniques used in Hapkido, which are also found in many other martial arts. These techniques are shown being applied from common positions you might find yourself in, including kneeling between an opponent's intertwined legs (Leg-Wrap Guard), kneeling at an opponent's side, or straddling an opponent's torso.

A

B

C

1. Entangled Front Shoulder Lock

Reclining opponent applies a choke with both hands. You are kneeling. Drop your chin and pull their arms downward to relieve pressure (A). Grab their L wrist with your L hand. Strike their L inner elbow at LU-5 or PC-3 with your R wrist. Pull their wrist and elbow in opposing directions, bending their arm (B). Drop your body across their torso, as you grasp your own wrist (C). Pull their fully-bent arm in *tight to their ribs.* Lock the shoulder by lifting their elbow, as you pull their wrist downward and inward by bending both your wrists (D). Their R hand is trapped under your chest.

Important Points

Make sure opponent's elbow is fully bent and pressed against the side of their body. Otherwise, the hold is far less efficient and may not work at all. When locking the shoulder (D), coordinate three actions: pull opponent's wrist downward and inward with your L hand; pull your L wrist with your R hand; and lift your R elbow. Bending your wrists (wrist-action) is crucial for increasing your range of motion when applying the hold.

D

D 1

2. Entangled Rear Shoulder Lock

Reclining opponent applies a choke with both hands. You are kneeling on your R knee (A). If needed, drop your L knee into their throat to release the choke (not shown). Grab their L wrist with your R hand. Grip their L elbow at HT-3 or PC-3 with your L hand. Pull in opposing directions, forcing their arm to bend (B). Drop your body across their torso (C). Push their bent-arm down and grasp your own wrist for support. Lock the shoulder: lift their elbow, as you pull their wrist downward and inward by bending both your wrists (D). Their R hand is trapped between both bodies.

Important Points

When compared to the previous technique, this hold rotates the arm and locks the shoulder in the opposite direction, similar to a hammer lock. When locking the shoulder (D), coordinate three actions: pull opponent's wrist downward and inward with your R hand; pull your R wrist with your L hand; and lift your L elbow. Bending your wrists (wrist-action) is crucial for increasing your range of motion when applying the hold.

B

A

C

Spear Hand

D

3. Knee Press, Spine Lock, Choke

Opponent traps you in a Leg-Wrap Guard (legs wrapped around your waist, ankles crossed), and applies a choke with both hands (A). Press your L fingertips (Spear Hand) into their throat at CO-22. At the same time, drive your R elbow outward into SP-10, just above the inner knee (B). The Spear Hand will release the choke; the elbow-gouge will loosen or release their leg-wrap. As opponent's legs release, wrap your R arm under their knee. Lift their leg across your body and turn them over (C). As you lift their leg, be ready to drop your head to avoid being caught in a Leg Interlock Choke (see *Chokes + Head Locks* chapter). Grab opponent's ankle (D) and pull it toward you, as you roll sideways onto their back. Allow their foot to slip down into your inner elbow (keep their foot extended). Strike the spine with your L elbow, wrap your L arm around the throat. Pull your hands toward each other, which will apply a choke, lock their bent-leg, and stress their spine (E).

E

B 1
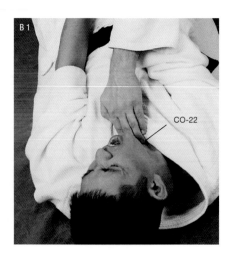
CO-22

B 2   (press SP-10)

A

B

4. Knee Press, Leg Lock, Rear Choke

Steps A–B are the same as the previous technique: Opponent traps you in a Leg-Wrap Guard (legs wrapped around your waist, ankles crossed), and applies a choke with both hands (A). Press your L fingertips (Spear Hand) into their throat at CO-22. At the same time, drive your R elbow outward into SP-10, just above the inner knee (B). As attacker's legs release, wrap your R arm under their L knee and lift it across your body (C). Grab their L instep with your L hand. Turn them over by sweeping their knee to the ground, as you twist and bend their L leg behind them. Straddle them and apply a Rear Naked Choke, catching their instep with your inner thigh as you enter. Pin their leg by pressing your inner thigh downward against their instep (E). If opponent tries to stay on their back during C, straddle their torso and apply a Knuckle Choke with one hand as you deliver a Descending Elbow Strike with the other hand (D1).

C

D   (Rear Naked Choke + Bent-Leg Lock)

D 1

A

B

(see B1 and B2, under technique 3

5. Twin Knee Press + Crab Lock

Opponent traps you in a Leg-Wrap Guard (legs wrapped around your waist, ankles crossed), and applies a choke with both hands (A). Press your L Spear Hand into the throat at CO-22. At the same time, drive your R elbow outward into SP-10, just above the L inner knee (B). The Spear Hand will release the choke; the elbow-gouge will loosen or release their leg-wrap. Gouge the R inner knee at SP-10 with your L elbow, as you wrap your R arm around the L knee (C). Rise to one knee and pivot left, as you lift attacker's leg and turn them over. As you lift the leg, allow your wrist to slip out to the ankle (D). Wrap the ankle in your armpit, with your wrist pressing up against the Achilles tendon. Keep attacker's foot extended to prevent counters. Step across and sit on attacker's lower back. Lean backward to stress their ankle, leg, and spine (E). The ankle lock is very effective, as long as attacker's foot remains fully extended. This reduces their leg strength and increases the level of pain at the Achilles tendon.

C

D

D1.

6. Chest Press + Reclining Arm Bar

You are straddling an opponent who is choking you with both hands. Plant both of your palms at the center of their chest and transfer all your weight to your hands. This compresses attacker's chest cavity and loosens the choke. At the same time, raise your L knee and bring your L foot forward (A). Using your hands for support, pivot your body 90° and swing your L leg over their head. Grab attacker's wrist and pull their arm straight as you sit backward (B). Lock opponent's elbow by pulling their wrist downward, as you press your R thigh into their elbow and lift your hips. To discourage counters: push your L thigh forcefully downward into the right side of opponent's head to keep it pinned; use your R foot to block their L arm; and keep their thumb pointing upward to reduce their biceps strength (C). These actions usually keep your opponent from turning toward you to relieve pressure on their elbow, or from grabbing their own R hand with their L hand to prevent the arm bar from being applied.

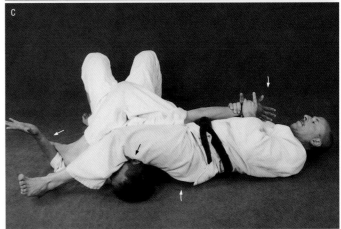

Sacrifice techniques are strikes, holds, or throws in which you will drop to the ground during the technique. Dropping your body is done for different purposes, such as to avoid an attack, initiate an escape or counter, power a throw by using the force of your falling body, or negate an opponent's leverage or mobility by forcing them to a ground position. Although these arts are commonly referred to as "sacrifice" techniques, this term is somewhat of a misnomer. "Sacrifice" implies that you are giving something up or assuming

SACRIFICE TECHNIQUES

greater risk in order to gain something, leading some martial artists to believe these skills should be reserved for desperate situations. In reality, many of these techniques require strong, purposeful actions. Just like any other technique, they are safe and highly effective when executed in appropriate circumstances, and pose greater risk when executed at the wrong time. There are many different types of sacrifice techniques, 29 of which are shown in this chapter in typical self-defense situations. Numerous other possibilities exist.

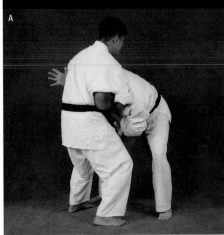

A

B

C

Spear Hand – 2 Fingers

1. Lift-Slam Throw

This throw is often used during close-range grappling, or to counter a Front Naked Choke (A). Relieve pressure by wedging your R Live-Hand forearm between attacker's elbow and armpit, as you pull downward on their wrist with your L hand (A). Hit the testicles as you reach between the legs and grip the buttock (B). Step to the side and pull attacker's hips to your chest to unbalance them. Lift and slam them to the ground (C). The impact of their fall often releases the choke. If not, straddle their waist to prevent movement. Thrust your Spear Hand into the base of the throat at CO-22 (D), angling your fingers behind the suprasternal notch to avoid crushing the windpipe (life threatening). You can also gouge the eyes with your fingertips and/or punch the ribs. Continue striking until the choke releases or you can pull your head free. As you escape, pin attacker's R arm with your L hand. Press their chin sideways to lock their neck, pin their head, and cut off their vision (E). Keep your head low as you withdraw, to guard against a possible left Hook Punch.

D

E

D 1

CO-22

A

B

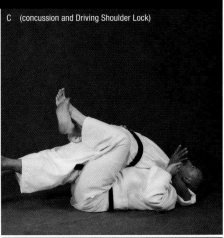

C   (concussion and Driving Shoulder Lock)

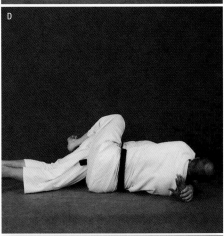

D

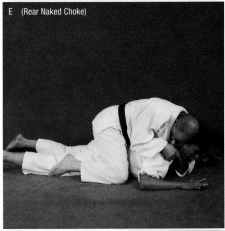

E   (Rear Naked Choke)

2. Concussion + Shoulder Lock

Attacker applies a Front Naked Choke. Relieve pressure by wedging your R forearm between their elbow and armpit, as you pull their wrist down with your L hand (A). Step close, lower your hips, lift your head, and sit backward (B). Attacker will usually release one hand to prevent a concussion when falling. Wrap their waist with your legs. Lock or separate their shoulder by pushing their hips away from you as you lift their wrist and arch your head back (C). In one continuous motion, shift your hips to your left, so you are no longer under attacker (D). Roll on top, apply a Rear Naked Choke (E).

Important Points

Often the only way to break this choke is to go to the ground. This radically alters attacker's use of body weight and leverage, providing the opportunity to counter, as shown in this technique. If the attacker has a secure hold, and you drop back quickly and forcefully, you will likely cause a concussion as their head slams into the ground. At the very least, it will loosen their choke hold.

A 1

C 1

E 1

A

B

C

D

Knife Foot

3. Blade-to-Leg Throw

Attacker grips your wrist and hand, and applies a Bent-Arm Wrist Lock (A). Step toward attacker and drop to your side (B). This blending movement gets you ahead of the wrist lock, relieving pressure. Hook your L instep against attacker's heel. Drive your R Knife Foot into their inner shin at SP-6 or LV-5, or into their inner knee at SP-9 (C). Attacker's leg will buckle as they fall backward to relieve pain (D). Twist and pull your hand free as they fall.

Important Points

This technique is often used if a Bent-Arm Wrist Lock is fully applied. As you drop, pull your hand toward your body. This unbalances attacker and reduces their leverage. You must be accurate when pressing their shin. If you don't hit a nerve, the throw won't work. Pressing the inner-knee outward is more certain, since the knee is weak in this direction. As attacker falls backward, execute a Back Shoulder Roll away from them to return to a standing posture.

A 1 (use free-hand to prevent lock)

C 1

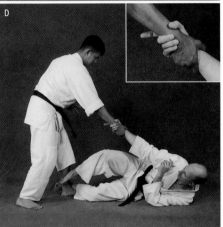

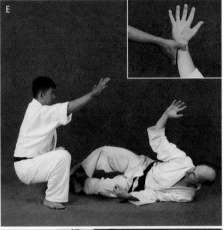

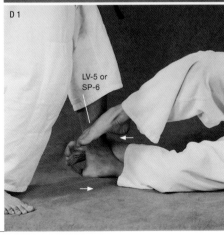

4. Shoulder Roll + Blade-to-Leg Throw

Attacker locks your elbow by pressing down with their L wrist, as they pull up on your wrist (A). Execute a Forward Shoulder Roll. This rotates your arm, completely negating the arm bar (B). As you exit your roll, grab their wrist and pull toward you. This helps you to pivot your body to face attacker (C). Hook your L instep behind their heel, and drive your R Knife Foot into their inner shin at SP-6 or LV-5 (D). Release your wrist hold as attacker falls backward to relieve pain (E).

Important Points

The efficiency of your ground-pivot depends on pulling your wrist toward you. If attacker holds onto your wrist, this helps. If they release your wrist during the roll, simply continue to a standing posture. You must be accurate when pressing their shin. If you don't hit a nerve, the throw won't work. Briefly hold their wrist as you press their shin, allowing pain to build. Then quickly release your grip, as they fall backward. Lever your hand free using a basic wrist escape.

LV-5 or SP-6

5. Drop Inside Shoulder Throw

Attacker applies a Rear Naked Choke from behind (A). Drop your chin to protect your throat. Reduce pressure by pulling attacker's arm downward with both hands, as you step back with your R foot, past their leg (B).
Pull their arm down as you drop to one knee, blocking their foot with your inner knee (C). This keeps attacker from stepping around to counter. Bend deeply forward, pulling them over your shoulder (D–E).

Important Points

Although standing throws are an option, this throw is most powerful when dropping. This allows you to use your entire body weight to assist. Make sure you trap their leg as you drop, planting your buttocks on the lower leg. Your bodies should be locked tight together as you throw; most problems result from excess space. Drive your head toward your L leg (E). If a strong attacker prevents you from bending forward, shift your body to their right side and redirect the throw in that direction.

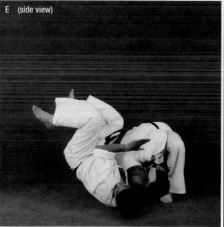

6. Drop Outside Shoulder Throw

Attacker grabs your belt, palm down (A). Grip their hand with both hands, trapping it in your belt. Cross-step forward with your R foot (B). Step across with your L foot. Pivot 180° as you lock and lift their elbow with your upper arm (C). Drop to one knee, planting your L foot deep between attacker's legs. Plant your shoulder in the armpit. Lock their elbow on your chest or shoulder (D). Bend forward and throw attacker over your shoulder (E).

Important Points

Grip attacker's hand, not the forearm (B). This prevents them from untwisting their arm as you pivot. If you can keep their hand trapped in your belt, this will assist the arm-twist as you pivot, particularly if your grips are poor. Lock attacker's elbow as you enter to hinder counters (C). Adjust your shoulder plant based on the relative sizes of your bodies. Against a much larger attacker, you can often execute this throw from a standing posture. Otherwise, dropping to one knee is necessary, in order to get your shoulder under their arm. This is a devastating throw. If an opponent cannot initiate their own fall, their elbow and shoulder will be severely damaged.

7. Neck Hip Throw

Attacker grabs clothing at your side (A). Step forward with your R foot, cross your wrists, and thrust them into both sides of the throat at ST-9, ST-10, and/or LI-18 (B–C). Grip behind the neck with both hands, plant your R foot deep between attacker's legs, and pivot 180°. Pull their head to your shoulder and plant your hips low in the center of their hips (D). Pull their head forward and downward, drop to your R knee, and bend forcefully forward, throwing attacker over your hips (E).

C 1 (alternate entry: pull hair, hit, wrap head)

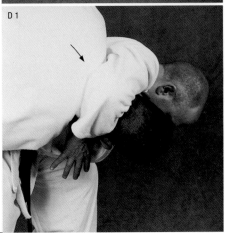

8. Drop Head Hip Throw

Attacker twists your arm behind your back, applying a Hammer Lock (A). Your wrist and shoulder are locked. Before the hold is tight: step backward with your R foot, turn toward attacker, and swing your free arm past their head (B). Wrap attacker's neck with your arm (C). Pull their head downward as you drop to one knee, blocking their foot with your inner knee (D). This keeps them from stepping around to counter. Bend deeply forward, pulling attacker over your hip (E).

Important Points

You must start before the Hammer Lock is tight. Otherwise, attacker can easily prevent you from turning. As you reach back to wrap their neck, you can also hit their head with an Outside Elbow Strike. Don't hit too hard or you will knock their head out of reach. As you execute your throw, attacker will usually release their arm hold. If they don't let go, or you feel your shoulder being locked, flip over and land on top of them as they fall.

Palm Heel Hand

9. Palm Heel + Rear Push Throw

Attacker applies an Armpit Arm Bar and steps in front to prevent escape (A). Strike sideways into their kneecap with your Palm Heel Hand, buckling their knee inward. Raise your upper body and thrust your arm backward into their chest (B). Sit backward, forcing a fall (C). Roll sideways on top of attacker and straddle their chest. Lock their neck and pin their head by pressing their chin sideways and downward with your palm. Strike with your free hand if necessary (D).

Important Points

Your initial strike will dislocate the kneecap, unbalance attacker, and provide a brief distraction to set up your throw. You can also remain standing during your throw: use your R knee to block their knee, and push backward into their chest with your elbow. Generally, standing throws only work if the arm bar is loose or sloppy, whereas sitting backward allows you to use your entire body weight to assist, even if the arm bar is tight.

D (side view)

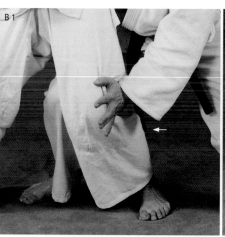

B 1

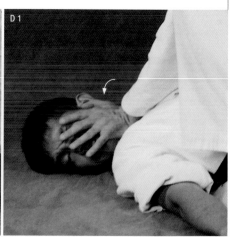

D 1

10. Gouge Eyes, Wrapping Throw

Attacker executes a Full Nelson Lock. If applied forcefully, it will break your neck (A). Reach backward with both hands (B) and gouge your thumbs into both eyes, as you raise one leg (C). Your fingers grip the sides or back of the head. As the hold loosens, drop your leg, bend forcefully forward, and pull your elbows to your hips, breaking the hold and trapping attacker's arms in your armpits. (D). Drop and turn, falling on top of them (E). Attacker's shoulder will usually be damaged.

Important Points

Pain releases the hold. You can also press the cheek at ST-2 or ST-3, or pull the hair or ears. If the head lock can't be broken, throw your own body in unison with attacker's, to prevent neck damage (D–E). As you drop and roll, lead their head or shoulder into the ground. Land on top of them to increase impact. You can also remain standing and throw over your hip, but only if attacker's grips are broken, or you may break your own neck.

11. Wrapping Throw

Step inside a straight or inside circular strike. Block outward with your L hand and grip attacker's wrist, as you deliver a R Inside Elbow Strike to the jaw at ST-4 (A–B). Continue to pivot as you wrap your arm over their upper arm, trapping it in your armpit. Pull their wrist across your body. Place your R foot in front of their far-foot to trap it (C). Drop and turn, landing on top of attacker as they fall toward their front or right front-corner (D–E).

Important Points

In this throw, you will use the spinning weight of your body to create a throw. You must lock attacker's arm tightly to your body before dropping. Your R leg may be placed outside or between their legs. This can be a very brutal fall for your opponent. They will fall directly on their back, as you land on their chest and shoulder. Shoulder injuries are not uncommon, even during practice. When training, grip loosely and reduce force.

12. Forearm Wrapping Throw

Attacker grabs clothing at your side (A). Turn your L foot outward, grip their wrist with your L hand, and raise your R hand (B). Step across with your R foot and pivot 180° as you hit downward into the biceps (N-UE-9) and inner elbow (LU-5 or PC-3), with your R Outer Wrist (C). Continue turning as you drive your wrist into the inner elbow. Plant your foot outside the leg (D). Drop to one knee and drive their elbow toward the ground to throw (E).

Important Points

You will use the spinning weight of your body to create this throw. You must pull attacker's arm tight to your body with your L hand, as you drop and press your R forearm into attacker's inner elbow. Your R leg may be placed outside or between their legs. This can be a brutal fall for an opponent, particularly if you land on their chest. Shoulder injuries are not uncommon, even during practice. When training, exercise caution and reduce force.

Outer Wrist

13. Front Drop Throw

From a relaxed stance (A), step forward with your L foot. Grip the back of opponent's collar or neck with your R hand. Grip their torso or arm with your L hand (B). Pull opponent toward their left front-corner. They will step forward with their L foot to recover their balance. As they step, block their L foot with your R leg, and drop to your R side (C–D). As you fall, your R hand pulls downward as your L hand pushes upward, forcing a fall (E).

Important Points

This throw requires good timing. As you drop from a standing posture, opponent must be unbalanced toward their front-corner, so you can make full use of your body weight. Your *turning and dropping* body weight, and the pull of your arms, are the source of power. Twist your body as you fall, landing on your side or front. Do not land on your back, or opponent may deliberately fall on top of you. Many other entries are also possible.

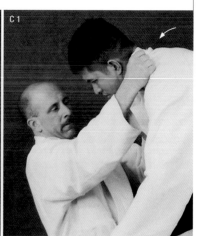

14. Rear Drop Throw

This throw can be used against a strike from any direction (jab punch is shown). Charge to attacker's right side, as you parry inward with your L hand (A–B). Step forward with your R foot and swing your L leg into the back of their legs, as you wrap your arms tightly around their waist and unbalance them toward their right side or right rear-corner (C). Forcefully twist your body and drop (D). Straddle and strike (E), or exit using a shoulder roll. Photo E shows the defender pressing his knuckles into the side of the chin at ST-4 (to pin the head sideways), as he raises his R hand to deliver a strike. Pinning attacker's head cuts off their vision and restricts movement.

Important Points

Drop throws are very fast and practical, and considered by many to be among the best punch defenses of any kind. Against a highly skilled striker, they are your best option, since they do not require you to *grab* a punch. They are usually executed off a parry or slip, by charging inward under an attacker's punch. For greater effect, forcefully kick your heel and lower leg into the back of the knees or calf when throwing (C).

Spear Hand – 2 Fingers

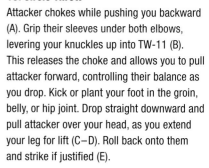

Upper Elbow

15. Circle Throw

Attacker chokes while pushing you backward (A). Grip their sleeves under both elbows, levering your knuckles up into TW-11 (B). This releases the choke and allows you to pull attacker forward, controlling their balance as you drop. Kick or plant your foot in the groin, belly, or hip joint. Drop straight downward and pull attacker over your head, as you extend your leg for lift (C–D). Roll back onto them and strike if justified (E).

Steps E–M show a devastating series of rapid strikes. This level of force is only used when justified by circumstances. To execute: Press your L Spear Hand (two fingers) into the base of the throat at CO-22, and raise your R hand. Deliver a Descending Elbow Strike to the head at M-HN-3, or cheek at ST-2 (F); then a Twin Inside Knife Hand Strike to the throat at ST-9 (G–H). Without retracting your L hand, push the chin sideways to lock the neck and pin the head, as you strike the groin with a Knife Hand (I). Grip the hair and lift the head (J). Slam the skull into the ground with a Palm Heel Strike to the face (K). Roll to your feet (L–M).

G (continued next page)

Important Points

When executing the throw, you must pull forcefully and drop *under* attacker. Most errors in execution result from dropping too soon, and failing to get your hips under attacker's hips. Do not execute this throw from a static position, since it is easily countered (attacker should be stepping forward). Plant your foot vertical, or angled outward (C1). *Angled* provides slightly better control of attacker's hips, but may produce greater stress on your knee. Circle Throws can also be executed by directing attacker to the side, rather than overhead. This is harder to counter, but less destructive to your opponent, which is why it is more common in competitive arts. If attacker is wearing light garments that stretch or tear easily, or is shirtless, grip their lapels or bare elbows. Generally, when dismounting an attacker to return to a standing posture, it is safest to direct a Forward Shoulder Roll over their head. Rolling sideways or backward is not usually recommended unless they are unconscious, since it is easy for an opponent to roll with you and immediately counter.

Knife Hand

Palm Heel Hand

16. Corner Throw

Attacker chokes while pushing you backward (A). Grip their sleeves or lapels (B). Unbalance attacker toward their right front-corner. Drop to your back, in front of and beneath attacker, kicking your R instep upward into the back of their L knee or thigh. As you drop, continue gripping their sleeves or lapels and pull them over your L shoulder, as you lift their leg with your R instep (C–D). Attacker will land on their side using a Side Fall, or their back using a Bridge Fall. Roll on top of them and deliver strikes or apply a choke, or roll away and return to a standing position.

Important Points

There are many variations on this throw, and it can be used in a wide variety of circumstances. Adjust the direction of your drop, based on attacker's foot placement. Ideally, you will want to drop perpendicular to the line formed by their feet. For example, in these photos the thrower is dropping toward their right rear-corner. You can plant your R foot anywhere in the area from attacker's L inner knee to their L buttock. You can direct a right-leg throw either over your left shoulder (most common); straight back; or over your R shoulder. Throwing straight back can easily lead to neck injuries, since an opponent will likely hit their head as they flip over.

17. Front Naked Choke Throw

Attacker delivers an inside circular strike (hook punch shown). Step inside with your R foot. Block inward with both Knife Hands or forearms, to the wrist and inner elbow (A). Grip their wrist with your L hand and pull it, as you hit the neck with your R Outer Forearm (B). Push attacker's head downward as you snake your hand around their throat. Join your hands, clamp tight C), and lift (C1), pressing your wrist or forearm into the windpipe. To throw, maintain the choke as you sit-out backward, forcing opponent to take a Bridge Fall (D–E).

Knife Hand

Important Points

This choke is very dangerous, since you place extreme stress on the cervical spine, and can easily damage the windpipe, leading to life-threatening injuries. Exercise caution. As you enter (C), be sure to protect your groin against a hand strike. Usually this is not an issue, since the entire technique is executed in a single, rapid, continuous motion. During practice: *do not* clamp the neck tightly; keep the hold very loose, or release it, during the throw. Direct the throw over your R shoulder, so attacker doesn't land on your face, breaking your nose. A variation of this throw can be executed by wrapping attacker's torso instead of their neck.

Outer Forearm

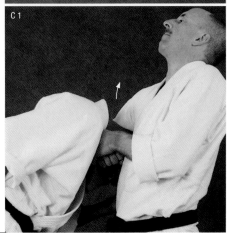

18. Reclining Front Naked Choke

Attacker charges forward to tackle you or apply a Two-Hand Reap Throw. As they rush in to scoop your legs, wrap your arm around their neck, placing your forearm across their windpipe. Join your hands and extend your wrist into their throat by using *wrist action*. Drop backward to your buttocks, pulling the top of their skull into the ground (B). Quickly wrap your legs around their waist, interlocking your ankles. Continue to choke as you push their hips away to increase leverage on the throat and cervical spine (C).

Important Points

This counter is used after your legs are scooped and you cannot avoid being thrown. Attacker's fall may give them a concussion (B). As soon as you drop, wrap your legs around their waist to keep them from flipping over onto their back to escape. Arching your back and extending your legs are very important, since this tightens the choke by forcing their hips away. You can choke either the windpipe (dangerous) or carotid artery.

A

19. Shoulder Turnover Throw

Attacker charges forward to tackle you or apply a Two-Hand Reap Throw. As they rush in to scoop your legs: lower your body, drop one foot back, and wrap both your arms under their armpits (A). This keeps them from grasping your legs. As attacker pushes forward, pivot 180°, lift their shoulder, and flip them over (B). Drop to your R knee, extend your L leg, and brace. Pull attacker's arms forward, as you lean backward (push their head toward their chest), locking their neck and shoulders (C).

B

Important Points

In this counter, you will use attacker's motion to flip them. Adjust the direction of your throw based on their foot placement. When locking the neck, press your R knee into their side, and extend your L leg for support (hinders escapes). Be careful: this lock exerts extreme stress on the cervical spine, similar to a Full Nelson. Alternate throw: wrap attacker's arms with your R arm under and L arm over, kicking your R leg out as you sit back (D).

C (neck lock)

D (alternate neck lock)

C 1 (opposite view)

20. Scissor Throw (disguised attack)

There are many different ways to execute a Scissor Throw, and many circumstances under which this throw can be used. Four possible options are shown on the following pages. In all versions, you will plant the back of one leg against a high target and the front of the other leg against a low target. You will then forcefully scissor your legs and twist your hips, unbalancing opponent backward. The photos at left show a disguised walking entry to set up a Scissor Throw to the chest and ankle.

To execute: Walk casually toward opponent's left side. Do not make any motions that signal your intent to attack (A). Plant your R foot near the side of attacker's L foot and pivot 90° as you slide your L foot behind attacker's far ankle (B). Plant both hands or your L hand only, as you forcefully swing your R leg into the waist or chest (C). Forcefully scissor your legs and twist your hips: your R leg pushes backward on their chest or hips; your L leg pushes forward on the back of both lower legs. Attacker falls backward (D). When entering this throw (C), you can also strike attacker's face with your heel.

21. Flying Scissor Throw

A Scissor Throw can also be applied by leaping into an opponent, without planting your hands. This requires good timing and must be well set up, to prevent counters. Their are several methods of entry. You can either jump from a stationary position (A–B), run and jump, or wrap your R arm around the back of the neck and grip the far shoulder for support, then jump. While airborne, plant your R leg against attacker's neck or head, and your L leg against their lower spine (C). Forcefully scissor your legs and twist your hips, throwing attacker backward (D).

Important Points

When applying this throw, your legs can also be planted on the chest and rear-thighs, chest and knees, or waist and knees. Proper breakfalls are essential to prevent injuries: you will land using a Side Fall or Back Fall; attacker will land using a Back Fall. If they fall incorrectly, whiplash and a concussion are likely. The photo below shows a Scissor Throw applied to the neck and head of one opponent, as you grip another for support (E).

22. Scissor Throw (against punch)

This throw can be used against a lead hand-strike from any direction. From a right-lead (A), cross-step forward with your L foot behind your R foot. Parry and grab attacker's lead wrist, before or during the strike (B). Swing your R leg across attacker's waist, as you unbalance them backward (C). Plant your L hand on the ground, as you place your L leg against the back of the knees (D). Forcefully scissor your legs and twist your hips, throwing attacker backward (E–F). You can follow with a Seated Axe Kick (heel down) to the face or solar plexus, if needed.

Important Points

This throw will will place you on the ground. If you do not possess strong ground skills (at least better than your opponent's), you will be no better off, unless the fall produces injuries. If attacker falls incorrectly, whiplash and a concussion are likely. Some throwers plant their hand with their fingers pointing in the same direction as attacker's toes, which reduces stress on your arm and shoulder when falling.

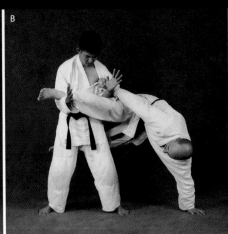

23. Scissor Throw (against throw)

As you execute a R kick, attacker traps your leg with a Two-Hand Wrap Block from *outside* (A). Before they can execute a throw or unbalance you, grab their shoulder or arm with your R hand, plant your L hand on the ground, and swing your L leg behind their legs (B). Forcefully twist your hips as you scissor your legs: your R leg pushes backward on their chest or hips; your L leg pushes forward on the back of both knees (C). Attacker falls backward (D–E). If justified, you can follow with a R Seated Axe Kick (heel down) to their head, face, or solar plexus.

Important Points

This counter is used if your kick is caught from the outside, or an attacker scoops your leg to throw. You must execute the counter very quickly, before attacker applies a throw. Hip rotation is crucial to create power.

If an opponent does not know how to fall, a whiplash or concussion is likely. Scissoring behind both ankles may cause their knees to hyperextend. If an attacker wraps your leg from *inside*, use the next two techniques.

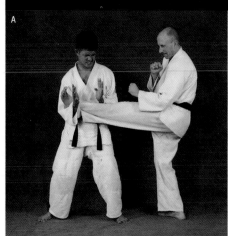

24. Reverse Scissor Throw

As you execute a L kick, attacker traps your leg with a Two-Hand Wrap Block from *inside* (A). Counter before they can execute a throw or unbalance you. Using your held-leg for support, jump upward, twist your body, and deliver a R Roundhouse Kick to the back of the head (B). Hit with your shin or instep, based on range. Scissor your legs, throwing attacker forward. Land on your side using a modified Front Fall (C). Deliver a Seated Axe Kick (heel down) to attacker's spine or lower skull (D).

Important Points

This counter is used if your kick is caught from the inside, or an attacker scoops your leg to throw. Your landing is the most difficult part of this counter and requires much skill in falling. Otherwise, you can easily hurt yourself in many ways, damaging your arms, wrist, shoulder, or knees. Take care to protect your knees as you fall. Slap with both forearms, landing on your side. You can also apply a Reverse Scissor Throw, in the opposite direction, by hitting into the back of both knees with the back of your R leg (plant your hand).

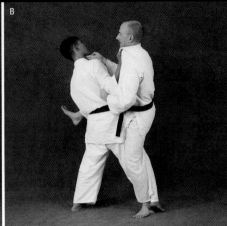

25. Legs-to-Hip Throw

Attacker lifts your R leg from *inside* and steps inward to reap your L leg (A). Press their throat at CO-22, or ST-9 and ST-10, with your R Spear Hand to keep them from driving forward (B). Grab their limbs or clothing, lift your support leg, and sit backward. Use your hand-holds to control your descent (C). As you drop to your back, grip both of attacker's ankles (D). Pull their ankles toward you as you forcefully extend your legs into their hips, forcing attacker to fall backward (E–F).

Spear Hand presses both
ST-9 and ST-10 (B)

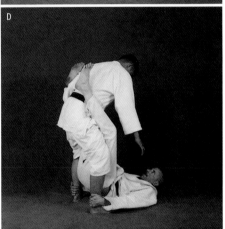

Important Points

Any time your leg is held high, drop quickly to avoid being slammed to the ground. Often a well-placed blow to the face or throat (B) can be used to force a Back Fall, without dropping your body. When gripping attacker's ankles (D), don't wrap your thumbs inside the ankle, since this slows transitions to ankle holds, and may cause your thumb to break if attacker kicks forward. After step F, either punch the groin, swing your heel down into the solar plexus or face, straddle attacker, or execute a Back Shoulder Roll and stand.

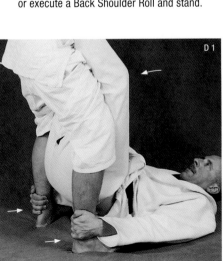

26. Falling Outside Crescent Kick

Attacker uses a Grab X Block to catch your Side Kick (A). As they twist your foot to apply a leg-twist throw, turn away to relieve pressure (B), and spin 180° in the air, executing an Outside Crescent Kick or Spin Kick to their head (C). In photo C, attacker's head is dropped to provide a better view. If an opponent is skilled, they will do this anyway to avoid your kick. In this case, use an Axe Kick later in your fall (D), or deliver a Roundhouse Kick upward into their face after landing.

Important Points

This self-initiated breakfall is a basic counter to any leg-twist throw, and a hallmark of Hapkido. You will finish in a Side Fall position, on your left side. In this counter, you are merely adding a kick onto the falling motion. It is very natural and easier than it looks. The fall rarely results in injury to yourself if you execute the breakfall properly. Even if you miss the kick, the velocity of your spin usually causes your opponent to release your foot.

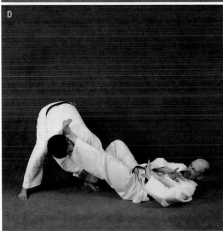

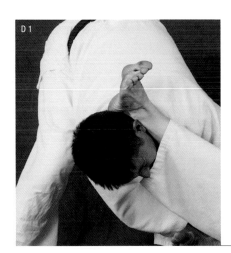

27. Drop Inside Hook Kick

This counter is used after you have been thrown. Attacker rushes inward, scoops your ankle, and locks your knee, forcing a Back Fall (A–B). As you land on your back, let your free leg swing up naturally (C). Pull your heel inward and down, by snapping your knee closed. Strike the cervical spine or base of the skull (D). Then deliver a Side Kick to the neck or head, driving attacker backward (E). You can also grab their arm and apply a Reclining Knee Arm Bar (see *Pinning Holds* chapter).

Important Points

This counter demonstrates how ground kicks can be used very effectively. Many possibilities exist. Your natural falling movements will often present a variety of opportunities. If required, you can repeat the combination shown, or shift to other ground kicks (see *Ground Kicks* chapter). If attacker's head is higher, execute a Seated Roundhouse Kick to their head, or a Front Toe Kick to CO-22 at the base of their throat.

A

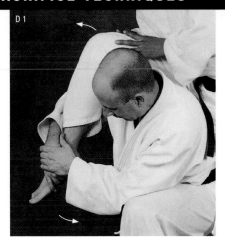

D 1

D 2 (alternate hold)

B

28. Leg Shoulder Throw

Step inside a Roundhouse Kick. Block outward with your L rear forearm, as your R lead hand wraps under the leg (A–B) and over the foot. Lift attacker's knee with your upper arm and grip their instep with both hands. Pivot as you step behind your R foot with your L foot, bring your R foot forward, and drop to your R knee. Plant your shoulder under the knee (C). Bend forward, pull the instep downward, and throw attacker over your shoulder (D–E).

Important Points

You can throw from a standing or kneeling position. In one fluid motion, step inward and pivot as you pull attacker onto your back and shoulder. How the held-foot is oriented, determines the fall. Pulling the foot inward forces a Side Fall (easiest landing). Pulling the instep straight downward (D1) forces a Front Fall (more difficult). Twisting the foot outward (D2) will likely break the knee during the throw, depending upon the throw's direction.

C

D

E

29. Leg Tackle Throw

Charge inward as you duck beneath a Spin Kick or Hook Kick, raising your R hand to block if needed (A–B). Grip attacker's ankle with your L hand, as you thrust your R Outer Forearm into the side or back of their knee (C). Pull the ankle upward to your L armpit (trap), as you drive their knee downward, forcing a Front Fall (D). Straddle attacker, pinning their leg behind them with your thigh, as you apply a Rear Naked Choke (E).

Important Points

This throw requires speed and precise timing. It is a good counter against high kicks, particularly turning kicks. The position of your hands and/or legs can be reversed. Take care not to scoop the leg up into your groin. Force a Front Fall if possible, since it is safer for you and eliminates many ground counters. Pin the leg by pressing your inner thigh downward against opponent's instep. Apply any rear choke, or pull the head backward.

Pin Leg

FURTHER READING

Philosophy and Religion

Chan, Wing-Tsit, trans. and comp.
A Source Book in Chinese Philosophy.
Princeton NJ: Princeton University Press, 1963.

Earhart, Byron H, edit.
Religious Traditions of the World.
San Francisco: HarperCollins Publishers, 1993.

Smith, Huston
The Illustrated World's Religions:
A Guide to Our Wisdom Traditions
San Francisco: HarperCollins Publishers, 1994.

Zimmer, Heinrich.
Philosophies of India.
Edited by Joseph Campbell.
Princeton NJ: Princeton University Press, 1969.

Medicine

Cohen, Kenneth S.
The Way of Qigong: The Art and Science
of Chinese Energy Healing.
New York: Ballantine Books, 1997.

Dox, Ida; John Melloni; and Gilbert Eisner.
The HarperCollins Illustrated Medical Dictionary.
New York: HarperCollins Publishers, 1993.

Kaptchuk, Ted J.
The Web That Has No Weaver:
Understanding Chinese Medicine.
New York: Congdon & Weed, 1983.

Maciocia, Giovanni.
The Foundations of Chinese Medicine.
London: Churchhill Livingston, 1989.

Netter, Frank H.
Atlas of Human Anatomy.
Summit, NJ: Novartis Pharmaceuticals, 1989.

Tedeschi, Marc.
Essential Anatomy for Healing and Martial Arts.
New York: Weatherhill, 2000.
——. *Essential Acupoints.* (Poster)
New York: Weatherhill, 2002.

Van Alphen, Jan, and Anthony Aris, editors.
Oriental Medicine: An Illustrated Guide
to the Asian Arts of Healing.
Boston: Shambala Publications, 1997.

General Martial Arts

Draeger, Donn F., and Robert W. Smith.
Comprehensive Asian Fighting Arts.
New York: Kodansha, 1980.

Farkas, Emil, and John Corcoran.
Martial Arts: Traditions, History, People.
New York: Smith Publications, 1983.

Haines, Bruce A.
Karate's History and Traditions.
Tokyo: Tuttle, 1968.

Nelson, Randy F., edit.
The Overlook Martial Arts Reader:
Classic Writings on Philosophy and Technique.
Woodstock NY: Overlook Press, 1989.

Tedeschi, Marc.
The Art of Striking: Principles & Techniques.
New York: Weatherhill, 2002.
——. *The Art of Holding: Principles &*
Techniques. New York: Weatherhill, 2001.
——. *The Art of Throwing: Principles &*
Techniques. New York: Weatherhill, 2001.
——. *The Art of Weapons: Armed and Unarmed*
Self-Defense. New York: Weatherhill, 2003.

Periodicals

Aikido Journal. Tokyo, Japan.

Black Belt. Valencia, California.

Dragon Times. Thousand Oaks, California.

The Empty Vessel: A Journal of
Contemporary Taoism. Eugene, Oregon.

Inside Karate. Burbank, California.

Inside Kung Fu. Burbank, California.

Internal Martial Arts. Collegeville, Pennsylvania.

Journal of Asian Martial Arts. Erie, Pennsylvania.

Taekwondo Times. Bettendorf, Iowa.

Tai Chi and Alternative Health.
London, Great Britain.

Japanese Martial Arts

Draeger, Donn F.
Classical Budo.
New York: Weatherhill, 1996.

Funakoshi, Gichin.
Karate-Do: My Way of Life.
Tokyo: Kodansha, 1975.

Inokuma, Isao, and Nobuyuki Sato.
Best Judo.
Tokyo: Kodansha, 1979.

Kano, Jigoro.
Kodokan Judo.
Tokyo: Kodansha, 1986 (first published 1956).

Kudo, Kazuzo.
Dynamic Judo: Throwing Techniques.
Tokyo: Japan Publications Trading Co., 1967.
——. *Dynamic Judo: Grappling Techniques.*
Tokyo: Japan Publications Trading Co., 1967.

Omiya, Shiro
The Hidden Roots of Aikido:
Aiki Jujutsu Daitoryu.
Tokyo: Kodansha, 1998.

Otaki, Tadao, and Donn F. Draeger.
Judo: Formal Techniques.
Tokyo: Tuttle, 1983.

Pranin, Stanley.
Daito-ryu Aikijujutsu:
Conversations with Daito-ryu Masters.
New York: Aiki News, 1995.

Ueshiba, Kisshomaru.
Aikido.
New York: Japan Publications, 1963.
——. *The Spirit of Aikido.*
Tokyo: Kodansha, 1984.

Ueshiba, Morihei.
Budo: Teachings of the Founder of Aikido.
Tokyo: Kodansha, 1991 (first published 1938).

Tohei, Koichi.
Aikido: The Arts of Self Defense.
Tokyo: Ritugei Publishing House, 1960.

Chinese Martial Arts

Frantzis, Bruce Kumar.
  The Power of Internal Martial Arts:
  Combat Secrets of Ba Gua, Tai Chi, and Hsing-i.
  Berkeley CA: North Atlantic Books, 1998.

Lee, Bruce.
  Tao of Jeet Kune Do.
  Santa Clarita, CA: Ohara Publications, 1975.

Yang, Jwing-Ming.
  Taiji Chin Na: The Seizing Art of Taijiquan.
  Boston MA: YMAA Publication Center, 1995.

Korean Martial Arts

Cho, Sihak H.
  Korean Karate: Free Fighting Techniques.
  Tokyo: Tuttle, 1968.

Chun, Richard, and P.H. Wilson.
  Tae Kwon Do: The Korean Martial Art.
  New York: Harper & Row, 1976.

Kimm, He-Young.
  Hapkido 2.
  Baton Rouge, LA: Andrew Jackson College
  Press, 1994.
  ———. *Kuk Sool Korean Martial Arts.*
  Baton Rouge, LA: Andrew Jackson College
  Press, 1985.

Lee, Joo-Bang.
  The Ancient Martial Art of Hwarangdo.
  (three volumes)
  Burbank CA: Ohara Publications, 1978.

Myung, Kwang-Sik, and Jong-Taek Kim.
  Hapkido. (Korean language)
  South Korea: 1967.

Suh, In Hyuk, and Jane Hallander.
  The Fighting Weapons of Korean Martial Arts.
  Burbank CA: Unique Publications, 1988.

Tedeschi, Marc.
  Hapkido: Traditions, Philosophy, Technique.
  New York: Weatherhill, 2000.
  ———. *Taekwondo: Traditions, Philosophy,*
  Technique. New York: Weatherhill, 2003.

BOOKS BY MARC TEDESCHI

Hapkido: Traditions, Philosophy, Technique

Acclaimed the most comprehensive book ever written on a single martial art, this text contains over 2000 techniques encompassing all forms of martial skills: strikes, holds, throws, weapons, meditation, and healing. Also includes in-depth chapters on history, philosophy, and anatomy, plus interviews with 13 renowned masters.

1136 pages, 8 1/2 x 11 in., 9000 b&w photographs
US $90.00 (hardcover), ISBN 0-8348-0444-1

Hapkido: An Introduction to the Art of Self-Defense

A concise overview of Hapkido in its entirety, with essential material for novices.

128 pages, 8 1/2 x 11 in., 680 b&w photographs
US $16.95 (softcover), ISBN 0-8348-0483-2

Taekwondo: Traditions, Philosophy, Technique

The most comprehensive text ever written on the world's most popular martial art—Taekwondo. Expertly integrates traditional and modern styles, sport and self-defense, in a single definitive text.

896 pages, 8 1/2 x 11 in., 8600 b&w photographs
US $90.00 (hardcover), ISBN 0-8348-0515-4

Taekwondo: The Essential Introduction

A concise overview of Taekwondo in its entirety, with essential material for novices.

128 pages, 8 1/2 x 11 in., 530 b&w photographs
US $16.95 (softcover), ISBN 0-8348-0537-5

Essential Anatomy For Healing and Martial Arts

This book familiarizes healers and martial artists with basic concepts of the human body, as defined by both Western and Eastern medical traditions. Includes principles of pressure point fighting, 20 essential self-massage and revival techniques, and detailed tables of acupoints in English, Chinese, Korean, and Japanese.

144 pages, 8 1/2 x 11 in., full-color
147 color drawings, 54 duotone photographs
US $19.95 (softcover), ISBN 0-8348-0443-3

Essential Acupoints (Poster)

A large, 7-color poster illustrating the 400-plus acupoints and 14 meridians that are the basis of Eastern medicine and martial arts. Also highlights Qi-flow, Yin-Yang, 5 Phases, and martial targets.

27 x 40 in., US $30.00, ISBN 0-8348-0510-3.

The Art of Striking

Outlines the core principles and techniques that define the art of striking in most martial arts. Contains over 400 practical strikes, including arm strikes, kicks, head butts, blocking and avoiding skills, combinations, and counters.

208 pages, 8 1/2 x 11 in., 1480 b&w photographs
US $35.00 (hardcover), ISBN 0-8348-0495-6

The Art of Holding

Outlines the core principles and techniques that define the art of holding in most martial arts. Contains over 155 practical holds, including joint locks, chokes, nerve holds, pins, combinations, and defenses against locks and chokes.

208 pages, 8 1/2 x 11 in., 1300 b&w photographs
US $35.00 (hardcover), ISBN 0-8348-0491-3

The Art of Throwing

Outlines the core principles and techniques that define the art of throwing in most martial arts. Contains over 130 practical throws, including hip throws, leg throws, hand throws, sacrifice throws, combinations, and counterthrows.

208 pages, 8 1/2 x 11 in., 1200 b&w photographs
US $35.00 (hardcover), ISBN 0-8348-0490-5

The Art of Weapons

Outlines the core principles and techniques that define armed and unarmed self-defense with common weapons. Contains over 300 practical techniques organized into in-depth chapters on the knife, short-stick, staff, cane, rope, common objects, and defense against handgun. Includes both offensive and defensive applications.

208 pages, 8 1/2 x 11 in., 1200 b&w photographs
US $35.00 (hardcover), ISBN 0-8348-0540-5

VIEW ONLINE

View samples or obtain information at:
www.tedeschi-media.com

HOW TO BUY

These books are available through retail book stores or direct from the publisher:

Weatherhill, Inc.
41 Monroe Turnpike, Trumbull CT 06611 USA
Sales: 800-437-7840; 203-459-5090
Fax: 800-557-5601; 203-459-5095
order@weatherhill.com

The Art of
GROUND FIGHTING

———

Designed and illustrated by Marc Tedeschi.

Principal photography by Shelley Firth and Frank Deras.

Creative consultation by Michele Wetherbee.

Editorial supervision by Ray Furse and Thomas Tedeschi.

Production consultation by Bill Rose.

The following individuals appeared with the
author in the photographs: Arnold Dungo,
Cody Aguirre, Jo-An Aguirre, and Michael Mar.

Also thanks to Merrill Jung for loaning
rare books from his personal collection.

The majority of the photographs were shot on
Plus-X Professional 2 ¼ film using Hasselblad cameras,
and were scanned from Ilford Multigrade prints
using an Epson ES-1200C flat-bed scanner.

Digital-type composition and page layout originated
on an Apple Macintosh 8500 computer.

Typeset in Helvetica Neue, Univers, Sabon,
Garamond, Weiss, Times, and Baker Signet.

Printed and bound by Oceanic Graphic Printing
and C&C Offset Printing in China.

Published and distributed by Weatherhill.

Weatherhill

PUBLISHERS OF FINE BOOKS ON
ASIA AND THE PACIFIC